TO: Jermaine
Thanks for listening
to the same stories
so patiently!
yours sincerely,
JB

To John, Malaika, Johnny, Imani
and my parents
Caroline McWatt Bowman and the late Henry Bowman

The Making of Modern Africa

Series Editors: Abebe Zegeye and John Higginson

Ominous Transition

Commerce and colonial expansion in the Senegambia and Guinea, 1857-1919

JOYE BOWMAN
Department of History
University of Massachusetts, Amherst

Avebury

Aldershot • Brookfield USA • Hong Kong • Singapore • Sydney

Published by
Avebury
Ashgate Publishing Limited
Gower House
Croft Road
Aldershot
Hants GU11 3HR
England

Ashgate Publishing Company
Old Post Road
Brookfield
Vermont 05036
USA

British Library Cataloguing in Publication Data
Bowman, Joye
      Ominous transition : commerce and colonial expansion in the
      Senegambia and Guinea, 1857-1919. - (The making of modern
      Africa)
      1.Africa, West - Commerce - History 2.Africa, West -
      Colonial influence   3.Europe - Colonies - Africa   4.Europe -
      Colonies - Economic conditions
      I.Title
      330.9'66'03

Library of Congress Catalog Card Number : 96-86716

ISBN 1 85972 154 0

Printed and bound by Athenaeum Press, Ltd.,
Gateshead, Tyne & Wear.

Contents

Figures and table

Abbreviations

AHU	Arquivo Histórico Ultramarino
AMNE	Arquivo do Ministério dos Negócios Estrangeiros
ANS	Archives Nationales du Sénégal
ANSOM	Archives Nationales Section Outre-Mer
BIFAN	*Bulletin de l'Institut Fundamental d'Afrique Noire*
BCGP	*Boletim Cultural da Guiné Portuguesa*
BOGP	*Boletim Oficial da Guiné Portugueza*
BSGL	*Boletim da Sociedade de Geographia de Lisboa*
PRO,CO	Public Record Office, Colonial Office
INIC	Instituto Nacional de Investigação Ciêntífica
JAH	*Journal of African History*

Acknowledgements

This study is the result of many years of research and fieldwork in Guinea-Bissau, Senegal, The Gambia, Portugal, France and England. Professors, colleagues, informants, friends and family assisted and encouraged me in a variety of ways throughout this project. To all I express my deepest gratitude. In most cases, I tried to follow their suggestions. I hope that I have done justice to their ideas. I admit that the opinions, interpretations and mistakes are my own.

Professors Agnes A. Aidoo, Christopher Ehret, Margaret Jean Hay, Willard Johnson, Boniface I. Obichere, the late Armstead Robinson, and Richard Sklar guided and motivated me at various stages of my career as a student. Subsequently, other scholars including Gerald Bender, George Brooks, Leon Forrest, Russell Hamilton, Allen Isaacman, Joseph Miller, Otto Olsen, Richard Ralston, Lars Rudebeck, and Ibrahim Sundiata offered crucial suggestions. Colleagues and friends at the University of Massachusetts at Amherst helped me to rethink this study. Their comments and support helped me to finish. This list includes Ernie Allen, John Bracey, Bruce Laurie, Barry Levy, Roland Sarti, Jean Sherlock, and Esther Terry. To all of you I say thank you.

Numerous other people have offered assistance over the years. Ingrid Bracey, Elsa Barkley Brown, Marsha Miles Brown, Joyce Ewen, Philip Hawkins, the late Dr. and Mrs. W. Lincoln Hawkins, Violin Hughes, Jacqueline LaFalle, Sidney LeMelle, Beverly LeMay, Reginald LeMay, Catherine Macklin, Waldo Martin,

Irma McClaurin, Tom Parrish, Marjorie Richardson, Carolyn Smith, the late Vernon Smith, and Jackie Wolf have shown their support in different ways. Without their contributions, I could not have finished.

I appreciate the technical support that Mary Rose and Gail Shirley at the Carter G. Woodson Institute provided. They helped me to learn how to use a computer — a real challenge. I am glad that they were patient with me. I owe Alice Izer in the Department of History at the University of Massachusetts-Amherst for producing the final draft. She managed to translate my materials into a finished product ready for the camera. I promise that I will not make any more changes! Noel Diaz and Phyllis Kawano are talented cartographers. They took various old and often ragged maps and tried to make sense of my directions — not a easy task! The editorial staff at Avebury, especially Anne Keirby, has been patient and accomodating. I also thank Professor Abebe Zegeye for his confidence in this project.

Scholars whose work takes them away from "home" to conduct research can readily appreciate the importance of local contacts. I was extremely lucky to have Raquel and David Soeiro de Brito in Lisbon. They welcomed me as family and made my trips to Lisbon enjoyable and comfortable. Isaú Santos, the director of the Arquivo Histórico Ultramarino, Alexandre Marques Pereira, the archivist at the library of the Sociedade de Geografia de Lisboa and their respective staffs assured that I had access to materials in their collections. The librarians at the Biblioteca Nacional were helpful as well. The late António Carreira and the late A. Teixeira da Mota shared information about Portuguese Guinea with me. They guided me to appropriate resources and suggested refinements in my study. I regret that they never saw the final draft. Ilídio de Amaral, Jill Diaz, Franz Heimer, and Maria João Queiroz were more than hospitable during my various research trips.

I owe special thanks to the Government of Guinea-Bissau for allowing me to carry out research there. Mário de Andrade, Mário Cissoko, Quémo C. Darame, Eduardo Ion Embaló, Gil Fernandes, and Tino and Milanka Lima Gomes made my visit not only possible, but productive. The staff at the Instituto Nacional de Ivestigação Cientifica in Bissau provided assistance and friendship. The American community in Bissau, especially Dean Curran, Carol Hazzard, and Jim Maher was warm and hospitable. But above all I owe thanks to my informants in Guinea-Bissau who shared their knowledge and understanding of their history with me. I have tired to relate their accounts as accurately as possible.

Research in Senegal would have been impossible without the hospitality and intellectual stimulation that I received from Susan Caughman, Gerry Goodrich, and Yvonne Jones. Professors Boubacar Barry and Sékéne Mody Cissoko imparted materials and ideas. I thank them for their interest in this study and my work. Also I extend my thanks to the Director of the Archives Nationales du

Sénégal, Saliou Mbaye, and his staff who were helpful and friendly during my stay in Dakar.

I remain indebted to many people in The Gambia as well. Bakary K. Sidibe was a continual source of information on the history of the region. His manuscripts and personal knowledge were invaluable. Without his help this work would not exist. Winnifred Galloway opened the doors of her home to me. She shared information with me about the history of the region, but more importantly, she helped me to understand many subtle cultural issues. I would also like to thank Sefu Lamine Bandeh of Sankulikunda for arranging interviews for me. I owe special thanks to my informants as well who trusted me with their traditions. I hope that I have done them justice. Omar Sidibe and Bakary Jammeh, my interpreters, translators, and friends, enabled me to collect the oral evidence. I also appreciate the cooperation of the President's Office of the Gambian government.

The reference librarians at the University Research Library at the University of California at Los Angeles (UCLA) were very helpful during the early stages of this study. Subsequently, librarians at the Alderman Library at the University of Virginia, and the W.E.B. DuBois Library at the University of Massachusetts at Amherst were always willing to help me track down material. The archivists and librarians at the Public Record Office, the Archives Nacionales, the Newberry Library, and the Northwestern University and Harvard University libraries helped me to complete my research.

I received financial support for this study from a number of sources. The original research funds were from the National Fellowships Fund, a Ford Foundation program. Supplementary support came from the Interdisciplinary Research Program on Angola, Mozambique and Guinea-Bissau at UCLA, as well as the UCLA Graduate Division. A Graduate Advancement Fellowship and a Teaching Assistantship in the Department of History at UCLA enabled me to complete the original dissertation. Research funds from the Social Science Research Council, the Carter G. Woodson Research Institute, the University of Virginia Faculty Grant Program, the University of Massachusetts Dean's Office, the Fundação Calouste Gulbenkian, and the National Endowment for the Humanities Travel Fund allowed me to complete my research project. The Department of Afro-American Studies at Northwestern University hosted me as a research affiliate in 1986-87. I appreciate this support.

The "African" proverb that "It takes a whole village to raise a child" has received quite a bit of attention lately. My experience of trying to finish this project and raise two small children bears witness to this folk wisdom. My husband, John Higginson, has given me unending support. I am eternally grateful to him. The other people of "my village" include Mrs. Luella Starks, as well as the teaching staffs at the Children's Learning Center (DeKalb, IL), New World and Grass Roots Child Care Centers (Amherst, MA), Hampshire

College Children's Center, Capacidad, Leisure Services, Crocker Care and Wildwood Afterschool Programs. I especially thank Grandma Christine Higginson and my oldest daughter, Malaika, for caring for Johnny and Imani. Without the support of "my village", life would have been crazier than even I can imagine. Thanks to each and everyone who took care of Johnny and Imani while I tried to finish one more piece of this project.

I feel lucky to have had an extended family to stick with me. My "fictive" kin have become part of this family. Arthé Anthony and Julie Saville always knew that there was a story to be told. Kandioura Dramé, *mon frère*, has provided inspiration over the years. He has helped me to decipher many of the cultural subtleties that I would have missed. Similarly, Lynda Morgan believed in me and this study. Although I know that each of them was curious, they never asked when it would be finished! They have been more than just friends. Fermino (Minoca) Pinto has become *meu irmão*. I have learned a great deal from him about Mozambique and the Portuguese colonial world. Merle Bowen, *minha irmã*, and I have helped one another negotiate the trials and tribulations of graduate school, fieldwork, manuscripts, teaching careers, and family life for almost twenty years. *Obrigada, camarada!*

My immediate family has provided support and understanding over the long haul. My father, the late Henry Bowman, and my mother, Caroline McWatt Bowman, always told me that if I worked hard I could do anything I wanted to in life. I could not have asked for better parents. My sister, Judy Bowman, has always been there for me. She is a real gem. Although they may not know it, my brother, Jon Bowman and his family have been a source of support as well. Thanks for sticking with me. My children, Malaika, Johnny, and Imani mean more to me than words can say. They give meaning to my life. I owe my greatest debt to my husband, John Higginson. It is not easy to balance two academic careers and a family. But, John has put aside his own work to help me complete this project. His understanding of the history of the world has helped me to reconceptualize my own work. I am glad that he never let me forget that this study needed to be written. I cannot thank him for all that he has done. Dedicating this book to John, my children and my parents is but a humble way of saying thanks.

1 From 'Free Trade' to the Imperialism of 'Free Trade': The Geographical and Historical Background of Nineteenth Century Guinea

Introduction

In the last half of the nineteenth century numerous forces combined to reshape the indigenous societies of the Senegambia region in West Africa. The abolition of the slave trade, the new emphasis on "legitimate commerce", and the various European efforts to colonize portions of West Africa resulted in a speedy commercialization of agriculture and compelled those still independent West African kingdoms on the northern savannah to incorporate the southern and coastal approaches of their region. For those societies governed by Islamic elites the advance of Christian infidels beyond the coast, particularly the Portuguese and the French, was especially ominous. Consequently, the expansion of states such as Futa Jallon and Sokoto was motivated as much by the prospect of religious conversion and revitalization as by the desire to control the terms of regional and international trade. In turn, Islam spread through the backlands of the Senegambia with an intensity that astounded contemporary African and European observers.

The various African societies of the Senegambia were largely unaware of the new discourse within European economic liberalism — which was focused on the abolition of slavery and modest legislative reforms that sought to ameliorate the most egregious features of European industrialization and which clustered around terms such as "political economy" and "Free Trade". Nevertheless, they were painfully aware of their own loss of economic momentum from the end of the eighteenth century onwards. Moreover, the spread of Islam from the cities and towns of West Africa to the countryside gave rulers and peasants alike a scaffolding for their outrage against European encroachment and the prospect of producing food and commercial crops on a scale unheard of by their forefathers.

Meanwhile the European powers had begun to reevaluate their economic and political objectives in Africa. After almost a century of propaganda in favor of Free Trade and the abolition of the slave trade it appeared that numerous Africans in the interior would welcome European rule with open arms, just as those in Sierra Leone, Gorée and other coastal enclaves had appeared to do. By the 1880s, the European powers determined that they wanted to divide the continent among themselves. However, the various powers agreed that each country had to be able to show "effective occupation" in the regions that they claimed. Such a quest proved initially more difficult than the European powers imagined.

Africans in the hinterland of West Africa were often willing to fight to maintain their independence. Moreover, French and Portuguese competition in the Senegambia was especially sharp. The French wanted to establish one large colony in West Africa. The Portuguese, on the other hand, attempted to hold on to Guinea for political as well as economic reasons. Their rivalry persisted well after both countries had signed the Berlin Agreement of 1885. In turn, this rivalry created a breach in European authority that was eagerly exploited in the short run by indigenous African rulers well into the twentieth century. For example, a year after the commencement of the First World War and some four years after Portugal's republican revolution, Portugal experienced stiff African opposition in many parts of Guinea. All of these factors contributed to rapid and dramatic changes in Portuguese colonial administration. Despite Guinea's size the Portuguese military occupation was illustrative of many of the more intractable problems associated with the European military occupation of most of Africa during the first part of the twentieth century.

The transition from the slave trade to "legitimate commerce" was the catalyst for a fundamental economic and social transformation of the Senegambia, particularly the southern or Guinea portion. The new demands of the Industrial Revolution meant that local Afro-European and European merchants were no longer primarily interested in slaves. Rather, they were concerned to divide their profit making activities between slaving and acquiring raw materials for European industry. Merchants and traders turned some of their attention to commodities such as palm products, peanuts, tobacco, rubber and cotton, while continuing their active presence in the slave markets of the Senegambian backlands. The net result was, by all accounts, a dramatic increase in the number of slaves leaving the Senegambian coast between 1820 and 1860, at the very same time that crops which could be sold on the world market — peanuts and coffee, for example — began to be commercially produced in the Senegambia. From the 1840s onward peanuts became the principal commercial crop of Guinea. Oil from peanuts was used to manufacture cooking oils, machine lubricants, soaps and candles — thus facilitating the expansion of European industry, while simultaneously enhancing the living standards of significant portions of Europe's burgeoning urban population.[1] But the persistence of the slave trade along side the production of export crops further exacerbated the clash between the ideology of Free Trade, as it had been expressed at the Congress of Vienna in 1815 and subsequent meetings of the European powers, and the prospects for the abolition of slavery. For how could commodities for a free market be produced by unfree labor?

Historical antecedents

African ruling and merchant classes in what became Portuguese Guinea were participating in the Atlantic Ocean's trading network as early as the late fifteenth century — exchanging slaves, gum, ivory, dyes and hides for European imports. By the beginning of the nineteenth century, these elites were firmly entrenched in the Atlantic commercial system as suppliers of both slaves and raw materials. In fact, the domestic economies of states such as Kaabu and Futa Jallon had become dependent on slave labor to a degree that would have been unimaginable to their rulers a century before. Consequently, the abolition of slavery and the slave trade threatened to overturn the existing configuration of political power within Senegambia. By the mid-nineteenth century, African, Afro-European, and European elites sought to control the terms and momentum of this ominous economic and political transition. Consequently, the trade in peanuts and the trade in slaves achieved a curious conjuncture throughout most of the second half of the nineteenth century.

In some parts of Portuguese Guinea, especially on Bolama Island and in the neighboring region of Forria, merchant elites reorganized themselves and their supporters to meet simultaneously the new demands for "legitimate commerce" and also those of the trade in human beings. Between 1840 and 1885 many of these merchants doubled as owners of plantations or *feitorias*, which employed both contract and slave labor to produce peanuts, coffee, sugar cane, tobacco and cotton.[2] By the 1860s, peanuts had become the most important of these exported cash crops.

The growth of so many plantations in the Guinean area of the Senegambia within such a compressed period begs several important questions: 1) Were the *feitorias* the catalysts for the dramatic increase in peanut production? 2) Were such increases a result of the owners' attempt to effect economies of scale on the *feitorias*, or did the aspirations of free peasant farmers affect the rate of increase? 3) Were there significant technical innovations associated with the increase in peanut production such as the introduction of plows, more animal power, and fencing? 4) If local peasants did in fact respond to the new commercial opportunities, did their response bring them into conflict with the plantation owners — and with burgeoning Portuguese colonial rule? 5) Were the *feitoria* owners interested in the reproduction of their work force, or did they assume that the labor supply was more or less unlimited?

As early as the 1840s peanut production in the Senegambia had resulted in the protracted abandonment of local food crops by a few African peasants and cultivators in some parts of the region such as the right bank of the Geba River. Yet the relative prosperity of some peasants was not achieved without great social costs. Chattel and domestic slavery in the southernmost part of the Senegambia and death and starvation farther north rose sharply in conjunction with new economic circumstances.[3] Moreover, a generation later, *feitoria* owners in what purported to be Portuguese Guinea had become a stiff source of competition for peanut growing Mandinka peasant farmers just north of the Casamance River in British controlled Gambia. This competition, combined with the expansionary wars of Fulbe and Mandinka warlords throughout the Senegambia, dangerously aggravated the subsistence problem in both areas, while giving rise to what one British observer described as "orgies of speculation" on the part of the various European commercial houses operating in the area.[4] The proverbial annual two tons of rice needed to feed a household and dependents while at work on the peanut crop could not be had from indigenous sources, particularly, where the local people, by dint of force, economic compulsion or choice had tied their fate to cash crops and foreign markets. The impact of the partly concealed subsistence crisis had a telling effect on the capacities of various people to resist subsequent European encroachment. As a result, major famines crisscrossed the Senegambia at the close of each generation after the initial commercial boom of the 1840s — in 1857, in 1876, in 1894, and in 1901.[5]

The spread of Islam from the mountains and plains east of the Senegambia also assisted the region's transformation, particularly in that part of it that became Portuguese Guinea. By the 1870s Islamic soldiers and missionaries were pressing in on the area just behind the Guinea coast from Futa Jallon in the south and from Fuladu in the north. The rulers of these states were interested not only in spreading Islam, but also in the apparent opportunities afforded by the production of cash crops such as peanuts. Islamic leaders disputed control of the most productive land with local land chiefs as well as with representatives of European merchant capital.

Moreover, lineage-based labor systems, which often used slaves to expand their labor force, were unable to meet the growing foreign demand for peanuts

4

and other cash crops. And Muslim leaders used their military power and the organizational capacities of their religion to build a new agricultural system based on tenancy in order to fill the vacuum created by the partial collapse of indigenous peasant agriculture and the initial instances of European encroachment. Muslim intervention underscored the transformation that began with European "legitimate commerce" and Free Trade. The peasantry's increasing attachment to commercial production became a barometer for this larger contest. Before fully examining the terms of this larger contest, let us turn to the geographical and cultural setting of the region that became Portuguese Guinea.

Geographical setting

The Republic of Guinea-Bissau, formerly Portuguese Guinea, is a small West African country, located south of Senegal and north and west of the Republic of Guinea (Conakry), between 12 20'N and 10 56'N latitude and 13 38'W and 16 43'W longitude. It is approximately 31,800 square kilometers. Guinea-Bissau has two distinct zones — the littoral and the interior. The littoral is comprised of a series of off-shore islands — Bissau, Bolama, Pecixe and Jeta — as well as a strip of coastal land. There is also the Bijagós archipelago, which is composed of eighteen smaller islands. The coast is made up of lowlands lying on a wide alluvial plain. These lowlands receive water from the sea at high tide and are also traversed by a number of disproportionately wide rivers.[6]

The interior of Guinea-Bissau consists of plains and some small hills. These hills are the foothills of Futa Jallon and the highest, measuring about 300 meters, are found near the border of the Republic of Guinea.[7] The Bafatá plateau serves as a transitional zone between the coast and the interior. And the meandering backland rivers extend the plateau for about another 40 meters. This smaller plateau, which is called Gabu, has fewer rivers than the Bafatá plateau. Farther south there are even smaller plateaus such as Oio and Forria. These smaller plateaus assist the transition from the mangrove swamps of the coast to the interior savanna and upland.

The region's river system is arguably its most important attribute in terms of human settlement and the movement of resources. The major rivers are the Cacheu-Farim, Mansoa, Geba-Corubal, Rio Grande de Buba, Tombali, Cumbija, and Cacine. The rivers enabled both Africans and Europeans to move easily between the coast and the interior. People tended to settle on their banks. Moreover, these rivers have hundreds of smaller branches. Consequently, the rivers have served as a means of transporting commercial items and as a communication network. Large vessels can readily negotiate the largest of the rivers, and thus reach the major centers of population. Small boats or *lanchas* are used where the rivers are shallow. Only a few of the smaller settlements in the northeastern part of the country cannot be reached by river transport.[8]

Despite its small size, Guinea-Bissau has a wide range of soils. Some of the most fertile soils in West Africa are found near the banks of the rivers, and some of the least fertile are found at the base of the foothills. The richest soils, near the rivers, are composed of deposits brought by invading ocean waters as well as the alluvium that the rains carry from the mountains. Because of the richness of this soil, these lands are the most densely populated. Rice is the principal crop. And the Balanta peasants who have lived on the banks of the rivers for centuries, continue to grow rice.[9] Needless to say, the Portuguese colonial government determined to exploit their efforts with all the means at its disposal.[10]

The soils of the foothills have undergone an especially damaging kind of leaching, whereby laterite soils are transformed into cement or "ferrous armor", which in turn, replaces the scarce topsoil once the torrential phase of the rainy season begins. Man's activities contribute to the creation of this "ferrous armor". The removal of natural vegetation cover exposes the soils directly to the rains and the sun and deprives them of organic materials which serve as natural fertilizers. Because these soils are less productive than those in other areas, large settlements of agricultural peoples are not found in this area. A variety of other types of soils exists throughout the country which fall somewhere between the two extremes of the alluvial river valleys and the "ferrous armor" of the foothills. Human settlement has waxed and waned with the consequent gradations of soil.[11]

In the coastal areas of Guinea-Bissau one finds a monsoon climate, characterized by a dense and ever-present humidity, even during the dry season. However, May and October are the hottest months owing to the increased humidity that accompanies the beginning and the end of the rains. In the interior zone, one finds a savanna-like climate which is somewhat less humid than the coastal areas. The temperatures of both zones are about the same, the yearly average being 26.1 C for the coast and 26.6 C for the interior. These temperatures are somewhat deceiving, since the humidity ratchets up the discomfort that comes with the high temperatures. The average rainfall between May and October on the southern coast is about 3,000 mm while in the interior the norm is about 1,500 mm.[12] In recent years, however, the rains have been sporadic, and Guinea-Bissau, like other countries in this area of West Africa, has suffered from the effects of drought. With respect to vegetation, the coastal areas are primarily composed of mangrove swamps with some tropical forest areas, whereas the interior is characterized by the tall grasses of the savanna.[13]

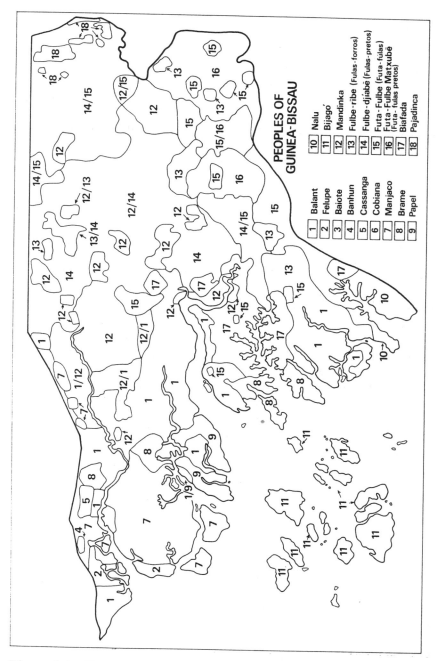

Figure 1.1   Peoples of Guinea-Bissau

7

The peopling of the Guinea regions of Senegambia

Guinea-Bissau has and has had an ethnically diverse population. The major ethnic groups present in the nineteenth century included the Balant, Biafada, Basserel or "Manjaco", Mandinka and Fulbe. Other groups found in smaller numbers included the Nalu, Sarakole, Soso and Jakhanke.[14] A detailed ethnographic analysis of these groups is beyond the scope of this study. However, a brief discussion of the major groups — the Biafada, Basserel or Manjaco, Mandinka and Fulbe — is essential.[15]

A) *The Biafada*

The earliest European travelers' accounts indicate that the majority of the ethnic groups in Guinea-Bissau today were present in the fifteenth century. The Balant, Biafada, Bijagó, and Basserel or Manjaco occupied the coastal regions while the Mandinka and Fulbe had spread themselves over the savanna and upland regions of the interior.[16] The Biafada were probably the autochthonous population of the littoral. When the Portuguese arrived in the fifteenth century, the Biafada occupied about one-third of the land area of present-day Guinea-Bissau.[17] As we shall see, the Biafada lost most of their lands during the nineteenth century, as Fulbe pastoralists conquered them and drove many of them off their lands. Today, their numbers are quite small, and many Biafada have been assimilated into Mandinka society.[18]

By the sixteenth and seventeenth centuries, the Biafada controlled a significant portion of the coast. They gained a large portion of their territory by driving the aboriginal Bijagó toward the archipelago and the smaller islands off the coast. According to Padre Manuel Alvares, who lived among the Biafada at the beginning of the seventeenth century, "the lands populated by the Beafada were of the patrimony of the Bijagó people".[19] Lemos Coelho, writing later in the same century, was of the same mind:

> This caste of negros [Bijagó], ..., were conquered by a caste of negros called Bikafares, people who came from the interior, but they do not say from which part. And seeing their defeat, they [the Bijagó] fled in canoes, which they also called *almadias* and came to assume the obligation of these islands [Bijagós Islands].[20]

Even after the Biafada had driven the Bijagó off the mainland, the latter continued to return to their former lands for religious purposes and to harry the Biafada interlopers.

By the end of the seventeenth century, despite occasional forays by the Bijagó, the Biafada had imposed their hegemony. The Biafada controlled up to twenty-five different territories on the mainland. They occupied Bolama and the larger

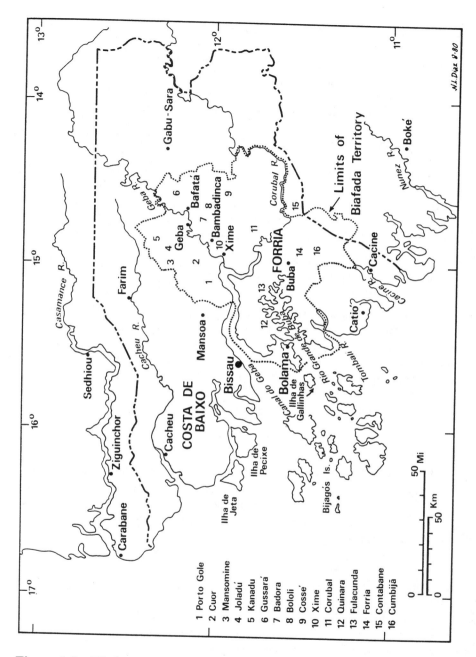

Figure 1.2   Biafada Territories

9

off-shore islands and exercised considerable influence over other coastal areas. For example, by the end of the period in question, the principal ruler of Bissau Island was obliged to receive his "barrette", the symbol of his royalty, from the Biafada paramount at Guinala.[21] Despite their influence on the coast, the Biafada recognized the suzerainty of the Mandinka state of Kaabu, and its ruler, the *Farim Cabo*. Biafada polities established agreements with Kaabu that reinforced their fealty to the latter state and insured peaceful coexistence throughout the seventeenth and eighteenth centuries.[22]

Biafada society, like neighboring ones, was a stratified agrarian society. It was no bucolic idyll. It included a noble class called *jagras*, who were the only members of society able to own land or hold political power. Portuguese observers in this period such as Alvares de Almada readily saw similarities between Biafada society and their own. However overdrawn such comparisons were, they identified the essential elements of the world of the Biafada:

> ... the lands belong to some *fidalgos*, to whom [other individuals] pay some taxes in the products that they have, as among us tithe; but as for the common people, they have neither lands nor inheritance.[23]

The institution of kingship existed, but the king's powers were limited. The king controlled the capital, and chiefs or notables, who were the king's subordinates, administered the outlying areas.[24] Moreover, among the Biafada, the hegemonic power of the king was further counterbalanced by popular symbolism in state ceremonies. For example, during the coronation ceremony, the king was bound and beaten in order, it is said, to remind him that he could not rule justly without experiencing punishment.[25]

B) *The Basserel or Manjaco*

Unlike the Biafada, the Manjaco were more removed from the tentative coastal centers of the Europeans and the new commercial activities, including slaving, that followed in their train. By the second quarter of the nineteenth century, however, many Manjaco settlements were swept into the illicit and rapacious current of the post-1807 Atlantic slave trade. By the 1860s enslavement had become an ironic port of entry into the world of Free Trade and "legitimate commerce" for thousands of Manjaco, many of whom later provided a large percentage of the ostensibly free labor force of the plantations or *feitorias* on the banks of the Senegambia's rivers.

The Manjaco live in the areas south of the Cacheu River and north of the Mansoa River, and on the islands of Jeta and Pecixe. They were part of a wider ethnic group which also includes the Brame and Papel.[26] "Manjaco" as a designation for a separate ethnic group only appeared in the eighteenth century. Philip Beaver, a British captain who established an agricultural colony on

Bolama Island, used the word to describe this coastal people. His confusion stemmed from the fact that he heard the word "Manjaco" in conversations. The Portuguese colonial presence — no doubt for fiscal purposes and administrative rationalization — assisted in the spread of the misnomer. As Bertrand Bocandé explained "Manjaco" means "say then", or "I tell you", and thus was a common phrase in the course of conversation.[27] The local people refer to themselves according to the *chão* or land that they come from, rather than by "Manjaco", Brame, or Papel. For example, people from Pecixe use Basiss, Ba-Ussis, Bussis (*ba* is the class prefix for the plural when referring to humans); those from Calequisse use Ba-Lequisse; and those from Caió use Ba-Hiú.[28] Hence Brame, Papel and Manjaco are all, in part, European caricatures of indigenous peoples.[29]

Like that of the Biafada, the world of the Manjaco, Brame and Papel was a hierarchical agrarian society, with several layers of government between local villages and principal centers of power. The paramount chieftain or king of Basserel ruled from the province of Calequisse. He also chose the rulers of the other two major provinces, Bula and Có — which the Portuguese called respectively Brame Grande and Brame Pequeno — and also the array of regional and territorial chiefs.[30] The king's field of selection for government officials was constrained by heredity and birth. Provincial and regional rulers were drawn from the upper aristocracy or *Batxatxa*, while territorial chiefs were selected from the lower aristocracy or *Babuçi*. The *Batxatxa* were chosen by an oracle of installment or *irã* at the king's capital in Calequisse.[31] Candidates awaited the king's pleasure without any kind of campaigning on their own behalf. On the other hand, *Babuçi* candidates for the territorial chieftaincies actively campaigned for future vacancies by presenting the king with gifts or adding to his largesse in some other way.[32]

Each regional and territorial ruler was assisted by a Council of Elders in resolving civil and administrative matters. However, regional rulers presided over numerous public ceremonies and indirectly adjudicated criminal cases. Moreover, they possessed certain exclusive rights and privileges, including the right to appropriate labor to work their agricultural lands and to build and repair their houses. They also received rent in kind for uncultivated lands and a portion of all the animals sacrificed at funerals.

In the various territories or *utxák*, the Council of Elders played a more explicit role in orienting the territorial ruler's administration, even though the council rarely convened as a body. Nevertheless, the members of the council, most of whom were *Batxatxa* aristocrats, had a voice in what went on in their area, and they readily expressed their opinions about the territorial ruler's decisions.

Each territory consisted of a number of settlements which were, in turn, composed of numerous extended households or *moranças*. Cousins, nieces, nephews and grandchildren could be members of a *morança*, even though

11

Manjaco society was and is a patriarchal society. Besides the aristocracy, Basserel or Manjaco society had three major professional divisions: a) peasants and professional craftsmen such as blacksmiths, weavers and potters; b) professional craftsmen with a public function (e.g. drummers, retainers of local notables, and messengers); and c) soldiers.[33]

The Manjaco economy centered on the cultivation of rice and millet. Peasants also hunted, fished, gathered various products such as salt and palm oil from the forest zones, and raised animals to supplement the cultivation of food crops. As early as the sixteenth century a fairly elaborate market system was in operation. Markets were held daily and alternated between the major settlements, which suggested a certain amount of regional economic specialization.[34]

By the seventeenth century, as the impact of the Atlantic trade began to be felt farther inland, the Manjaco peasantry also began to cultivate maize. Consequently, cultivation of peanuts and the intensification of slaving in the Manjaco country in the mid-nineteenth century were simultaneously the culmination of an earlier current of agrarian transformation and the commencement of a pattern of economic activity that would ultimately destroy much of the peasantry.

By the 1850s, by dint of slavery, other forms of economic compulsion, and the political strategies of their rulers, an increasing number of young men left the Manjaco country for other parts of the Senegambia and West Africa.[35] For example, many young men of Basserel and Boboe went to work for European traders on the coast in order to "acquire enough wealth to satisfy the King of Basserel".[36] They worked on Portuguese, French and English ships and traveled along the coast as well as back and forth to Europe. While the majority of these young men were unskilled laborers, many became ship builders, stevedores, and caulkers. Manjaco also migrated to the coastal forest to tap palm trees and cultivate the lands using their own "pam-pam" method of dry rice agriculture.[37] Moreover, once peanut production experienced a marked increase in the mid-nineteenth century, Manjaco came to dominate the labor force on the *feitorias*. In the latter part of the century, as these *feitorias* closed and peanut production declined, large numbers of Manjaco migrated north to the Casamance region of Senegal to cultivate peanuts, disappearing into the Mandinka population in the process.

C) *The Mandinka*

By the fifteenth century the Mandinka were pressing on the eastern border of the Senegambia in the area between the Gambia and Geba rivers. Some Mandinka groups left their homelands in Mali prior to Sundiata's consolidation of the Mali state in 1234. The majority, however, spread west in search of new lands during the latter thirteenth and fourteenth centuries, when Mali embarked upon a phase of imperial expansion.[38] Within a century of their initial occupation of large portions of Senegambia, the Mandinka transformed many of the large swamps of the interior into arable land by means of dikes, drainage ditches and artificial dams — techniques that their ancestors had used to tame large stretches of land adjacent to the Niger River. After the eighteenth century, however, Mandinka efforts to transform more swampland were frustrated by several overarching factors. There were no currents to help man-made diversions carry off stagnant swamp water, and the salinity of swamp water made wet rice cultivation difficult, if not impossible, south of the Cacheu River. Moreover, a dearth of fertilizer and the consequent dependence on crop rotation kept agricultural output low in the less well endowed regions of the south. This was a chronic problem for the West African cultivator as far south as the Akan country of modern day Ghana; hence the dependence on *lougan* or "slash and burn" agriculture. These arduous and lengthy journeys also undermined agricultural output. The astounding growth of the Atlantic slave trade in the eighteenth century further accentuated these disadvantages for Mandinka settlers south of the river.

Mandinka who settled north of the Cacheu River had another decided advantage over their kinsmen in the south as far as agriculture was concerned in the form of cattle and livestock. Livestock were a ready source of fertilizer and power and their explicit use in agricultural work meant that nubile Mandinka and indigenous women, over time, were relegated to a less autonomous role in the economy and in the quotidian affairs of village settlements. However, nubile women, who remained an important potential source of labor in spite of their lost autonomy, came to be appropriated by Mandinka warlords or *kafo-tio* and land chiefs or *sate-tio*. This appropriation was carried out directly or through secret societies. Biafada and Balant women in particular were assimilated to the culture of the victorious Mandinka, which meant that a dramatic and widespread transformation of patterns of inheritance and, more parenthetically, ownership of local means of production was effected. Consequently, by the end of the eighteenth century, Mandinka domination had sunk deep roots in the lands between the Cacheu and Gambia Rivers.

The Mandinka established several states in the Senegambia. On the eve of the nineteenth century, Kaabu was the most powerful of these Mandinka states.[39] Its ruler, the *Farim Cabo*, collected tributary payments from the other Mandinka states, and from the Biafada and Balant communities, as well as taxes from his own subjects. The *Farim Cabo*'s agents collected taxes and exercised the necessary force to garner village labor for war and large infrastructural purposes; but in one sense the central political authority was in fact carrying out political decisions that had been made in more centrifugal fashion in the villages and *kabilo* or territorial wards. Local leadership and partly visible forms of association such as age-grade and secret societies played an important role in decisions of state.

Mandinka society had three major divisions in the nineteenth century: freeborn (*foro* or *horo*); slaves (*dyo* or *jongo*); and artisans (*nyamalo*) and praise-singers (*jali* or *griot*). Among the freeborn, the extended, patriarchal family, called the *lu* was the base of society. The *lu* consisted of a male head, the *fa*, his wives and children, the children's wives and children, as well as the *fa*'s junior brothers and their families. War captives as well as other foreigners' dependents were often part of this family.[40] An extended family of three or four generations then, was more like a small lineage, which in turn belonged to a more extended lineage.

Mandinka settlements were usually large and contained several different lineages, which made up the territorial wards. Lineages living together in these settlements usually belonged to different clans. The stability of a given territorial ward therefore was reinforced by cross-cousin marriages in the patrilineal line and by the fact that women remained in their father's villages after they married.[41] Mass Mandinka conversion to Islam in the nineteenth century reinforced the male line of descent as the most powerful component of Mandinka identity.

Leadership at the village and territorial level was premised on a set of putative relationships to the land, with emphasis on the oldest claims to rights in land.[42] For example, the head of a given village or territorial ward was the patriarch of the oldest lineage. A group of elders, who served as the chief's advisors, checked his power, and without their approval, the chief was powerless. The elders were intimately involved in everything that the chief did, including settling disputes, collecting taxes, and recruiting labor; for in most instances, they were also members of his *kafo* or age group association.[43] Village chiefs generally made decisions at open trials which the public could attend. They held these trials at the *bentang*, a platform usually under a large *baobab* tree, which served as a central meeting place.[44] Even though the public did not make decisions on the cases being heard, their presence certainly influenced the moral climate in which the chief and his retainers made their decisions.

Another important social and political organization within Mandinka society was the *kafo* or age-group. The age-group associations of the villages and territories maintained religious shrines and public spaces and served as the police and military. In fact, the mobilization of men and, on occasion, the entire society for military service was the principal purpose of the age-group association.[45] Theoretically, the Mandinka warlords or *kafo-tio* were elected by the other members of the age-group; but, in fact, such a designation could not undermine the authority of the heads of the oldest lineages. Consequently, the territorial ruler also doubled as regional warlord.[46]

14

The freeborn community often held chattel and domestic slaves. Slave labor intervened in virtually every aspect of economic activity. However, chattel and domestic slaves possessed different rights and privileges within Mandinka society. Slaves who were captured in war or purchased were treated as private property. These slaves had few rights and very little hope of assimilation. On the other hand, slaves who had lived in the same community for at least two generations were considered pawn family members. Domestic slaves worked for their masters for a set number of days during the week and for themselves on others. Such slaves were able to purchase freedom for themselves and their children and, on occasion could amass large amounts of property and moveable wealth. They often held important positions within the state and were intermediaries for Mandinka aristocrats in their dealings with Europeans.[47] They often took Mandinka names. More importantly, their personal rights were protected and they "could not be sold elsewhere or killed without a public trial".[48]

The third caste in Mandinka society consisted of the artisans (*nyamalo*), namely blacksmiths, leatherworkers, potters, weavers, dyers, and goldsmiths, as well as the praise-singers (*jali* or *griot*). Like certain slaves, members of this caste also used their positions to acquire wealth. Each group in this caste played a role in the functioning and stability of the society. For example, the *jali* or *griot* was responsible for reciting the community's histories and traditions. Artisans not only manufactured items used by their community but often had ritual functions. For example, blacksmiths not only forged tools and weapons but also circumcised male adolescents who were deemed men at a certain point by the more senior age-group associations. Blood rituals designed to ward off the inadvertent pollution of people who required their services formed the practitioners of these professions into ostracized if not inferior castes with limited rights in terms of land ownership and political participation. The partial separation of precolonial artisans from village and territorial institutions of power meant that their families often kept their fields and livestock separate from those of a given village or ward.[49]

Like the majority of their neighbors, the Mandinka were primarily farmers. By the middle of the nineteenth century they were producing peanuts, sesame, and rice for commercial purposes, and maize, millet, manioc, and sweet potatoes for local consumption. Other vegetables were grown in smaller subsistence plots, which predictably, were the province of women. Men were responsible for the heavy labor, like clearing the land, and for cultivating maize, peanuts, manioc, and sweet potatoes; women cultivated rice, millet, cotton and vegetables. Mandinka men also raised livestock and hunted to supplement these food crops, while maintaining hegemonic control over external commercial activities such as collecting and marketing palm oil and rubber, for the latter activities were seen as logical extensions of hunting and foraging.[50]

15

D) *The Fulbe*

The Fulbe are part of an ethnic group found throughout West Africa, stretching from the Senegambia to Chad and south to Cameroon. Their language, Fulfulde, is part of the West Atlantic group of the Niger-Congo family of African languages.[51] Every group the Fulbe came in contact with called them something different. And this may have something to do with the varying nature of their relationships with more sedentary agricultural peoples; for the Fulbe were pastoralists when they first entered the Senegambia region. For example, the Mandinka called them Fula, while the Hausa and British called them Fulani. The Portuguese described them as Fulos, while the Wolof called them Poel — from which the French derived Peul. They call themselves Pullo or Fulbe.[52]

Like the Mandinka, the Fulbe originated in the grasslands east of Senegambia.[53] Some time between 1464 and 1512, under the leadership of one Temalá and his son, Coli Tenguêlá, the Fulbe streamed into the Mandinka occupied lands of the Senegambia. One of Temalá's subordinates, Dulo Demba, was the leader of the first group of Fulbe herdsmen to cross the Gambia River. Two centuries later, when Afro-Portuguese and Portuguese merchant adventurers wondered about their own initially unsuccessful efforts to establish permanent settlements south of the Gambia River, one of their number, André Dornelas, compared the Portuguese efforts to those of the Fulbe:

> ... He [Dulo Demba] entered into the kingdoms of the Mandingas, victorious, and arrived at the wide Gambia River, 150 leagues from the mouth. Seeing it wide and profound this Fulo king ... blocked the river, with a large multitude of stones which the Fulos emptied there.[54]

According to Dornelas, the Fulbe continued to move southward, until they finally arrived in the Biafada kingdom of Guinala. Consequently, the Biafada kingdoms united to repulse the Fulbe:

> There was a pitched battle, in which there were many deaths on both sides, because the Fulos were very skillful horsemen and good archers. Nevertheless, they [the Fulbe] were defeated, and their king Dulo Demba, killed ...[55]

Doubtless Dornelas's disquisition on the circumstances attending the arrival of the Fulbe in the Senegambia two centuries before was warped at crucial points; but in his mind, and those of his compatriots, the Fulbe occupation was something of a precedent for their own better equipped but abortive effort — an effort in which trade, slaving, war and diplomacy were merely different aspects of the same enterprise.

The arrival of the Fulbe had little effect on the political stability of the Mandinka state system, but it did result in large numbers of Fulbe settling in the Mandinka regions of the Senegambia. The pastoral Fulbe had no large scale political institutions at this point. Rather they lived within the various Mandinka states and paid tribute and taxes to their rulers.[56]

Between the seventeenth and the nineteenth centuries the number of Fulbe herdsmen in the Mandinka state of Kaabu rose markedly.[57] In return for tribute and taxes in kind, the Fulbe received limited rights in land and protection from their Mandinka overlords.[58] But by the second decade of the nineteenth century, relations between the Mandinka and Fulbe had begun to sour and the mounting tensions brought latent conflicts among the Fulbe themselves to the surface.

Three major groups existed among the Fulbe of the Senegambia: the "free" Fulbe or *Fulbe-ribê*, the Futa Fulbe of Futa Jallon and Futa Toro, and the "captive" Fulbe or *Fulbe-djiábê*. "Free" Fulbe and their herds were concentrated in Forria and in the Gabu region of Kaabu. The Futa-Fulbe, on the other hand, were grouped around Futa Jallon and Futa Toro and in many instances, had abandoned their herds to become merchants and Islamic clerics and scholars. The "captive" Fulbe consisted of domestic slaves or former domestic slaves of the Fulbe herdsmen of the north or the Fulbe merchants of the south.[59] The differentiation by group was less important than that by caste.

By the outset of the nineteenth century, well before their mass conversion to Islam, all Fulbe of the Senegambia were becoming increasingly sedentary. Because of their proximity to the Mandinka, the Fulbe took many of their cues about farming and settled life from these people. The Fulbe *galle* or compound, for example, was often composed of a group of brothers and their families under the control and direction of an elder. This elder, usually the oldest male member of the group, was the spokesman for the compound, judge for internal disputes, and distributor of the group's communal wealth.[60] In many ways he was not unlike the Mandinka *fa*. The compound also included people from outside the families of a group of brothers. Such persons were often without family connections of any sort. They became part of a given compound at the discretion of the elder.[61]

The Fulbe villages were somewhat autonomous at least in terms of internal affairs; but the compound was the building block of their autonomy. The oldest male descendant of the founding father was in charge at the village level. But his authority was not without important nuances and constraints:

> He had an assistant beside him and a council of notables who were the elders or heads of compounds. Their primary collective role was to preserve social order. Their powers were of mediation rather than of command, and the limits of their actions were severly restrained by Mandingue domination ...[62]

Fulbe villages were made up of a series of compounds. Members of the various compounds in a given village worked the communal fields that provided basic subsistence for the elders and notables.[63] The male and female members of a compound were divided into four age-group associations or *girde*. Both male and female components of the age-group association worked in common on a given task, without distinctions between gender or age. This rough and ready equality at work was mitigated, however, by the presence of household or domestic slaves among the Fulbe.[64]

Fulbe immigrants crossed into the Senegambia with household slaves. As in Mandinka society, these slaves had certain rights invested in their persons which customary law upheld. Once married, Fulbe household slaves were allowed to accumulate personal wealth and to work several days a week for themselves.[65] Of course, much of the Fulbe canon about the treatment of slaves was determined by whether a given slave had been born within a Fulbe compound or had been captured or purchased.[66] For the Fulbe readily recognized that even if a domestic slave had been born among them, he or she was also a descendant of the former "masters of the land", and was due certain courtesies and rights on that basis. The children of domestic slaves were entitled to the same education as the children of their masters; and if such slaves amassed enough wealth, they could purchase their freedom.

The plight of war captives and chattel slaves, *nangaabe* and *soodaabe*, was another matter. They were responsible for performing the heavy labor in the fields and other work that was deemed inappropriate for anyone within the moral condominium of the Fulbe compound.[67] Nor were their personal rights protected by any formal procedure. They were outcasts in every sense of the word, even though they were an integral part of the Fulbe division of labor. Along with craftsmen such as dyers, weavers, goldsmiths, blacksmiths and potters, who were marginalized because of their alleged supernatural powers, chattel slaves and war captives existed on the outer edge of the Fulbe world. Unlike craftsmen, however, chattel slaves were marginalized because they were without any power at all.[68]

The end of the "Imperialism of Free Trade" and the economic transformation of the Senegambia and Guinea

The first fifty years of the nineteenth century drastically changed the relations of power among and within the indigenous societies of the Senegambia. This transformation was enacted partly by the ravages of the Atlantic slave trade of the eighteenth century and partly by the uncertain portents that accompanied the spread of commercial capitalism beyond the confines of western Europe and the United States between the British suppression of the slave trade in 1807 and the end of the American Civil War in 1865.[69]   Also, the agency of the great economic and moral crusades of the nineteenth century — Free Trade and the abolition of slavery — changed dramatically once the representatives of various European states were drawn out of their coastal enclaves and into the interior of Africa. The indigenous peoples of the Senegambia and their rulers viewed European initiatives in this era, however lofty their ostensible motives, with circumspection and even hostility. Doubtless, the spread of Islam in the Senegambia greatly reinforced African skepticism. Nevertheless, Europeans, often in spite of themselves, tended to contradict their much vaunted apparent ideals by what they actually did.

If we were to turn to a prominent European figure in order to see how the major European powers perceived world affairs just before the Great Slump or Panic of 1873 brought the era of economic liberalism to its strangely ambiguous close, we could make no better choice than the Viscount Palmerston, the man who succeeded Castlereagh and Canning as British Foreign Minister in the 1840s, and who gave new meaning to the term "Imperialism of Free Trade".[70] Palmerston might have summed up world affairs from the 1848 revolutions to the end of the 1860s in this fashion: The only world affairs that mattered were those between the five European "great powers" — Great Britain, Russia, France, Austria and Prussia — whose conflicts might result in a major war. The only other state with sufficient guile and power to count, the United States, was negligible, since it had just experienced a major civil war and confined its interests to the two Americas and the Pacific; and no European power had active ambitions in the Americas other than economic ones — and these were the concerns of private businessmen and not governments.

In Palmerston's view Portugal and its constellation of coastal African enclaves, which were perceived as dubious redoubts against the predations of African and European slavers, formed part of a netherworld of states whose importance was determined by their relationship to one or all of the great powers at a given moment, or by their capacity to excite the passions of the latter countries' leaders by altering the global balance of power and material advantage. While Palmerston might not have explicitly assented to Alexander Herculano's conclusions about Portugal's population at midcentury — "In civilization we are two rungs below Turkey and about the same distance above the Hottentot ..." — his silence could have been taken as decorous agreement. Nevertheless, Palmerston was most concerned that Portugal maintain its national integrity, after the liberal revolution of 1836, just as he would be in the instance of Belgium in 1839. But the inconclusive triumph of liberalism among the governing circles of Portugal between 1836 and 1856 must have confirmed him in the former belief, even though the second generation of liberals under the leadership of Fontes de Mello did consolidate Portugal's national debt, return Portuguese currency and commercial paper to the money markets of London and Paris, and ease the reservations of the great powers about Portugal's commitment to end the slave trade.

After the 1860s, however, this view of *realpolitik* would be forsaken for a more nuanced one.[71] The march of industrialization increasingly made wealth and industrial capacity the decisive factors in international power; hence devaluing the relative standing of France and Russia, while greatly enhancing that of Prussia, soon to become Germany, and Great Britain.[72] Moreover, the emergence of Japan and the United States as independent powers, after the 1868 Meiji Restoration and the American Civil War of 1861-65, created the possibility of a truly global economic order for the first time in history.[73] The increasing tendency of European businessmen and governments to expand their activities to Africa, Asia, Latin America, and the Pacific islands greatly reinforced this possibility.[74] Consequently, the formal international power structure — which had been most exemplified by the Concert of Europe, the loose federation of nation-states and empires that was formed after the 1848 revolutions had destroyed the Holy Alliance — began to diverge from the real one, insofar as the major powers, including Japan and the United States, began to feel themselves unduly constrained by the rules of conduct stipulated by the Concert. Furthermore, international politics became more or less the preserve of those rapidly industrializing countries that jointly exercised monopoly over world trade, while continuing to engage in a vicious and ongoing round of economic competition among themselves.

The foundations of the new power structure were laid in the latter part of the 1860s and early 1870s. It was an era when the revolutionary aspects of an industrial economy and republican ideals were modified to suit the aspirations of the powerful. Economic liberalism and the European bourgeoisie appeared to have triumphed over aristocratic prerogatives and over the insistence of the lower classes that some of the precapitalist conventions designed to shield them from complete destitution be retained within the new capitalist order. However, the Franco-Prussian War of 1870 and the financial panic several years later exacerbated the fear of a general European war among observers of international affairs. Moreover, the economic troubles that followed the Great Slump of 1873, particularly the continued fall of prices through the 1880s and 1890s, attenuated the triumph of a liberal bourgeoisie in all the European countries and the United States. In the poorer countries of Europe, such as Portugal, this attenuation held up a liberal revolution in their legal structures and political institutions until well after the turn of the century.[75]

Meanwhile, from the mid-nineteenth century onwards, the volume of commodities from the Senegambia increased on world markets. But the actual manner in which items such as peanuts and coffee were produced became that much more anarchic. This anarchic character found its most paradoxical expression in the simultaneous existence of various forms of unfree labor along

20

side free labor in the European enclaves and among the more resilient African states. Yet the control that merchants, plantation owners, paramount chieftains, and other wealthy persons exercised over the slaves and free workers whose efforts engendered the commercial boom was merely formal and therefore highly contingent. As a result of the abject social condition of large portions of the peasant population and the spread of Islamic holy war and famine throughout the Senegambia, African and European rulers appeared to be losing momentum toward the end of the 1870s. Under these circumstances, it was virtually impossible for owners of significant forms of property to establish uniform criteria for the achievement of economies of scale in the agrarian states of the Senegambia and the coastal and riverain European enclaves. Because the emphasis was on output rather than the per capita productivity of labor — merchants everywhere were more or less agreed that commercial booms were temporary — African workers, whether slave or nominally free, were exhorted to produce peanuts and coffee under the most outmoded and brutal circumstances and on a scale unimaginable by the previous generation. For example, as late as the 1860s, African workers on plantations on the Pongo and Cacheu Rivers, whether they were enslaved or not, were often sold overseas along with the coffee or peanuts they produced.[76] The source of the brutality here was not only the increasing number of such instances, but the degree to which they breached the moral limits of economic exploitation as set down by African and Islamic tradition as well as by European liberalism. Consequently, merchants and planters were more or less agreed that the commercial boom of the 1860s and 1870s could not last.

This, of course, meant that legal and social relationships in the Senegambia during the period in question were simultaneously retrograde and unprecedented, since the labor needed to produce the new cash crops, whether it was in the persons of slaves or peasants, was not likely to be acquired on the basis of a contractual or customary relationship — relationships which would have countenanced the possibility of a dynamic rearrangement or transformation of the factors of production, at least in theory. On balance this did not mean that the kinds of labor forces in question did not change, or that there was no agency of change at all, but simply that such transformation was not compelled by the structural nature of the new economic organization or by any marked change in the economic expectations of the owners; for all manner of people who possessed power and wealth in the Senegambia were quite willing to combine the economic advantages that a market economy gave to employers with the cultural and political advantages of slaveowners and autocrats. When some kind of transformation did, in fact, take place, it was the result of moral outrage and the altered political contents of the aspirations of the workers themselves who, in turn, were chattel slaves, indentured servants, partly proletarianized peasants and the like. These changes in consciousness

21

were often wrought in highly particular local idioms, however, and in the Senegambia during the last half of the nineteenth century, Islam became the most powerful of revitalizing local idioms.

Notes

1. For more information on "legitimate commerce" see: A.G. Hopkins, *An Economic History of West Africa*, New York, Columbia University Press, 1973, pp. 125-35; Allan McPhee, *The Economic Revolution in British West Africa*, London, 1926; reprinted New York, 1970. See also: Boubacar Barry, *La Sénégambie du XVe au XIX Siècle — Traite Négrière, Islam e Conquête Coloniale*, Paris, Éditions L'Harmattan, 1988, pp. 190-94.

2. "Provincia da Guiné Portugueza (Abandono completo das suas fazendas agrícolas)", *As Colonias Portuguezas*, 5, 31 de dezembro 1887, p. 138.
   In Mandinka, "Forria" means "Free land". See: Alberto Xavier Teixeira de Barros, *Breves Apontamentos sobre a História do Forria*, Lisbon, Imprensa Nacional, 1896, p. 6. '
   For more information on cash crops other than peanuts, see AHU, Cabo Verde, Pasta 88: Governor General to Ministro e Secretário d'Estado dos Negócios da Marinha e Ultramar, 12 April 1878.

3. David Eltis, *Economic Growth and the Ending of the Transatlantic Slave Trade*, New York and Oxford, Oxford University Press, 1987, pp. 60-66.

4. Michael Watts, "Manufacturing Dissent: Culture and Production Politics in a Peasant Society", paper presented to the seminar "Political Economy and Popular Culture in Africa", Stanford University, Hoover Institution, 1989, p. 9.

5. For examples see: Odile Goerg, "Échanges, réseaux, marchés. L'impact colonial en Guineé mi-XIXè-1913", Thèse de 3è cycle, Paris-VII, 1981; Watts, "Manufacturing Dissent"; and Christian Roche, *Conquête et résistance des peuples de Casamance*, Dakar, Les Nouvelles Éditions Africaines, 1976.

6. Information on the geographical setting is from: Réné Pélissier, "Guinea-Bissau: Physical and Social Geography", in *Africa South of the Sahara 1978-79*, London, Europa Publications Lts., 1978, pp. 445-52; Raquel Soeiro de Brito, "Guiné, Cabo Verde e São Tomé e Principe: Alguns aspectos da terra e dos homens", in *Cabo Verde, Guiné, São Tomé e Principe*, Lisbon, Universidade Técnica-Instituto Superior de Ciências Sociais e Política Ultramarina, 1966, pp. 15-232; and A. Teixeira da Mota, *Guiné Portuguesa*, 2 vols., Lisbon, Agência Geral do Ultramar, 1954, 1,

pp. 3-105.

The name Portuguese Guinea is used throughout this study for the pre-1973 period. In discussions of the post-1973 period Guinea-Bissau is used. The Republic of Guinea (Conakry) is the contemporary name for French Guinea (Guinée Française).

7. Reuben K. Udo, *A Comprehensive Geography of West Africa*, New York, Africana Publishing Company, 1978, p. 171.

8. For more information on the river system see: Teixeira da Mota, *Guiné*, 1, pp. 57-73. Also: Réné Pélissier, "Guinea-Bissau", p. 445.

9. For more information on Balant agricultural techniques see: A. Teixeira da Mota, "Agricultura de Brames e Balanta vista através de fotografia aéres", *BCGP* 5, April 1950, pp. 131-72; and Teixeira da Mota, *Guiné*, 1, pp. 209-99.

10. Ernesto J. de Carvalho e Vasconcellos, *Guiné Portugueza: Estudo Elementar de Geografia Física, Económica e Política*, Lisbon, Tip. da Cooperativa Militar, 1917, p. 62.

11. Teixeira da Mota, *Guiné*, 1, pp. 43-55.

12. Brito, "Guiné, Cabo Verde", pp. 16-17.

13. Réné Pélissier, "Guinea-Bissau", p. 445.

14. Teixeira da Mota, *Guiné*, 1, pp. 184-5. For more information on the languages see: Joseph Harold Greenberg, *The Languages of Africa*, 3d ed., Bloomington, Indiana University Press, 1970; and Diedrich Westermann and M.A. Bryan, *The Languages of West Africa*, rev. ed., Folkestone and Landon, Dawsons of Pall Mall for the International African Institute, 1970.

15. For more information on ethnographic material generally see: Teixeira da Mota, *Guiné*; Marcelino Marques de Barros, "Guiné Portugueza: breve notícia sobre alguns usos, costumes, línguas e origens dos seus povos", *BSGL* 5, 1882, pp. 117-21; António Carreira, "Organização social e económica dos povos da Guiné Portuguesa", *BCGP* 16, October 1961, pp. 641-736; António J. Dias Dinis, "As tribos da Guiné Portuguesa na história", *Portugal em Africa*, 2nd ser., vols. 3 and 4; A. Teixeira da Mota, *Inquérito Ethnográfico*, Bissau, 1947; Landerset Simões, *Babel Negra*, Porto, 1935.

16. Alvares de Almada, "Tratado Breve dos Rios de Guiné do Cabo Verde", in *Monumenta Missionária Africana, Africa Ocidental*, ed. António Brásio, 2d ser., vol. 3, Lisbon, Agência Geral do Ultramar, 1964; Walter Rodney, *A History of the Upper Guinea Coast*, Oxford, Clarendon Press, 1970, p. 6; and Teixeira da Mota, *Guiné*, 1, pp. 141-42.

17. A. Teixeira da Mota, *Fulas e Beafadas no Rio Grande no Século XV (Achegas para a Ethnohistória da Africa Occidental)*, Argupamento de

Estudos de Cartografica Antiga, Série Separatas No. LX, Lisbon, Junta de Investigação do Ultramar, 1970, pp. 5-6; and Almada, "Tratado Breve", pp. 322-23.

18. A great deal of confusion surrounds the Biafada. As A. Teixeira da Mota explained, part of the confusion stems from the fact that the Mandinka called the Biafada "Djola". The Feulpe and Baiote, found in the Cacheu region are also called "Djola", however, as are their relatives in the Casamance region. At one time the assumption was that all were part of the same ethnic group. For Mandinka speakers "Djola" is a term applied to all littoral people. Further confusion about the Biafada resulted because many authors included them as part of the larger Mandinka family. The term Djola (Diola) and Dyula should not be confused. They refer to two completely different groups of people. See: Teixeira da Mota, *Guiné*, 1, pp. 150-51 and 171; and Westermann and Bryan, *Languages*, pp. 17 and 35.

19. A. Teixeira da Mota, "Actividade Marítima dos Bijagós nos Séculos XVI e XVII", in *Memoriam António Jorge Dias*, Lisbon, Instituto de Alta Cultura; Junta de Investigações Científicas do Ultramar, 1974, pp. 243-44.

20. Teixeira da Mota, "Actividade Marítima", p. 244.

21. Teixeira da Mota, "Actividade Marítima", p. 244.

22. A. Teixeira da Mota, "Un document nouveau pour l'histoire des Peuls au Sénégal pendant les XVème et XVIème siècles", *BCGP* 24, October 1969, p. 818; and Almada, "Tratado Breve", p. 327.

23. Almada, "Tratado Breve", p. 332.

24. Rodney, *Upper Guinea Coast*, pp. 29-30.

25. Rodney, *Upper Guinea Coast*, p. 30.

26. "The linguistic affinities, the actual practices of their funeral ceremonies, of their enthronement of kings, their superstitions, and a certain number of rules of common law existent and common to these tribes, constitute the principal basis for this assertion". António Carreira, *Vida Social dos Manjacos*, Centro de Estudos da Guiné Portuguesa, no. 1, Bissau, 1947, p. 24. See also: INIC, "Resposto ao Inquérito Ethnográfico elaborado pelo o Governo — Cacheu", p. 1.

27. Bertrand Bocandé, "Notes sur la Guinée Portugaise ou Senegambie Meridonale", *Bulletin de la Société de Geographie* (Paris), 3d ser., no. 11, mai et juin 1849, p. 340; Philip Beaver, *African Memoranda: Relative to an Attempt to Establish a British Settlement on the Island of Bulama*, London, C. and R. Baldwin, 1805.

According to António Carreira, "the word "manjaco" comes from "ma", which means *I* or *we*, and *dj*, which means "say" or "said" — and comes from *pe-dj*, where *pe* represents a class prefix — and *co*, a particle which reinforces the affirmative". See: António Carreira, "A etnonimia dos povos entre o Gambia e o estuario do Geba", *BCGP* 19, July 1964, p. 260.

28. Carreira, "Etnonimia", pp. 261-62.

29. Teixeira da Mota, *Guiné*, 1, p. 146. Other terms like "Bantu", "Kaffir", and "Frafra" have come into use in similar ways. Although the use of "Manjaco", "Brame", and "Papel" is a misnomer in some ways, the Portuguese internalized these terms and forced the local people to use them also. These terms appear in nineteenth and twentieth century written records. The local people use these terms when dealing with Europeans, and refer to their *chão* only with one another. Thus, in spite of the inaccuracies of the terms, I will use it as the nineteenth and twentieth century writers did and as the people themselves do now.

30. Teixeira da Mota, *Guiné*, 1, pp. 147, and 311-12; Carreira, *Vida Social*, pp. 25-6 and 113; *BOGP*, Annex 4, 30 de dezembro de 1911, p. 3; *BOGP*, Annex to no. 3, 1928, p. 18.

31. According to Teixeira da Mota, *irã* is a Crioulo word which refers to "dynamic spirits, their qualities and their symbols" within a given society. He goes on to explain that it was one of the first words Europeans learned when they arrived in the area. The local people quickly learned that they could avoid explaining certain religious ideas and beliefs by referring to them as *irã*. "Thus, whatever incomprehensible matter [existed in] the mind of the Europeans, automatically passes to being linked with *irã*". (Teixeira da Mota, *Guiné*, 1, pp. 244-45).

   The *Irã da reinança* refers to the *irã* associated with the King. Usually a shrine existed in honor of the *irã* where people went to perform certain rituals, offer presents or ask advice on important matters. (Carreira, *Vida Social*, pp. 113-15).

   For further information on the subject of *irã* see: Alexandre Barbosa, "Louvam-se irãs", *BCGP* 5, April 1950, pp. 257-62; Augusto J. Santos Lima, "O Iran", *BCGP* 2, January 1947, pp. 173-77; and Amadeu Nogueira, "O Irã na circunscrição de S. Domingos", *BCGP* 2, July 1947, pp. 711-16.

32. The ceremonies for choosing a successor to the King of Bassarel himself were elaborate. A large number of nobles under the direction of the *Kaãdjã*, the principal counsel to the king, made the selection. The only eligible contenders to the throne were the king's brothers, born of the same mother, and members of the *Batxatxa*. If the last king had no brothers who qualified, then his successor was chosen from among the sons of his mother's eldest junior sister. Once selected, the candidate had to be approved by the *Irã da reinança* and if the *Irã* agreed the candidate actually began his duties as king. For more information on Manjaco

society generally, see: Carreira, *Vida Social*, pp. 93-99 and 112-33.

33. Within each *utxák* were a number of *povoações* (settlements), whose chiefs were known as *Nãtximetu*. The *Baçie* chose the *Bãtximetu* from among those with a certain amount of capital at their disposal. The nominee usually paid a fixed amount in money, cattle, and *panos* (cloth). The exact amount varied from one area to another depending upon the local situation. The *Bãtximetu* had many of the same responsibilities as the *Baçie* but on a more local level. They were responsible for settling family disputes with their *povoação* as well as regulating relations between families. They were also entitled to extract a certain number of days' labor each year from the people of their *povoação*.

There were numerous *moranças*, the houses of one family head, usually located in one compound. The family, which was the basic social unit, consisted of the head of the household as well as his wife or wives and their children. Relatives were also incorporated into the *morança*, including nieces and nephews, cousins, grandchildren, and other members of the extended family. Manjaco society was and is a patriarchal society in which inheritance passes from brother to brother, rather than father to son, sometimes through the mother's line, but at other times through the father's line, depending upon the region. See: Carreira, *Vida Social*, pp. 99-112.

34. "The Manjaco of the Costa de Baixo are actually known as *Babok*, which means those who painfully walk from market to market. Such a system presupposes security and stability of territorial organization". See: Teixeira da Mota, *Guiné*, 1, pp. 312-13.

35. For more information on the Manjaco generally see: Edward Eric Gable, "Modern Manjaco: The Ethos of Power in a West African Society", Ph.D. dissertation, University of Virginia, 1990. For more information on the history and development of migration in the Senegambia region, see: Lucy Colvin, et.al., *The Uprooted of the Western Sahel: Migrants' Quest for Cash in the Senegambia*, New York, Praeger, 1980.

36. Bocandé, "Notes sur la Guinée Portugaise", p. 340.

37. The "pam-pam" method refers to the cultivation of unirrigated rice in areas where dense shrubs exist. For more information on this method, see: Teixeira da Mota, *Guiné*, 1, pp. 299-308.

38. Upon arrival in the Senegambia region and on the upper Guinea Coast, these Mandinka established several states including Braço, Kaabu, Niani, Wuli and Kantora. Kaabu emerged as the powerful state and its ruler, the *Farim Cabo*, received taxes not only from surrounding Mandinka states, but also from neighboring groups, including the Biafada and Balant. Kaabu in turn recognized Mali's supremacy until the latter's fall. Although

the Mandinka were not an indigenous group in Portuguese Guinea, once they established themselves there, they became a major power and played a dominant role in the economic, social and political life of the region. See: Teixeira da Mota, *Guiné*, 1, pp. 154-56 and B[akary] K. Sidibe, "The Story of Kaabu: Its Extent", paper presented to the Conference on Manding Studies, SOAS, London 1972, p. 9.

39. Other states included Niani, Braço, Wuli and Kantora.

40. António Carreira, *Mandingas da Guiné Portuguesa*, Centro de Estudos da Guiné Portuguesa, no. 4, Bissau, 1947, p. 68; Yves Person, *Samori — Une Revolution Dyula*, 3 vols., Dakar, IFAN, 1968-75, 1, pp. 54. For more information on the Mandinka see: Carelton T. Hodge, ed., *Papers on the Manding*, Bloomington, Indiana University Press, 1971; and *Manding — Focus on an African Civilization*, 3 vols., papers presented to the Conference on Manding Studies, SOAS, London, 1972.

41. "The stability of the Mandinka *kabilo* was reinforced by a preference for marriage by cross-cousins in the patrilineal line (marriage was forbidden between uterine cousins) and by virilocal rules of residence". Quinn, *Mandingo Kingdoms*, p. 12.

42. The village was the next level of unity above the family level. Yves Person explains that the village was "a territory and not a group of buildings". See: Person, *Samori*, 1, p. 57.

43. In the nineteenth century the *çatéu-tio* became known as the *alkali*. Once Islam was established the *alkali* shared power with the almamy, who was the religious leader of the village. Quinn, *Mandingo Kingdoms*, pp. 13-14; and Carreira, *Mandingas*, p. 68.

44. Carreira, *Mandingas*, p. 68; Quinn, *Mandingo Kingdoms*, pp. 13-14; and Person, *Samori*, 1, pp. 57-8.

45. Person, *Samori*, 1, pp. 64-72

46. Age-grades joined unattached members of society together and thus served as a unifying force. Persons, both male and female, initiated together were members of the same *kafo* and felt a binding commitment toward one another throughout their lives. Quinn, *Mandingo Kingdoms*, p. 14; and Curtin, *Economic Change*, pp. 36-7.

47. "[These] slaves could hold positions of considerable responsibility. In Wuli, the King's head slave collected the state's customs from European traders". Quinn, *Mandingo Kingdoms*, p. 16. See also: Curtin, *Economic Change*, pp. 36-37 and Leary, "Islam, Politics", p. 45.

48. Quinn, *Mandingo Kingdoms*, p. 16. For more information on slavery in Africa, see: Suzanne Miers and Igor Kopytoff, eds., *Slavery in Africa — Historical and Anthropological Perspectives*, Madison, University of Wisconsin Press, 1977; Claude Meillassoux, *L'esclavage en Afrique*

précoloniale, Paris, François Maspero, 1975; Walter Rodney, "African Slavery and other Forms of Social Oppression on the Upper Guinea Coast in the Context of the Atlantic Slave Trade", *JAH* 7, 1966, pp. 431-43; John Grace, *Domestic Slavery in West Africa: With Particular Reference to the Sierra Leone Protectorate, 1896-1927*, London, Frederick Muller Ltd., 1975; Allan G.B. Fisher and Humphrey J. Fisher, *Slavery and Muslim Society in Africa*, London, C. Hurst & Co., 1970; Suzanne Miers and Richard Roberts, eds., *The End of Slavery in Africa*, Madison, University of Wisconsin Press, 1988; Paul E. Lovejoy, *Transformations in Slavery — A History of Slavery in Africa*, Cambridge, Cambridge University Press, 1983; Claire Robertson and Martin Klein, eds., *Women and Slavery in Africa*, Madison, University of Wisconsin Press, 1983; Claude Meillassoux, *Anthropologie de l'esclavage: le ventre de fer et d'argent*, Paris, Presse Universitaire de France, 1986.

49. "... these distinctions operated to bar members of the inferior castes from certain economic and social privileges within the community such as ownership of land, political office and the tax revenues and benefits associated with holding office". Quinn, *Mandingo Kingdoms*, p. 16.

50. Carreira, *Mandingas*, pp. 128-46. Some Mande speakers, like the Dyula, were actively involved in long-distance commerce. As early as the ancient empire of Ghana, if not before, the Dyula began to establish themselves as traders and to develop an identity separate from the other Mande speakers. They adopted Islam earlier than other groups in West Africa, and thus were not only responsible for spreading goods, but also new political and religious ideas. The term Dyula comes from the Mande word *juula* which means trader. For more information on the Dyula and their role in West Africa see: Person, *Samori*, 1, pp. 95-122; Curtin, *Economic Change*, pp. 75-91; Robert R. Griffeth, "The Dyula Impact on the Peoples of the West Volta Region", in *Papers on the Manding*, ed. Carelton T. Hodge, Bloomington, Indiana University Press, 1971, pp. 167-81.

51. Greenberg, *Languages of Africa*, p. 8.

52. Curtin, *Economic Change*, pp. 18-22. For a more complete list of other terms used for Fulbe groups see: Thierno Diallo, *Les Institutions Politiques du Fouta Dyalon au XIXè Siècle*, Dakar, IFAN, 1972, p. 26.

53. For more information see: Teixeira da Mota, "Document nouveau", pp. 801-09 and 818-19. A complete analysis of Fulbe immigration is beyond the scope of this study, but clarification of the major issues is essential. Scholars once assumed that the Fulbe migrations were led by Coli Tenguêlá, who left the Songhai state after the Fulbe were defeated. He received credit for conquering Futa Jallon and Futa Toro. Recent evidence indicates that it is a mistake to attribute all of these conquests to a single

person, Coli Tenguêlá. It seems that two people were responsible for these migrations, Temalá and Coli Tenguêlá, father and son. Temalá ruled for forty-eight years (1464-1512) and his son, Coli Tenguêlá, ruled for twenty-five years (1512-1537). Furthermore, it was previously assumed that Temalá was the king of the Fulbe as well as the King of Tekrour. As Teixeira da Mota explains, however, Temalá, King of the Fulbe, and the King of Tekrour were two distinct people, confirming Tekrour only came under Fulbe hegemony under Coli Tenguêlá after 1512.

Another area of confusion, now clarified, involves the debate over the origin of Temalá's migration. The assumption was that Temalá left from either Futa Toro or Futa Jallon, because it was said that he came from "Futa". But a reexamination of the sources indicates that Temalá could have left from another region, known at that time as Futa Kingui. "Futa" is the term that the Fulbe applied to the areas they occupied. See: A. Teixeira da Mota, Introduction to *Fulas do Gabú* by José Mendes Moreira, Centro de Estudos da Guiné Portuguesa no. 6, Bissau, 1948, pp. 17-18; Rodney, *Upper Guinea Coast*, p. 11; Louis Tauxier, *Moeurs et Histoire des Peuls*, Paris, Payot, 1937, p. 95; and Jean Boulège, "La Sénégambie du milieu du XV siècle au debut du XVIIè siècle", Thèse du 3ème cycle, Faculté des Lettres et Sciences Humaines de l'Université de Paris, 1968, pp. 185-88.

54. André Dornelas, *Descrição da Guiné*, cited in Teixeira da Mota, "Document nouveau", p. 816.

55. Dornelas, *Descrição*, cited in Teixeira da Mota, "Document nouveau", p. 816.

56. Teixeira da Mota, *Guiné*, 1, p. 157.

57. Mendes Moreira, *Fulas*, p. 26 and Teixeira da Mota, *Guiné*, 1, pp. 273-74.

58. Paul Pélissier, *Les paysans du Sénégal: les civilisations agraires du Cayor à la Casamance*, St. Yrieix, 1966, p. 524; Bertrand Bocandé, "Notes sur la Guiné Portugaise ou Sénégambie Meridionale", *Bulletin de la Société de Geographie* (Paris), 3d ser., no. 12, juillet et aôut 1849, pp. 58-59.

59. Mendes Moreira, *Fulas*, p. 62 and Leary, "Islam, Politics", pp. 48-9. Clerics by necessity became Islamicists and scholars in as much as they sought to quickly assimilate the sounds of spoken Fulfulde to Arabic letters. This, in turn, gave rise to an important body of literature which stimulated the popular sentiment for the Islamic *jihad* of the nineteenth century. See: Richard Roberts, *Warriors, Merchants, and Traders*, pp. 84-87 and David Robinson, *The Holy War of Umar Tal: The Western Sudan in the Mid-Nineteenth Century*, Oxford, Clarendon Press, 1985, pp. 12-16.

60. Curtin, *Economic Change*, p. 31. See also: Paul Pélissier, *Paysans du Sénégal*, pp. 528-29.

61. Leary, "Islam, Politics", p. 49.

62. Leary, "Islam, Politics", p. 50.

63. The *galle* was also an economic unit responsible for organizing people for economic production, defense, communal help and social control. "Within the galle labour was communal, permitting allied or associated households to work together for the common good. In this system, each household within the galle worked in cooperation and conjunction with the others. Whether the relationship was based on family ties or mutual agreement, labour and responsibilities were shared and alternated among the families ..." (Leary, "Islam, Politics", p. 49). See also: Jean Girard, "De la communauté traditionelle à la collectivité moderne en Casamance", *Annales africaines*, 1963, pp. 139-40.

64. Diallo, *Institutions*, pp. 111-14. See also: Chaikhou Balde, "Les associations d'âge chez les Foulbe du Fouta Djalon", *BIFAN* 1, janvier 1939, pp. 89-109.

65. "Slaves could become wealthy within this society because, once married, they were allowed to work two out of seven days a week on their own account". (Leary, "Islam, Politics", p. 48).

66. Diallo explains that the "house" slaves "... were considered almost as members of the family of their master and were often treated as such. They were the former masters of the land. They could neither be the object of exchange nor sale". Diallo, *Institutions*, p. 107. See: L.J.B. Berenger-Feraud, *Les Peuplades de la Sénégambie: Histoire-Ethnographie-Moeurs et Coutumes, Legendes, etc.*, 1879, reprinted, Nendeln, Germany Kraus Reprint, 1973, p. 137.

67. Diallo, *Institutions*, pp. 107-08.

68. For more information on the various divisions in Fulbe society see: Diallo, *Institutions*, pp. 88-91 and 110. See also: Meillassoux, *Anthropologie de l'esclavage*.

69. E.J. Hobsbawm, *The Age of Capital, 1848-1875*, New York, Scribener, 1975; and E.J. Hobsbawm, *The Age of Empire, 1878-1914*, London, Weidenfeld and Nicolson, 1987.

70. See: George F.E. Rude, *Debate on Europe, 1815-1850*, New York, Harper and Row, 1972; Hobsbawm, *Age of Capital*; and Trevor Lloyd, "Africa and Hobson's Imperialism", *Past and Present*, no. 55, May 1972, pp. 130-53.

71. See: Ronald Robinson and John Gallagher, *Africa and the Victorians*, London, Macmillan; New York, St. Martin's Press, 1961. The principal defect of Robinson and Gallagher's thesis is that they do not sufficiently

understand or appreciate the magnitude of this transition.

72. See: Samuel Clark, "Nobility, Bourgeoisie and Industrial Revolution in Belgium", *Past and Present*, no. 105, November 1984, pp. 140-75.

73. See: Paul Kennedy, *The Rise and Fall of the Great Powers*, New York, Random House, 1987, pp. 245-49; Thomas C. Smith, *The Origins of Modern Japan*, Stanford, Stanford University Press, 1959.

74. V.G. Kiernan, *Imperialism and its Contradictions*, New York, Routledge, 1995; V.G. Kiernan, *History, Classes and Nation-States*, Cambridge, Polity Press; New York, Blackwell, 1988; Hobsbawm, *Age of Capital*; and Hobsbawm, *Age of Empire*.

75. Rondo Cameron, "A New View of European Industrialization", *Economic History Review*, 38, 1 (February) 1985, pp. 1-23; Charles Moraze, *The Triumph of the Middle Class*, London, Weidenfeld and Nicolson, 1966; Charles Moraze, *The Nineteenth Century, 1775-1905*, London, Allen and Unwin, 1976.

76. Barry, *La Sénégambie*.

2 Competition between Two States: Kaabu and Futa Jallon

Islam and the Mandinka aristocracy of Kaabu before 1831

By the nineteenth century Kaabu and Futa Jallon, the two most powerful states in the Senegambia, were intimately involved in the international commercial economy. Both tried to adjust to the new and unprecedented demands of the world market. Consequently, the transition from the slave trade to "legitimate commerce" directly affected the internal political institutions of both states. However, Futa Jallon, an Islamic state that was affected by the wave of revolutionary Islam coursing through West Africa during the nineteenth century, was more successful in weathering this commercial transition. In fact, Futa Jallon's attempts to extend its control over the Senegambia during the latter half of the nineteenth century, under the rubric of a revitalizing form of Islam, hastened Kaabu's decline.

Kaabu was founded during the last half of the thirteenth century, a generation or so after Sundjata transformed the various Mandinka and Malinké states in the back country of the Niger River into the most powerful state in the Western Sudan. The oral traditions of several peoples of West Africa claim that Tiramang Traoré, one of Sundjata's generals, wanted to conquer the grasslands of the Senegambia, including the Casamance region of present day Senegal — so much so that he threatened to commit suicide if Sundjata refused him permission to carry out the expedition. Emperor Sundjata granted Tiramang

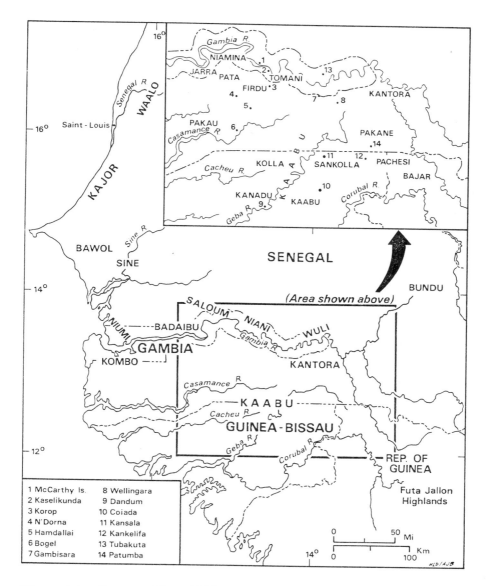

Figure 2.1   Senegambia c. 1880

Traoré permission to go, but before the expedition could leave a levy of horses had to be raised among Mali's vassals. Sundjata sent a detachment of soldiers and merchants to Jolof to acquire horses. The king of Jolof, ostensibly a subject of Sundjata, killed the entire expedition, except for one person who was sent back to inform Sundjata of the king of Jolof's unfavorable disposition. Sundjata was furious and sent Tiramang Traoré with a larger detachment of soldiers to conquer Jolof and also the other western lands. Traoré was successful, and Sundjata made him ruler of the new western provinces.[1]

After their formal military victory, the Mandinka aristocracy turned its attention to the subjugation of the indigenous peoples of the grasslands and littoral of the Senegambia — the Djola, Biafada, and Basserel or Manjaco. Large numbers of these people were driven or fled to the coastal areas that they occupy today. Others like the Biafada preferred to remain in their homelands, assimilating various aspects of Mandinka culture and outwardly accepting Mandinka rule. Farmers, hunters, merchants and religious leaders streamed into the newly conquered lands during subsequent centuries.[2]

Mandinka settlement in the Senegambia preceded the thirteenth century rise of Mali. Many early Mandinka settlers left the lands surrounding the headwaters of the Niger River in order to escape the cycle of drought and famine in that part of the Western Sudan where Sahelian scrubland meets the desert. Trade and the prospect of acquiring new sources of salt, iron, kola nuts, wild grasses, spices and fish also spurred Mandinka settlement. This process of gradual settlement and westward expansion continued until the end of the sixteenth century. It was only partly based on conquest.[3]

By the seventeenth century the Mandinka state of Kaabu and its aristocracy dominated the grasslands and littoral of the Senegambia. Europeans on the coast understood very little about the internal workings of Kaabu, but they knew it controlled much of the hinterland. European initiatives inevitably encountered Kaabu's formidable presence farther inland. If one can believe the accounts of the seventeenth century Portuguese merchant adventurers, Kaabu's power extended well beyond the northern bank of the Gambia River. Consider Teixeira da Mota's summary of Duarte Pacheco Pereira and Alvares de Almada:

> The chief of the territory of *Cabo*, or the *Farim Cabo*, was one of the most powerful rulers who exercised the power over the creeks of the river [the Gambia River] ...[4]

The first four kings of Kaabu were related to Tiramang Traoré and were responsible for building the state. The exact relationship of these four kings to Tiramang Traoré is not clear, but probably the first three were relatives through marriage, while the fourth was actually Tiramang's son.[5]

Ostensibly, after this point, all Mandinka princes or *nyancho* were descendants of Balaba, the autochthonous female oracle, and Tiramang Traoré's grandson.

Four daughters were produced from this union. These four daughters married into the ruling houses of the Mandinka provinces of Jimara, Saama, Pachana and distant Saloum.[6] The descendants of these four daughters, and those of their daughters, granddaughters, and so on, were *nyancho*. The female *nyancho* did not necessarily marry any one person but rather:

> ... adopted a prince or king as her husband until she grew tired of him or until it became expedient to leave him. All children born to any such union were given her surname — Sane or Mane — and not that of the father.[7]

Nyancho men who married non-*nyancho* women produced the generality of the Mandinka aristocracy or the *koringo*. A *koringo* could not become king but could sometimes attract a *nyancho* woman and thus produce *nyancho* children. Another group of *koringo* were those people who aligned themselves mostly through marriage to the ruling Sane or Mane families.[8] Although they were not *nyancho*, it was not unusual for *koringo* to become provincial rulers in one of the eight provinces of Kaabu.

Toward the end of the sixteenth century the Fulbe incursions into Futa Jallon and Kaabu compelled the Mandinka *Farim Cabo* to think of his fealty to the emperor of Mali as a mere formality. A definite pattern of succession to the office of *Farim Cabo* or King emerged. And while the entire Mandinka aristocracy was composed of about forty-four families, only those members of the aristocracy who traced their origins in the male line to Tiramang Traoré's grandson and Balaba and whose family name was either Mane or Sane could become king. Blood ties within the latter two houses of the aristocracy gave them a natural sense of unity. By the seventeenth century, in varying degrees and depending on the specific circumstances, the problems of the Houses of Mane and Sane came to be identified with the problems of Kaabu itself.[9] Yet the protracted nature of succession was only partly reflected in the alternative possession of kingship by these two collateral lineages; for only Mane and Sane families from the provinces of Jimara, Saama and Pachana could, in fact, rule — and all such rulers had to be *nyancho*.[10]

The *nyancho* believed that their stratum of the aristocracy possessed specific qualities, including courage and a sense of personal freedom, that were worthy of emulation by the general population and other Mandinka aristocrats:

> The *nyancho* were considered to be part spirit and part human. They were animists, never muslims, who scorned weakness among themselves and in others; death to them was better than defeat or the unthinkable brand of "Cowards". A *nyancho* would often kill himself rather than face the prospect of slavery, torture or any other form of humiliation, especially at the hands of those he considered his inferiors ... All men were equal to the extent that they were all born male. But they surpassed one another only to the extent that they surpassed in qualities of *keyaa* (manliness). There

35

was freedom to exercise these qualities by anyone to whom the possibilities existed. These possibilities were infinite for some, and for them public renown came easily; for others the possibilities were extremely limited and public renown was practically an impossibility. This can be illustrated by comparing a very brave slave warrior with a free man or a noble warrior. Whereas the noble warrior would publicly receive full credit for his valour, the slave was like a planet shining only when light reflected upon it — a slave could only shine in the reflected glory of his master. According to the dictates of Mandinka culture until he freed himself, a slave's valour would not receive public recognition. He was destined by his station to be always a follower, never a leader. The man who displayed *keyaa* was a *jarinteo*, a daring man, the man of courage. Even the man who dared do wicked things was admired as a *jarinteo*, if he did them with style.[11]

The *nyancho* ethic had three main principles: *keyaa* or manliness, *soninkeyaa* or filial piety, and *nganaya* or heroism. Manliness referred to "appropriate" treatment of social inferiors, bravery, courage, physical endurance, and a sense of forbearance. Only by exemplifying these qualities could a *nyancho* prove his worthiness. To demonstrate filial piety, the *nyancho* worshipped at various totemic ancestor shrines or *jalang*.[12] Each *nyancho* lineage possessed a shrine at which its issue were obliged to worship. The shrine varied depending upon the lineage; but it was usually a baobab or silk cotton tree with a corpse of the lineage's totemic animal — a snake or crocodile, for example — buried inside it. When a *nyancho* consulted an ancestral shrine he was obliged to make an offering of animals and palm wine.

The *nyancho* exhibited two other important features in their princely code of personal and aristocratic honor — horsemanship and *mansaya* or the disposition to rule. Both were indispensable. For the *nyancho* on horseback, fortified with sword, matchlock rifle, leather and chain mail jerkin and the conviction that no enemy could stand against him, "was the pride of his lineage and the whole elite class".[13] This martial spirit often compelled the *nyancho* to range far beyond his own province in search of moveable wealth. The ability to ride on horseback was essential. Booty collected in raids enabled the *nyancho* to provide for families and retainers.[14] It also reinforced their conception of power, along with the disdain that their stratum of the aristocracy displayed for the accumulation of personal wealth.

The *nyancho* dressed in a special fashion. They wore a hand woven cloth that was different from that of commoners, and the bulk of their clothing, livery, and sandals were orange colored. But it was *mansaya*, disposition to rule or rulership, that distinguished *nyancho* from the rest of Kaabu's subjects, including the lesser aristocracy. *Mansaya* was the *nyancho*'s quintessential attribute. Its possession meant license to live off the general populace. Its loss meant that a *nyancho* and his lineage forfeited prestige and respect, and lost all hopes of producing a *Farim Cabo*. "... Traveling in search of *mansaya*" became synonymous with *nyancho*.[15]

Nyancho were usually quiet and withdrawn, and rarely seen in public, except when they appeared in full regalia at the *Farim Cabo*'s court in Kansala and when they worshipped at their ancestral shrines. Their consumption of palm wine and, by the nineteenth century, stronger European spirits made them even more withdrawn and unpredictable.[16] But as long as *nyancho* worshipped at the ancestral shrines in full public view of Kaabu's subjects, and as long as princely excesses and acts of personal vengeance were mitigated by heroic deeds on behalf of the sovereign and the state, allegiance to the princes on the part of the lesser aristocracy was more or less assured. *Nyancho* ideology, however flamboyant, tended to support the state and the primacy of the *Farim Cabo* at Kansala. But by the nineteenth century that ideology was becoming skewed by the centrifugal effect of the new economic and political realities spreading from the Atlantic coast and from the Islamic redoubts along the Niger River. These new circumstances provoked a sharp crisis within the Mandinka aristocracy and among the princely aristocracy in particular — so much so that the princely ideal began to depart radically from the exigencies of rule. After 1830, for example, upon the accession of King Siibo, the *nyancho* were presented with choices that would have never occurred to their ancestors, or that would have translated to something just short of sedition.[17]

As mentioned earlier, only the provinces of Jimara, Saama, and Pachana supplied Kaabu with kings. The rulers of the remaining five provinces were *koringo* — even if they were *nyancho* by birth.[18] At the head of each province was a *faring mansa* or king's client, who the king installed at his court in Kansala. The *faring mansa* was usually a son, a relative or staunch supporter of the king. Although often a Sane or Mane, the provincial ruler could also be a local person, and not necessarily a Mandinka. While the king exercised very little direct supervision over the provincial rulers, they were obliged to send a large portion of the taxes and tribute they collected to Kansala.[19] They also raised a portion of Kaabu's armed forces from provincial levies.

Occasionally provincial rulers were obliged to demonstrate their loyalty to the sovereign with some spectacular display; but they were also obliged on a more consistent basis, to command the respect of the provincial population and local princes. The respect and compliance of the princes was indispensable, particularly if a given provincial ruler was not himself a prince. Otherwise the provincial ruler could be faced with a test of wills that could damage his ability to govern on behalf of the sovereign.[20] Even in instances where a given provincial ruler convinced the local *nyancho* that it would be unwise to openly contest his authority, the provincial administration would often grind to a halt for lack of princely involvement. Worse yet, were instances where princely aristocrats broke with their reclusive pattern and perversely interfered with the flow of local revenue to the sovereign at Kansala. The number of such instances increased markedly in the outlying provinces such as Badora, Tumanna, and Bajar during the reigns of Siibo and Jahnke Wali. For example, by 1831, princely disaffection with the central authority was so pervasive in Badora and Tumanna that King Siibo had already declared that no *nyancho* from these provinces should ever become *Farim Cabo*. On the eve of the Fulbe uprising and Kaabu's war with Futa Jallon in the 1860s disaffection among the *nyanchos* of the outlying provinces had turned into outright hostility.[21]

The king took care to surround himself with loyal subjects who carried out his wishes and who served as intermediaries between him and his people. Included among these loyal subjects was the king's *jali* or herald who relayed messages and orders to the provincial rulers and who served as the official keeper of family stories. The king also had non-Muslim and Muslim advisors, as well as a special smith and personal slaves. In addition to these professional men who performed specific duties for the king, provincial rulers and other officials were obliged to make periodic visits to Kansala. This kind of court etiquette, combined with the belief that the king was clairvoyant, buttressed the paternalistic image of the king as *mama* or "grandfather" of Kaabu's subjects. A king's greatness was judged by the number of people who frequented his court.[22]

Kaabu's location athwart a number of different trade routes linking the Atlantic Ocean with the cities and towns of the Western Sudan assured it an important place in both the overland and seafaring networks of international trade. As early as the sixteenth century, commercial traffic on the Geba, Cacheu, Casamance and Gambia Rivers came under Kaabu's political control. By the seventeenth and eighteenth centuries regular caravans from Kaabu were making their way to the cities and towns along the Niger River, as far north as Segu and perhaps Jenne. Certainly merchants from the northern entrepôts had occasion to visit Kaabu. By the nineteenth century Kaabu assisted in linking the products and initiatives of African merchants operating primarily in the transaharan area with those of European commercial houses and plantation owners in the European enclaves of St. Louis, Bathurst, Bolama Island, and on the Pongo River, until the military expansion of Islamic warrior-clerics such as Al-Hajj Umar Tal and others contested the appropriateness of such connections.[23]

Two major groups of merchants moved along Kaabu's commercial routes, Dyula traders and merchants and the African representatives of European commercial houses on the Atlantic coast. Both groups benefitted from Kaabu's stability and obeyed its king, providing him, in turn, with the goods he wanted in exchange for his protection. Ivory, hides, wax, camwood, raw cotton, tobacco, gold and slaves were exchanged for kola nuts, salt, iron bars, and copper rings, with cotton cloth serving as the main currency.[24] Until the second third of the nineteenth century Kaabu's rulers kept goods and merchants moving along routes that ran through a relatively peaceful and stable country.

The king, the provincial rulers and the princely aristocracy benefitted immensely from the state's active and *rentier* economic activities. The *nyancho*, in particular, while uninterested in amassing wealth for its own sake — "he would have sooner died than handle a hoe" — had to expropriate large amounts of wealth in the form of slaves, grain, cloth and livestock in order to maintain his own standard of living and that of his retainers.[25] And by the nineteenth century the international commercial economy had transformed the manner and rate of the *nyancho*'s expropriation of commoner wealth. The new economic circumstances, which began to assume a coherent form in the 1820s, compelled the local princes to make it possible for the free Mandinka peasantry to engage in a greater amount of self-exploitation by way of the production of cotton cloth and, to a lesser extent, tobacco. The princes also distributed war captives among the peasant households of a given province. In turn, these war captives assumed a greater role in the production of subsistence food crops such as dry rice, thus releasing the peasant man and woman to cultivate and weave cotton. Men and women often produced cotton cloth in common, without any palpable sexual division of labor.[26] Doubtless this kind of rearrangement of the productive capacities of Kaabu's population was more prevalent in the outlying provinces than in Saama, Pachana or Jimarra, where local princes were more likely to become king, but during the first half of the nineteenth century the demands of the *nyancho* in general seemed insatiable.[27]

The *Farim Cabo*, however wise or foolish, did not differ from other *nyancho* in this respect. For the continued domination of the king and Kaabu's entire aristocracy was based on the formal vertical political structure and also on the horizontal dispersion of the princes throughout the provinces and the tributary dependency of Saloum north of the Gambia River. As a result, the king's power was multi-layered. And the power of a given provincial ruler could be enhanced or checked by the extraterritorial surveillance of the king's putative cosanguinal kin. Such a system worked well enough as long as control over the domestic agricultural economy and tributary revenue were the principal basis of political power. But, once the demands of the Atlantic slave trade and international commerce began to overshadow and transform the domestic economy, many of Kaabu's political institutions became redundant.[28]

In the wake of political devolution the maintenance of the king's power and the primacy of his authority were often at the expense of the princely aristocracy in the outlying provinces. Moreover, many of the *nyancho* who became redundant in this period reacted with uncharacteristic indifference and hostility to the interests and prerogatives of the sovereign at Kansala. For example, not only did many *nyancho* of Badora and Tumanna, and perhaps those of Pachesi and Bajar as well, attempt to weigh in against the succession of Siibo to the throne in 1830, but many also converted to Islam in the years just before and just after Siibo's succession. Some of these *nyancho* concealed their conversion until the eve of the war with Futa Jallon in the 1860s. Others, like a number of local princes in Badora and Pachesi, publicly converted to Islam among their ancestral shrines at Bijini and Tambb Dibi, thus breaking definitively with the authority of the king and their ancestors.[29] Instead of marching to Kansala with the first outbreak of war and rebellion in the 1860s, they marched across the Gambia River to aid the Islamic marabouts or warrior-saints of the small Mandinka kingdom of Niumi during the Soninke-Marabout wars. The most illustrious of their number, Kelefa Sane, was killed in the fray of battle in the latter 1860s.[30]

During the reigns of Siibo and Jahnke Wali the responses of the princes in the outlying provinces to calls for assistance from the monarchy became, at best, desultory — even among those princes who, unlike those of Badora, protested their declining fortunes in a fashion more consistent with aristocratic traditions.[31] Their inaction during the war and rebellion of 1865-67 was particularly striking, for it deepened the rift within the princely aristocracy and set Mane against Sane even within the three core provinces of Kaabu.[32]

Before the nineteenth century, through appropriate political alliances and a series of judicious marriages, it was entirely possible for a *nyancho* from one of the least politically favored areas of Kaabu to see his issue become king within several generations — or even one generation under the most propitious circumstances.[33] But by the nineteenth century local princes were faced with the more immediate problems of their increasing redundancy and their declining political and economic fortunes. *Nyancho* lost ground to the lesser aristocracy and commoners in their attempt to maintain control of the state and formal political authority. Moreover, provincial rulers began exercising more power at the expense of the king in Kansala, particularly in the outlying areas. Smoldering feuds and rivalries among the princely and lesser aristocracy turned into interprovincial wars. For example, the *nyanchos* of Kantora attempted to foment a civil war; those of Sankolla and Tumanna fought against themselves as well as the *koringo* aristocracy; those of Wuropana and Jimara followed suit shortly before the death of Siibo.[34] As commoners and members of the lesser aristocracy replaced the local princes in positions of formal authority, Kaabu lost some of the vigorous eloquence of a state ruled by an aristocracy with a martial tradition. It was not that the *nyancho* ceased to believe in their code of honor; but throughout the nineteenth century, that code of honor became more an instrument of retaliation and personal revenge than a means for powerful self-assured men to govern themselves and others.

It was the Fulbe communities within Kaabu that increasingly felt the brunt of the vengeful impulses of the princes; for without the customary restraints that historical ties to the land provided, the Fulbe were the most vulnerable group of people in Kaabu. Fulbe and Mandinka traditions maintain that the Mandinka aristocracy extracted tribute and taxes from the Fulbe with increasing brutality and atrocious displays of force.[35] For example, by the nineteenth century, Mandinka overlords often expropriated Fulbe millet, the principal subsistence of the latter people, to cure tobacco.[36] Fulbe subjects who were thought to be assertive or uncommonly self-righteous were the targets of aristocratic vituperation. In some instances a Fulbe was wrapped in straw and set alight, and "... as he danced in pain, all the women and children would clap in time to his movements and sing ... until he fell or until they poured water on him".[37] The customary rights of Fulbe came to be routinely ignored in this period and many Fulbe compounds lived in a constant state of submission and terror.[38] But the crisis within Kaabu's aristocracy, which assumed its most dramatic form in the small-scale instances of civil war that followed Siibo's death in 1850, provided a window of opportunity for disgruntled and potentially insurgent Fulbe leadership inside Kaabu. By the 1860s the growing strength of the Fulbe state of Futa Jallon to the south, combined with the alacrity and zeal of the latter state's merchants and Muslim clerics, had flung that window wide open.

Futa Jallon and the Fulbe of Kaabu before 1850

By the eighteenth century, despite Islam's deep and ancient roots in the cities and towns of West Africa, the number of Muslims in the countryside of the Senegambia was still relatively small. Up to this point Muslims were content to be subjects of non-Muslim rulers. Even though such Muslims were often influential advisors to these rulers, they had limited political, economic and social rights. By the outset of the nineteenth century this situation had changed dramatically. Zealous Muslim clerics, under the protection of the partly clandestine Islamic brotherhoods, exhorted Muslims in both town and country to commit *heshira*, or to remove themselves from communities of non-believers. By the first decade of the nineteenth century these self-induced Muslim removals had become a revolutionary tide that threatened to engulf the institutions of non-Islamic states throughout West Africa. Islam became arguably the most important political force on the West African savannah, including that part of the savannah that stretched into the Senegambia. The overriding issue was adapting the political institutions of non-Muslim societies to those of Islam. The number of Islamic converts grew immensely; and by the 1830s and 1840s, in the Senegambian states of Futa Jallon, Futa Toro and Bundu, the initial call to *heshira* had been transformed into an onrushing Islamic revolution or *jihad*.[39]

Jihad is understood to mean a "striving for the cause of Allah" among Muslims. Such efforts have both an internal and external aspect. Consequently, *jihad* encompasses more than the mere eradication of unbelievers: Quite explicitly it calls for the establishment of an "Islamic moral order in society, for which a force of arms may be necessary, although warfare is not always a prerequisite".[40]

Islamic law stipulates that, under certain conditions, *jihad* is obligatory for believers. Muslims living in "pagan" lands had a clearly defined obligation to leave these lands (*heshira*) and to wage an unremitting war of words and aggressive force against unbelievers. The holy book of Islam, the *Koran*, laid down an uncompromising set of prescriptions for believers:

> Those who have believed and migrated and striven with their belongings and their persons in the cause of Allah, and those who have given them shelter and help, are friends one of another. But you are under no obligation towards those who have believed and have not migrated, until they migrate.[41]

Believers were required to "... declare [a] *jihad* upon those who refused to submit or to pay the tax of humiliation until all peoples were brought into the fold of Islam".[42] Believers had an obligation to:

> Fight in the cause of Allah against those who fight against you, but transgress not. Surely, Allah loves not the transgressors. Once they start the fighting, kill them wherever you meet them, and drive them out from where they have driven you out; for aggression is more heinous than killing.[43]

In the second half of the twelfth century the Dialonké, a people related to the Mandinka, left their home in Mali. Incessant conflicts with their neighbors, the Songhai, compelled them to move westward across the grasslands to the mountainous upland of Futa Jallon, in what is now the Republic of Guinea. This mountainous region is also the source of the Niger, Gambia and Rio Grande Rivers.[44] These attractive natural features drew successive waves of Dialonké farmers and Fulbe pastoralists into the area for well over six centuries. Gradually the Dialonké, and later the Fulbe, drove the autochthonous Baga farmers to the coastal regions.[45]

The Dialonké, like the Baga, were farmers. They lived in village settlements and their political organization centered on the elders of the oldest putative lineages to which a given family could belong. The absence of a centralized state was not a liability to settlements of farmers under peaceful conditions. In fact one could argue that the absence of coercive liens from distant rulers may have been a positive benefit to farmers. Moreover, Dialonké settlements did not exist in isolation from each other in spite of the relative autonomy of their economic organization.[46] Such contact was indispensable in a situation where vast geographical space threatened to vitiate human attempts to alter the natural environment.

From the fourteenth through seventeenth centuries Fulbe moved into Futa Jallon in search of new pastures for their herds. Up to the middle of the eighteenth century, the Dialonké farmers and Fulbe herdsmen were able to work out a mutually beneficial relationship. The Dialonké retained the most fertile lands and ceded the steepest uplands to the Fulbe. Just before the rainy season Fulbe herds came down from the highlands to graze on the grass and stubble left by the previous year's crop, and to provide the Dialonké's fields with a source of animal fertilizer. Dialonké and Fulbe also exchanged and bartered a portion of their surplus moveable wealth — Fulbe traded the products of their herds for those of Dialonké's fields.[47]

While there were fundamental differences between Dialonké and Fulbe, the arrival of recent Fulbe converts to Islam in Futa Jallon's highlands at the outset of the eighteenth century further exacerbated these differences. The brash intervention of the Europeans at the coast in the economies of hinterland African societies and the European demand for animal hides also served to transform the Fulbe predilection for animal husbandry into a distinct commercial advantage. Fulbe exportation of hides to the coast and to the towns farther east, along the Niger River, became a source of tension between Fulbe and Dialonké. The burgeoning enmity between the two communities was at least in part a consequence of the number of hides that were exported; for unlike Mandinka aristocrats in Kaabu, the Dialonké elders and chiefs had no institutional means of placing a lien or tax on Fulbe hides or slaughtered animals. Moreover, Fulbe herds were growing larger and pressing down on Dialonké lands at the base of the highlands well before the rainy season. Finally, the new markets for hides and the consequent accumulation of wealth in a number of Fulbe compounds released a marked number of Fulbe men from the drudgery of herding and subsistence cultivation. Some of these men became merchants and traders; others, by the commencement of the nineteenth century, entered the service of the new religion as *ulama* or Muslim religious teachers. Large merchant families such as the Diallo-Huilabe and the Qadiriyya and Tijaniyya Muslim brotherhoods dominated public life in these regions of Futa Jallon where Fulbe were greatly concentrated. None of the new men, whether they had converted to Islam or not, were inclined to continue with the existing arrangements between themselves and the Dialonké notables.[48]

Once a portion of the Fulbe in Futa Jallon came to understand some of the implications of their new economic position, the prospect of changing the political and social status of all Fulbe became that much greater. However, the control of valuable goods and wealth by a stratum other than the Fulbe clan heads and elders grated sharply against the prerogatives of Fulbe clan and compound leaders. Consequently, the emergence of indigenous Fulbe merchants and Islamic clerics was not initially sufficient to compel all Fulbe to embrace Islam or to break the bonds of subservient clientage to the Dialonké; moreover, by the eighteenth century a number of Dialonké and Mandinka speaking peoples had converted to Islam as well. All Muslims were forced to tolerate the injustices and the oppressive measures that the Dialonké elders and non-Muslim Fulbe imposed on them. Perhaps the most intolerable restriction, from the vantage point of the new converts, was their inability to pray. But as their numbers grew, particularly in the central and southern regions of Futa Jallon, Muslims began to pray openly and to teach from the *Koran* in public. These actions were in marked contrast to an earlier period, when newly arrived Muslims secretly practiced their religion and attempted to increase the number of converts through quiet persuasion. The non-Muslim Dialonké and Fulbe leadership displayed a wide range of responses to the new, more aggressive tack of Futa Jallon's Muslims:

> Some, scandalized by such an audacity, obliged the Muslims to gather up and take away the dirt on which they had prayed. Others full of admiration took pride in imitating them, others still were satisfied to keep their distance with a suspicion mixed with fear. Others finally, arrogant and contemptuous, overpowered them with their sarcasms, but their bantering arrogance revealed their fear.[49]

By the second decade of the eighteenth century the Muslim population of Futa Jallon, particularly Muslim Fulbe, no longer believed that the peaceful conversion of unbelievers was possible. In 1725 they declared a *jihad* against Futa Jallon's unbelievers and established a theocratic state. By the end of the eighteenth century this new state possessed two important centers of power — Timbo, which was established in the 1720s, and Labe, which was founded in the 1760s after several generations of protracted armed conflict with northern Dialonké chiefs and elders. But the bloodiest battles of the war were in the strongholds of non-Muslims Fulbe herdsmen in the central and southern regions.[50] Dialonké and Malinke notables in the south converted to Islam some time before the outset of the *jihad*. Those who refused to convert during the eighteenth century were reduced to servitude or forced to resettle in coastal swamps on the Atlantic coast.[51]

In the uncertain and warlike atmosphere of the eighteenth and nineteenth centuries, which was further exacerbated by the post 1820 resurgence of the slave trade south of the Gambia River and the spread of Islam, the benefits of the earlier Dialonké and Fulbe pattern of political organization fell away rapidly.[52] Both were rolled over by the military machine of the primarily Fulbe Islamic *jihad*. But the *jihad* in Futa Jallon was more than a communal ethnic conflict in Islamic drag; for as we have mentioned earlier, the Dialonké notables of the south were converted to Islam by a combination of diplomacy,

44

missionary work, and force well before the commencement of the *jihad*. Islamic courts were adjudicating communal conflicts in the south as early as the 1720s. On the other hand, some of the fiercest military conversions were reserved for the non-Muslim Fulbe herdsmen of central Futa Jallon. To be sure, Fulbe who converted to Islam played a principal role in the creation of the new theocratic state; but Muslim successes should be attributed more to the Islamic intervention in both Dialonké and Fulbe traditions and conventions.

In some instances this intervention, particularly juridical intervention, dramatically redefined the relationship of the individual to the collectivity in terms of matters such as marriage, inheritance and taxation, while simply imposing an Islamic gloss on others such as circumcision and burial. Islam chose to govern the habits of the active adult population of Futa Jallon over those of children and the dead.[53] In time the new Islamic state sought to recast the world of children and also that of the dead, but only after it was firmly in place.

For example, the men from Timbo and Labe — in short, the men from the towns — chronicled the conjuncture between religious conversion and the expansion of Fulbe herdsmen out of Futa Jallon's highlands, and the political groundswell that followed in the wake of these events during the eighteenth and nineteenth centuries. In some instances Islamic scholars and professional military men chose to sidestep the bucolic idiom of Fulbe herdsmen and Dialonké farmers in recording these experiences. Yet many of the *tarika* or official chronicles of this era were rendered in the Fulfulde language with Arabic script.[54] Many took decades to complete because they had to be submitted to a painstaking political distillation by way of the new Islamic courts, which, in turn, made them more palatable to merchants, soldiers, the *ulama* or religious teachers and state officials. Even though many of the latter people were less than a generation removed from the world of the herdsmen, with its hordes of flies, cow dung and excruciatingly dull and lonely hours, they had, in the course of the *jihads* of the eighteenth century, become different people.[55] Each chronicle and, more immediately, each decision by a Muslim *qadi* or judge became therefore a means to memorialize religious conversion and the profound social transformation that had swept over Fulbe communities from what is now northern Nigeria to the Atlantic Ocean, while simultaneously conferring a wider ranging legitimacy on the state structures that grew out of the process.[56]

The Islamic Fulbe state of Futa Jallon continued consolidating its power throughout the first two decades of the nineteenth century. Muslims continued to fight those who refused to convert to Islam, but after the eighteenth century such conflicts were sanctioned and encouraged by the state. But the new Islamic state realized that it had to do more than convert unbelievers; it had to establish its legitimacy among those of its subjects who were not yet Muslims.

The victors drew up a constitution and formed a confederation of nine provinces, which were, in part, military precincts. Each province was organized around a preexisting Fulbe community or *dîwal* — Timbo, Fode Hadji, Fougoumba, Kebali, Bauria, Labe, Timbi, Kollade and Koin.[57] The provincial rulers were military leaders or *alfas* as well as Islamic scholars and clerics. The provincial ruler of Timbo took the position of *Almamy* of Futa Jallon, the head of the confederation and the local army of the faithful. The institutionalization of the religious zeal expressed during the initial *jihads* brought the more explicit efforts at conversion to a close.

In theory the *Almamy*'s powers were somewhat limited. His principal duties were to coordinate and direct war against outsiders. Furthermore, whenever one of the lesser provincial rulers wanted to declare war or establish commercial relations outside of the confederation, he was obliged to consult with the *Almamy*. The *Almamy* also served as a mediator in solving problems among the different provinces and had a voice in the nomination of each provincial ruler.[58] The Council of Elders or *Kekung* provided a ballast for the power of a given *Almamy*, however, and could, under certain circumstances, countermand his decisions or depose him. Limiting the power of the *Almamy* or deposing him became an exceedingly difficult matter if he possessed the local charter or *wird* of one or both of the Islamic brotherhoods. The political intervention of these clandestine conclaves of learned men was, in some respects, the crowning achievement of the *jihads* of the eighteenth century and, in some ways, mitigated the constraints that the new state's institutions imposed upon its rulers.[59]

Under certain circumstances, however, the state Council of Elders could choose to ignore the institutional array of power and the constraints of Islamic erudition, opting instead to exercise their customary right to confine the *Almamy*'s prerogatives to military matters. During the reign of *Almamy* Sori, for example, from 1761 to 1784, the strength of the Council increased considerably — so much so that it wrested control of the Islamic courts from the erudite men of the Islamic brotherhoods and confiscated the property and wives of several provincial rulers.[60] Meanwhile *Almamy* Sori's army experienced numerous military victories; and tribute in the form of horses, cattle, rice, kola nuts, captives and gold flowed into his home province of Timbo. Given his greatly strengthened position, *Almamy* Sori determined to stanch the power of the Council by the end of the 1770s. When, in 1780, Sori was called before the Council on the basis of a series of fabricated charges, he responded by marching with his army to the Council's meeting place and summarily executing those of its members who opposed him. He then convened a council of notables and jurists, which no doubt contained members of the Council of Elders who had escaped execution, that confirmed him again as *Almamy*.[61]

Futa Jallon developed an elaborate economic system that allowed it to survive until the late 1890s. Initially, a significant portion of the state's economy depended upon the slave trade. In this trade, slaves as well as gold, hides, ivory and beeswax were sold on the coast for guns and gunpowder. Slaves also cultivated cotton and wove cotton cloth, which doubled as a commercial item and a regional currency throughout the Senegambia. Such slaves were often the by-products of the first wave of the Islamic holy wars of the previous century. By the nineteenth century, however, Fulbe rulers "prohibited the recruitment of slaves from within the boundaries of Futa Djalon", and thus embarked on wideranging campaigns in search of captives.[62] By the middle of the nineteenth century Futa Jallon's, and more specifically the province of Labe's, predilection for slave raiding threatened Kaabu's sovereignty as well as its position as the regional linchpin of intercontinental trade.[63]

A generation after the renewed regional impetus of the slave trade in the Senegambia in the 1820s the domestic economies of Futa Jallon and Kaabu were characterized by the cultivation of cotton and subsistence crops such as millet and rice, the raising of cattle, and the manufacture of cotton cloth and iron tools and weapons with a combination of slave and free peasant labor. Horses were of particular value, and one horse could be exchanged for ten chattel slaves or ten cows. This rate of exchange suggested that the price of chattel slaves in the hinterland economies of the Senegambia was falling in spite of the increased deployment of household and chattel slaves in all phases of economic activity.[64] On balance, then, the trend in slave prices in Futa Jallon and Kaabu appeared to follow the secular trend of slave prices in the overseas trade through the Atlantic.[65] The only exception to this apparent rule of thumb was the exchange of war captives among aristocratic Fulbe families, where chattel slaves circulated among the various lineages within a given *galle* or compound.[66]

The central paradox of the Senegambian economy at this juncture therefore was that the price of war captives was falling precipitously against the price of commercial products, particularly raw cotton and cotton cloth produced by free peasants and domestic slaves in Kaabu and Futa Jallon. This paradox was further aggravated by British merchants flooding local markets in the Senegambia with cotton cloth from Great Britain and India, and by the commercial production of coffee and peanuts by various forms of unfree and dependent labor in the coastal and riverain European enclaves.[67] The paradoxical economic situation worked to expose further the internal cracks within Kaabu's aristocracy and political institutions, while becoming the source of a powerful centrifugal political tendency among the provincial rulers in Futa Jallon.

The rapid growth of the army, Islamic courts and networks of aristocratic retainers put great stress on Futa Jallon's fiscal and commercial resources in the nineteenth century. As a result, Futa Jallon's ruling class felt compelled to resort to unconventional methods of acquiring revenue, while ratcheting up the level of taxation on the common farmer and herdsman.[68] The *Almamys* of the nineteenth century imposed unprecedented tax levies on Futa Jallon's population; but even more striking than the new taxes was the inclination of some *Almamys* and provincial rulers to commandeer the *zaaka*, a fund for the destitute and elderly that was distributed at the various mosques during Friday prayers. Doubtless this self-serving manipulation of an apparent expression of religious piety made for a certain amount of cynicism and disaffection among Futa Jallon's population, or so outside observers such as the English merchant James Watt surmised as early as 1794.[69]

The nineteenth century also saw a marked increase in the activities of the *yelle mansa*, irregular armed bands organized by the least favored sons and nephews of the *Almamy* and the provincial rulers — and often sponsored by the *Almamy* himself. These armed irregulars were often used to settle the *Almamy*'s personal scores. They engaged in conflicts that the regular army would have been reluctant to participate in because of the factional nature of the politics that underscored such conflicts. Moreover, these armed bands of retainers ranged beyond the state's borders, seizing captives and pillaging the countryside of neighboring Kaabu. Attacks by these bands occurred with alarming regularity after the 1840s, when the *Almamy*'s need for revenue for the state's infrastructure and slaves to work the domanial estates or *runde* of the ruling class became linked to a second wave of Islamic expansionism animated by the warrior-cleric Al-Hajj Umar Tal.

Al-Hajj Umar was no stranger to Futa Jallon's political intrigue. Umar spent five years of his early career as a religious scholar and teacher, from 1820 to 1825, at various mosques and religious schools in Futa Jallon's two largest provinces of Labe and Timbo. He, in fact, was an eyewitness to the bloody civil wars between the House of Soriya and that of Alfaya for control of the post of *Almamy*. He might have even been residing in the capital of Timbo in the bloody years of 1824 and 1825, when control of the capital seesawed back and forth between the armies of the two opposing forces. Umar saw past the bloody circumstances of this five year period, however, and came to the conclusion that the key to controlling the future course of Futa Jallon and the spread of Islam in the region was the ability to socialize and educate the children of the aristocracy.[70] It was to such an end that Al-Hajj Umar devoted much of his energy and substantial ability in the years between 1840 and 1846, from the town of Jegunko on the eastern edge of Futa Jallon, often with the blessings and protection of the reigning *Almamys*.[71]

Meanwhile the hit-and-run attacks of the *yelle mansa* on Kaabu's outlying provinces placed increasing pressure on the provincial rulers and the regular army of Futa Jallon to mobilize themselves for a full scale war with Kaabu, especially after many members of the *yelle mansa* bands began to perceive themselves as "holy warriors" or *talibé* rather than bandits.[72] Alfa Ibrahima of Labe was the first provincial ruler to experience some of the mounting pressure, since his was the largest province of Futa Jallon and was just adjacent to Kaabu's Badora and Tumanna provinces. Doubtless Ibrahima was apprised of the crisis within Kaabu's aristocracy, since one of its most palpable expressions was the embracing of Islam by a number of local Mandinka princes in the provinces closest to Labe such as Badora. Moreover, religious teachers and *jihadists* from Labe may have well been actively fanning the smoldering flames of aristocratic and Fulbe communal discontent in Kaabu as early as the succession crisis that accompanied Siibo's death in about 1850, just after the Umarian mission in Futa Jallon. Combined with Ibrahima's understanding of the political situation in Kaabu was his own disaffection from the *Almamy* at Timbo, as well as the growing importance of many of Labe's mosques and Islamic schools once the Umarian *jihad* began to gain momentum, even though Ibrahima himself displayed no explicit signs of disloyalty to the *Almamy* and did not thwart the movement of armed irregulars crossings his lands into Kaabu.[73]

In theory a provincial ruler needed permission from the *Almamy* before embarking on any war. The conquered lands then came under the *Almamy's* control, but, in fact, the *alfa* or provincial ruler became the real master of the conquered lands.[74] In 1850, when Alfa Ibrahima formally petitioned the Almamy to invade Kaabu, Fulbe forces under the control of the *Almamy* and also troops loyal to Alfa Ibrahima had engaged in a protracted series of military forays against Kaabu for almost a decade; for members of the Sane branch of the princely Mandinka aristocracy had readily enlisted the aid of Alfa Ibrahima and other Futa Jallon notables. Consequently, the columns of soldiers from Futa Jallon, who had previously confined themselves to raiding Kaabu's border provinces, became a force in the internal affairs of the latter state well before Alfa Ibrahima's choreographed petition to the *Almamy* at Timbo.[75] The more or less permanent intervention of soldiers from Futa Jallon in the affairs of Kaabu after Siibo's death emboldened the nascent leadership of the Fulbe communities inside Kaabu, while simultaneously providing a justification for the harsher policies exercised by the Mandinka ruling class against their Fulbe subjects.[76]

War, European commerce and the internal uprising of the Fulbe of Kaabu, 1847-1867

The decade after Siibo's death found the administrative influence of Kaabu disintegrating all along its western border. To be sure, the periodic raids of armed irregulars from Futa Jallon and the restiveness of Fulbe communities inside Kaabu further destabilized the border situation in the 1850s; but the raids and the consequent war between Futa Jallon and Kaabu were, in fact, the final plunge in a generation long slide — which, in turn, had been precipitated by a series of telling internal and external events. For example, in 1834 victorious liberal revolutionaries in Portugal imposed a new administrative framework on the Portuguese settlements in the Cape Verde Islands, and on those at Cacheu, Geba and Ziguinchor on the estuaries of Cacheu, Geba and Casamance Rivers in the Senegambia. These fragile redoubts of Portuguese influence were now declared to be military precincts, sub-precincts and warrant areas, which were to be staffed with a Governor-General, a governor, military prefects and warrant officers.[77]

This absurd new arrangement in the Portuguese enclaves in Senegambia was as ineffectual as it was bold; for liberal forces were still engaged in mopping up the last pockets of armed supporters of the previous regime in Lisbon. Moreover, there was no physical infrastructure for such an administrative reorganization. In fact, the extent of the Portuguese presence on the Senegambian mainland did not stretch beyond a handful of contentious clans of Luso-African merchants and their armed African and mulatto retainers. Representatives of these clans and however many armed volunteers they could muster at any given time came to fill the new positions and the new military dress uniforms, for which, of course, they had to pay, since the metropolitan government of Mousinho de Silvera was virtually bankrupt.[78] Consequently, up to this point, the Portuguese settlements existed at the pleasure of the *Farim Cabo* and more local African authorities, and because of the absence of a vigorous French presence in this particular part of the Senegambia. They would have continued to exist in this disingenuous manner during the latter part of the 1830s and 1840s — in spite of their new military uniforms — had it not been for the much exacerbated crisis among Kaabu's rulers and the consequent unrest of the Fulbe communities, and also the increased French commercial interests in the lands between the Pongo River and the Portuguese settlement at Ziguinchor.

The conflict between the French and the Portuguese in Kaabu's western periphery came to a head in mid March 1837, when a French war schooner, the *Aigle d'Or*, and its crew seized the Portuguese settlement of Ziguinchor and sealed off the estuary of the Casamance River for other European vessels operating in the Atlantic Ocean.[79] Immediately Francisco de Carvalho Alvarengo, Ziguinchor's Luso-African warrant officer and its most successful merchant, gathered up as many armed men as he could muster and hastily made his way southward to Cacheu, to inform the ailing governor Honório Barreto, his maternal cousin, of the French encroachment. During Alvarengo's absence the French built a number of fortifications upriver from Ziguinchor at Sedhiou (Seju) and encouraged French merchant-planters to settle in the vicinity.[80]

Honório Barreto was 24 years old at the time of the French seizure of Ziguinchor. He had been a student in Portugal in the latter 1820s, when memories of the French occupation of Portugal during the Peninsular War were still fresh in the minds of the Portuguese people, and when the rule of the infant Queen Maria was insured by war ships of the British Vice Admiralty docked in the harbor of Oporto.[81] In 1831, three years before Barreto became *provedor* or warrant officer of Cacheu, a French fleet blockaded the Tagus River, effectively cutting Lisbon off from the outside world while threatening to reduce an eighth of the city's buildings to rubble. Some version of all of these events must have been churning around in Barreto's mind as he wrote a stinging rebuke of the French actions, replete with fulsome exhortations about the sanctity of Portuguese national sovereignty, and attached it to a formal plea for military assistance from the British resident governor at Bathurst in the Gambia. The British — and the Portuguese Governor-General — chose not to answer the plea for help; and Barreto was left to stew in his own recriminations while French planters and slaves settled in among the Mandinka peasants of Ziguinchor and Sedhiou.

Despite the ignorant dismissals of Honório Barreto's observations about the Portuguese position in the Senegambia in metropolitan circles, largely because he was an *homen de cor*, or "person of color", Barreto was, above all, a Portuguese patriot — and remained so throughout his twenty-six year tenure as a government official. Since he was also an African, his devotion to Portugal was a distinct disadvantage in an African setting. And since many Africans were well aware of Portugal's weak position in the Senegambia in relation to France, and even to a declining Kaabu, Barreto's Portuguese patriotism made him look doubly foolish to potential African colonial subjects. As early as the mid 1840s, Barreto's writings reveal that he, more than anyone, was painfully aware of his own liabilities, and also those of Portugal:

> It is quite easy for some functionary, entombed in his office and without any purpose other than maintaining his job, to invent the facts, — to the point of construing a virtual paradise on earth, for which only praises are due. To this end, they cast aspersion on my abilities: they give orders that they know will never be executed; then the said orders are rushed to the metropolitan government, which determines, or if it deems necessary to determine, whether such orders are being carried out. To live in Portuguese Senegambia is to live without any security. At this very moment its inhabitants are harried by the native rabble. They are attacked and killed with impunity, while in Lisbon the Government Gazette claims that order reigns in all the Portuguese possessions and that they are flourishing.[82]

As Barreto bemoaned the indifference of metropolitan Portuguese officials, Al-Hajj Umar, whose Islamic missionary efforts had taken him by then into Forria, the no man's land between Kaabu and Futa Jallon, was exhorting all Fulbe and Muslims in Kaabu to leave the northern and eastern provinces and come south to Geba and Forria. In short, he commanded them to commit *heshira*, to remove themselves from the community of unbelievers. In the midst of Umar's call to *heshira*, the mass conversion of the Fulbe of Kaabu to Islam began.[83]

Before Al-Hajj Umar's arrival in Forria in the latter 1840s only a small number of Fulbe in Kaabu had converted to Islam. Even among the *Fulbe-ribê* or "Free-Fulbe", who had come from Masina during the first waves of Islamic proselytization beyond the cities and towns of West Africa in the eighteenth century, the number of Muslims was well below nineteenth century figures. In fact, as shown earlier, many Mandinka, particularly in the outlying provinces of Kaabu, had converted to Islam before the commencement of the mass conversions of the mid-nineteenth century.[84] As a result, at least initially, Umar sought to pitch his message to a variety of people in the Senegambia. He claimed that the thirteenth century of Islam (1785-1885) was a special time,"... when Muslims expected revival, turmoil and possible final judgement ..."[85] Most of the Mandinka princes, to whom Umar first addressed his appeal, were incredulous, with the possible exception of the *nyancho* Sama Koli Sane, who had already converted to Islam and who, for his own reasons, wanted to overthrow the reigning *Farim Cabo*, Jahnke Wali. Doubtless even he was skeptical of the more apocalyptic features of Umar's message.[86] But for many Fulbe of Forria and Geba, who had experienced an increasing catalogue of abuses at the hands of Kaabu's officials, and at those of the Mandinka princes in particular, the apocalypse was already at hand.

The Fulbe response to Umar's message north of the Geba River was not so unilateral. Before the 1850 battle of Berekolong, between Kaabu and Futa Jallon, only Fulbe from Kanadu responded to Umar's call for a mass exodus from the more central provinces of Kaabu. But, even Fulbe from Kanadu came south for a variety of reasons, the rockiness of Kanadu's soil being perhaps the most immediate one.[87] Despite increasing abuse at the hands of Mandinka overlords, there were a number of countervailing reasons for many Fulbe to ignore Umar's message. A number of Fulbe communities in Kaabu had, by this time, ceased to be redoubts of herdsmen engaged in some subsistence cultivation and had become fixed peasant villages. Well before the intersection of the wars between Kaabu and Futa Jallon and the Fulbe uprising in Kaabu, many Fulbe had become peasant farmers who paid their taxes to their Mandinka rulers with millet and *fortaro*, a particular kind of cotton cloth made by the more settled Fulbe communities. Moreover, Fulbe smiths made hoes and rifles, which were called *longko* and fashioned after the European flintlock rifle;

during the uncertain times of the 1840s and 1850s, Fulbe peasant farmers often thought it expedient to go to their fields carrying both. In other words, up to the beginning of the 1850s, many of these transformed Fulbe communities, which were composed largely of *Fulbe-djiábê* or former "slave Fulbe" believed that they had sufficient resources to defend themselves against the grossest forms of abuse, and that they were not in need of external assistance.[88] The raids of the *yelle mansa* on Kaabu's outlying provinces and the peripatetic Umar disabused a growing number of them, particularly those in the vicinity of Forria, of this belief.

A month before Ramadan in 1846 or 1847, Al-Hajj Umar arrived in Jalaba, just south of the Luso-African settlement at Geba. Tradition claims that the Fulbe peasants around Geba did not oppose the presence of the *cristões* or "Christians" at Geba because they felt that such people might be a counterwieght to the excesses of the local Mandinka princes.[89] This was, in fact, not wrong, since the European merchants at Geba did sell locally produced and imported gunpowder. Moreover, by 1850, the number of *nyancho* between Geba and Sankolla without any formal means to support their entourages had risen to five.[90] Nevertheless, Umar's presence was not a welcome one — perhaps because he had tried initially to convert the local Mandinka princes.[91] After failing to convince the Mandinka overlords and alienating many of the Fulbe in the vicinity of Jalaba, Umar was relegated to the margins of the Fulbe settlement, and it was there that he encountered Molo Eggue.

Molo was the son of Malal, a man from Wasulun. A Fulbe noble, Samba Eggue, bought Molo's paternal grandfather; but eventually, Molo's father was manumitted. Molo's father married a woman from his former master's family — a woman who was "blemished" or who no one else wanted. A *Fulbe-djiábê* without close connections to his mother's family, Molo was without a definite place in the world of the Fulbe of Kaabu in his own right. He was obliged to make a place for himself. He became an animal hunter.[92] Hunting was an important skill in mid-nineteenth century Senegambia. Hunters provided a measure of protection to a given settlement of peasant farmers by killing dangerous animals that threatened their families and their fields. The more adept hunters often had a number of loyal apprentices. In times of war these apprentices and their masters might be conscripted as auxiliary soldiers, for their knowledge of a specific terrain could make the difference between winning and losing a battle or a skirmish. Moreover, hunters often supplied local notables with valuable economic resources such as rare animal skins and ivory. What Molo might have lacked in inherent status therefore was, in some ways, made up for by his reputation as a great hunter.[93] Consequently, after his initiative among the Mandinka princes failed, Umar could not have made a better choice for conversion than Molo Eggue.

53

Molo's career as a hunter did not end abruptly after his encounter with Al-Hajj Umar; for while he himself was proof of the growing self-sufficiency of the Fulbe communities in Kaabu's more removed provinces, it was not clear that this self-sufficiency could translate into an uprising against Mandinka overlords. Nor was it certain that Umar initially expressed a desire to foment rebellion, much less to put Molo at the head of one. If Umar did express such a desire, it must have been in a veiled and disingenuous manner, replete with allusions to the more apocalyptic passages of the *Koran* and the arcane glosses on such passages that Umar himself and other members of his Tijaniyya Islamic brotherhood had written; for it was not until 1852, some six years after his encounter with Molo, that Umar declared *jihad* on all unbelievers in the Senegambia.

But some of the intensity of Molo's relationship with Umar must have been present at the very outset of the encounter; for Molo recounted to his contemporaries that on the day before he met Al-Hajj Umar he dreamed that his compound was on fire. Molo's wife, Kumba Wude, claimed that while Umar was in their compound the goats did not disturb her store of pounded millet, suggesting, in turn, that Umar had the power to make even the most ravenous of animals observe Ramadan.[94] Molo was convinced of Umar's greatness, and on the basis of this personal conviction he converted to Islam. Whether his conversion compelled him to project himself as a leader of the Fulbe in Kaabu is another matter; but certainly he could not have ignored the growing number of Fulbe streaming into the vicinity of Geba and Forria from the north in this period.

Tradition holds that Umar took leave of Molo and Kumba Wude soon after he converted them. Molo asked Umar to pray for him and his wife, and to listen to two requests. The first was that Umar enlist divine intervention in reducing the hardships that the Fulbe endured under the Mandinka; for, in Molo's estimate, the Fulbe were merely the passive agency of their rulers' desires. The second request was of a more immediate and personal nature — Molo and Kumba Wude wanted a child. Umar listened to these requests and promised to pray for them. He told Molo Eggue that "this land's bravery, its popularity, its wealth will all be in your hands. If you do not say anything, it will not happen ..."[95] Umar went on to explain that Allah had placed Kaabu's fate in Molo's hands. He instructed Molo to keep a sheep in his compound among his goats, and that Musa should declare war on Kaabu on the day that the sheep was taken and slaughtered by Mandinka officials. Umar also predicted that Molo and Kumba Wude would have a son, and he should be named Musa, a diminutive of the Prophet Muhammad's name.[96]

After making these predictions Al-Hajj Umar made his way to Futa Jallon. As custom dictated, Molo Eggue offered to take his guest part of the way. Since Umar had to travel through Geba, Molo decided to show him his base of operations there. Geba and Jangjanbureh (Georgetown) were two of the main centers where Molo Eggue took his skins and ivory to trade for European goods and gunpowder.[97] When they arrived in Geba, the marabout told Molo Eggue that when the war against the Mandinka finally began, he should buy his gunpowder from the Luso-African merchants at Geba.[98] After several days they moved on towards the Corubal River, where the marabout left Molo Eggue.

On the eve of the 1850 Battle of Berekolong, Molo Eggue perceived that war between Futa Jallon and Kaabu was imminent. He began to build up a constituency broader than his own group of apprentices, while secretly attempting to enlist the assistance of the most notable Fulbe elders in attempting to foment a Fulbe uprising behind the formal battle lines. The elders feared that any actions taken against the Mandinka would lead to the annihilation of the Fulbe. Consequently, they refused to help Molo and threatened to turn him over to the local princes if he approached them again.[99]

As a result of his unsatisfactory encounters with the Fulbe elders, Molo was obliged initially to recruit his forces among Fulbe, Mandinka and northern Tukolor who had already converted to Islam. However, it is not clear that Molo's forces directly participated in the Battle of Berekolong, even though their assistance after the initial victory would have been crucial for logistical purposes. Just before 1850 he sent Mamadu Samba to Saama and one Yaronding to Pachana to raise a guerilla army in the very heart of Kaabu.[100] Meanwhile, Demba Marem in Forria, an unknown much like Molo Eggue, had raised a guerilla force that engaged in joint operations with Molo Eggue's men. Demba, however, was also in direct communication with Alfa Ibrahima of Labe.[101] Molo himself began a kind of guerilla war at Bijini in 1854, several years after Berekolong and well after Al-Hajj Umar's declaration of *jihad*. But even though Molo aligned himself with Futa Jallon, once Al-Hajj Umar declared *jihad* in 1852 from his fortress town of Dingiray in southeastern Futa Jallon, Molo was able to retain some degree of autonomy. Some time after Umar's 1852 declaration, Molo received the title of *alfa* or governor.[102] Molo and his lieutenants and confederates became a third force in the war between Kaabu and Futa Jallon.[103]

The Battle of Berekolong in Sankolla was the first major battle between Kaabu and Futa Jallon. Having received the *Almamy*'s permission to engage in the campaign Alfa Ibrahima believed that Berekolong, situated in the very center of Kaabu's provinces and fortified with a series of turreted walls, was "the key which one had to possess if one wanted to occupy Kaabu".[104] Nhalem Sonko, the *nyancho mansa* or provincial ruler of Sankolla, governed from Berekolong. Nhalem had come from a long line of local princes and his military exploits were known even in Futa Jallon. His personal bravery contributed to the mystique surrounding Berekolong. Alfa Ibrahima presented Nhalem Sonko with an ultimatum of either conversion to Islam or war. Nhalem chose the only acceptable option for a *nyancho*, namely that he and his people "preferred death with arms in hand, to accepting the domination of the Almamy and his god".[105] The war began.

Alfa Ibrahima's troops advanced against the fortress at Berekolong in September 1850, toward the end of the rainy season when the supply of food in towns would have been at its lowest. Even so, Ibrahima's army engaged in heavy fighting for five days. Portuguese accounts claimed that Alfa Ibrahima died in the fighting. But evidence from indigenous and French sources, as well as recent monographic work, demonstrate that Ibrahima left immediately after the fighting. He took the *nyancho* princess Kumancha Sane with him as part of the spoils of war. Later she bore him a son Yaya, who, as we shall see, became *alfa* of Labe and sworn enemy of further European encroachment in the Senegambia.[106]

Despite the dramatic flourish of its beginnings, the war between Futa Jallon and Kaabu dragged on for another seventeen years. There were a number of reasons for the war's protracted nature. For example, the fact that Al-Hajj Umar did not declare *jihad* until 1852 made Futa Jallon's victory at Berekolong a somewhat hollow one, particularly since the momentum of the war rested with the military forces that were auxiliary to Alfa Ibrahima's 6,000 men — the bands of *yelle mansa* and the irregular forces of Fulbe from Kaabu itself under the leadership of men such as Molo Eggue and Demba Marem. Both groups, more than the regular army of Futa Jallon, saw themselves as *talibé*, or holy warriors, directly inspired by the fiery, apocalyptic preaching of Al-Hajj Umar, who, despite his great influence, held no office of state in Futa Jallon. Also, handing over Berekolong and other occupied areas in Forria to the descendants of former slaves was doubtless a source of great consternation to Alfa Ibrahima and his subordinate military commanders. Yet they were not in a position to do otherwise. The actual prosecution of the war was held up by the tension between the enthusiasm of the military leaders of the irregulars and the more conservative position of the rulers of Futa Jallon and the Fulbe elders inside Kaabu, many of whom were skeptical of the war's religious overlay. Few of the Fulbe elders had converted to Islam before the commencement of the war. In fact, only a minority of Fulbe in Kaabu had converted to Islam before 1860.[107]

Between 1852 and 1854 a large portion of Muslim Fulbe were also swept up into Umar's campaign against the Bambara state of Kaarta, which lay in the western backlands of the Niger River, east of Futa Jallon and Kaabu. And this too contributed to the protracted nature of the war against Kaabu. Tens of thousands of Muslim Senegambians volunteered for Umar's holy war in the east, in spite of the growing strength of Molo Eggue and Demba Marem, and Futa Jallon's determination to control the economic activity of the hinterland between the Pongo and Gambia Rivers.[108] By the outset of 1856 the majority of Umar's soldiers in the Niger corridor were Senegambians. As early as January 1855 Umar's *jihad* had acquired a distinct west-to-east orientation.[109]

By May 1856, Kaarta finally fell to Umarian forces. But in the succeeding years the difficulties of administering Kaarta from faraway Dingiray multiplied; for while many of the Senegambian *talibés* were reasonably good soldiers, in spite of a penchant for torturing the more intransigent unbelievers, there were simply too many of them in Kaarta.[110] Moreover, in the wake of the Umarian victory, the French governor at St. Louis, Louis Faidherbe, despatched troops under Paul Helle to occupy the town of Medine in order to secure French control of the Upper Senegal River valley. In the ensuing clash of 1857 the Senegambians bore the brunt of Umar's first defeat. Umar did not occupy Medine, although he did capture two French cannons, but the battlefield outside the town's walls was strewn with the bodies of soldiers from Futa Jallon and Kaabu.[111] Thousands more chose to remain in Kaarta, as Umar and his sons recruited a fresh army from Futa Toro for the campaigns farther east in the Middle Niger. After the 1857 defeat at Medine, the west-to-east orientation of Umar's first army broke down, as thousands of partly disillusioned *jihadists* either marched southward to Futa Jallon or remained in the vicinity of Kaarta until the early 1860s.[112]

Meanwhile Molo Eggue and his subordinates continued to chip away portions of Kaabu's outlying provinces. Doubtless a standing army of three thousand men under the command of the Alfa of Labe gave Molo's more mobile forces the opportunity to consolidate the territorial gains they had made between 1854 and 1860. But in 1862 Jimara, one of the three central provinces of Kaabu, and its adjacent *koringo* territories fell to Molo Eggue's army.[113] Molo was now in control of a territory that was a little over 100 miles from the French garrison at Medine at its outer limits. In short, Molo controlled the approaches to Kaabu from the Atlantic coast in the west and from the north. To the east was the Umarian *jihad* state, and to the south lay Futa Jallon.[114] Kaabu's capital at Kansala and the last two remaining princely provinces were effectively cut off from the outside world.

Between Al-Hajj Umar's departure from Kaabu in the latter 1840s and his call for *jihad* in 1852, a coterie of Fulbe leadership had emerged within the outlying provinces of the latter state that was relatively independent of both the Fulbe communal elders and the rulers of Futa Jallon. Their forces were reasonably well armed and convinced that the toll of abuses against the Fulbe of Kaabu had no reasonable justification. Their conversion to Islam underscored that belief. *Jihad* or holy war meant not only a war with the unbelieving rulers of Kaabu, but also a profound redistribution of authority within Kaabu's Fulbe communities during the course of the war. Subsequent regimes, including the French and Portuguese colonial administrations, stood or fell on the basis of how they addressed this internal redistribution of authority in the Fulbe areas.[115]

After 1862 this redistribution of authority was further embellished by a belief among the *jihadists* that the French advance down the Senegal River and toward the headwaters of the Niger River under Faidherbe was, in fact, the second phase of the *baraka* or divine providence, which had been initiated by Al-Hajj Umar, that would precede the Islamic millennium.[116] Al-Hajj Umar's death in 1864 deepened this conviction among the Fulbe *jihadists*. Under these circumstances the intervention of the *Almamy* of Futa Jallon himself, Abdul Khonsu, in the final war against Kaabu in 1867 had as much to do with compelling the irregular military forces and wayward Labe to submit to his authority as it did with the conquest of a powerful neighboring state ruled by infidels.

When the Fulbe forces finally launched their offensive against what remained of Kaabu in 1867, they realized that a series of uncoordinated attacks might give the *Farim Cabo*, Jahnke Wali, enough time to regroup his forces and fight the various Fulbe armies one at a time. Consequently, Molo Eggue and Demba Marem's armies in the west, the bulk of the veterans from the Umarian campaigns under the command of one Bokar Sada at Bundu in the east, and a twelve thousand man army from Futa Jallon in the south, converged on Kansala, the capital of Kaabu, at the same time. Once this force of approximately thirty thousand men began to march, the fissures within Kaabu's aristocracy began to widen. There were spectacular betrayals among both the lesser and princely aristocracy. The *nyanchos* of Tumana laid down their arms at Kofara, on the border between Pachesi and Tumana.[117] Some, in fact, joined the invading forces. Those of Badora were deeply divided over the war and the policies of Jahnke Wali. A handful of them and their retainers fought valiantly on the eastern edge of the province, while those who had converted to Islam before the commencement of hostilities crossed the Gambia River to fight in the marabout war of the Jahanke Mandinka Muslims.[118]

Perhaps the most spectacular betrayal was that of Chica Embaló, a Fulbe notable who, some time after 1864, took the name Bakary Quidali. Chica Embaló had been one of the Fulbe notables who did not defect to the Fulbe rebels after Berekolong. Even after three thousand regular troops of Futa Jallon occupied a portion of Forria, he remained loyal to the *Farim Cabo*. But in 1864 a group of Mandinka princes expropriated a large number of his cattle and parcels of skins that he had been selling to European merchants in the area and to merchants from Futa Jallon. This incident marked the turning point for Chica Embaló, whose family, according to tradition, had collaborated with the rulers of Kaabu from the inception of the state. In 1867 he was one of the twelve military governors or *alfas* who marched on Kansala.[119]

The fall of Kansala remains an important part of Mandinka oral tradition. According to that tradition, Jahnke Wali, the king, sent his son and a nephew out to survey the size of the approaching army. His son, Sankole Demba, returned first with an estimate of the size of the enemy's army:

> He dismounted and scooped sand into his hand and said to the Mansa, "Grandfather, can you count this?"

> "No, I don't know how many grains of sand you hold," replied Janke Wali.

> "Nor can I count the number of men in the Fula army," said Sankole Demba. "I therefore advise that we fight them outside the fort and not from within. Those of us who must die, must die; but those in the fort would live after us."[120]

Jahnke Wali distrusted his son's judgement believing that cowardice had made him exaggerate the size of the approaching army. When Jahnke Wali's nephew returned with the same story, however, the Mansa began to believe the force was indeed large and would perhaps be the greatest challenge he had ever faced.[121]

The Fulbe armies took their position on the outskirts of Kansala, surrounding the town's walls. The battle did not start immediately, however, because both sides received warnings not to shoot first. Kaabu's soldiers broke the impasse by firing the first shots. The siege of Kansala began. The Fulbe built ladders to climb over the walls. Mandinka defenders atop the walls attempted to decapitate the invaders as fast as they scaled the walls. Nevertheless, the Fulbe continued their relentless attack. The relentlessness of the *jihadists* had a marked effect on aristocratic Mandinka women. Presumably they preferred death to concubinage, for many of these women, according to Mandinka tradition, committed suicide by jumping into the town's wells:

> The *nyancho* women watched the Soninkes kill and kill the Fulas until they grew tired of killing, but the Fulas kept coming. When the women saw the Fulas begging to jump into the fort, the first Fulas who had ever come into the fort unbound, they knew the worst had come.[122]

Jahnke Wali, convinced that what remained of Kaabu's army could not defeat the extraordinarily large Fulbe army, ordered his sons to "put fire to the seven gunpowder stores", thus ending the war and the Kaabu state.[123]

The siege of Kansala was both costly and difficult. Thousands of Fulbe soldiers lost their lives. Two-thirds of the *Almamy's* 12,000 man army died. Several thousand of Jahnke Wali's soldiers were killed and some 15,000 were captured and taken to Futa Jallon as slaves.[124]

The origins of Fuladu

The *Almamy* appointed loyal supporters as rulers in the newly conquered areas. He expected these local officials to send part of the annual taxes they collected to Futa Jallon as tribute. Ostensibly the *Almamy* had some influence on local affairs, but, for the most part, as long as these officials in the outlying areas continued to send tribute, they remained relatively autonomous. Perhaps the most significant consequence of the fall of Kaabu was the creation of new Fulbe spheres of influence — one in Fuladu under Alfa Molo and then his son Musa Molo, one in Forria under Demba Marem or Bakar Demba, and one in Gabu (formerly northern Forria and Geba) under Bakary Quidali.[125] With Futa Jallon's support, Alfa Molo consolidated his state of Firdu or Fuladu. The other two spheres of Fulbe power were nominal clients of Fuladu. Fuladu paid annual taxes and tribute to Futa Jallon, including part of any booty collected in the wars it fought. In addition, Fuladu provided soldiers for the central army whenever they were needed. In return, Futa Jallon provided protection for and spiritual leadership to Fuladu.[126] Often the relations between client and patron were strained. For example, shortly after the battle in Kansala, the *Almamy* of Futa Jallon denounced Alfa Molo and installed one of his sons as ruler in Fuladu.[127] The cause of the confusion may have been a question of doctrine, or a fear of losing this valuable territory. Whatever the source of confusion, the *Almamy* and Alfa Molo resolved the matter quickly, and Alfa Molo resumed his position as head of state.

Alfa Molo approached his relationship with Futa Jallon pragmatically. He recognized the powerful position of the latter state and the role it played in his successful fight against Kaabu. Throughout most of his reign, Alfa Molo readily sent tribute and a share of the spoils collected in war to the *Almamy*. He encouraged the people living in the areas he conquered to convert to Islam and he recruited Islamic scholars from the towns of Futa Jallon to take up residence in Fuladu.

Alfa Molo recognized that Fuladu's legitimacy was partly determined by its readiness to spread Islam. But Molo's acts of faith were motivated in part by his desire to maintain Fuladu's borders and to insulate it from external attack. He believed that by securing Fuladu's borders he could consolidate his rule and initiate an internal economic reorganization of the region.[128] As we shall see, however, conflicts within Fuladu, and between Fuladu, Futa Jallon, and the Europeans persisted. By 1881, after Alfa Molo's death and further encroachment by the Europeans, Fuladu's existence was challenged by a myriad of forces.

But even before the 1880s, Fuladu was beset by a series of problems that had been bequeathed to it by the prewar circumstances. For example, in the 1850s, the fate of Futa Jallon, Kaabu, and the French and Portuguese enclaves in the

Senegambia had begun to turn on whether any of them could establish comprehensive control over the Forria. After the fall of Kansala in September 1867, the Forria became even more central to the political and economic fortunes of states in the Senegambia. This was particularly so for the fledgling state of Fuladu. For at the outset of the 1860s, with the in-migration of the Fulbe from the north and the prolific expansion of plantations and commercialized peasant agriculture along the banks of the rivers in this former no man's land, the region's economic center of gravity began to shift to the backlands between the Rio Grande and Gambia Rivers.

Notes

1. B[akary] K. Sidibe, "The Story of Kaabu: Its Extent", paper presented to the Conference on Manding Studies, SOAS, London, 1972, pp. 6-7; Sékéne Mody Cissoko, "Introduction à l'histoire des Mandingues de l'ouest: l'empire de Kabou (XVIè-XIXè siècle)", paper presented to the Conference on Manding Studies, SOAS, London, 1972, pp. 2-3.

2. Donald R. Wright, *The Early History of Niumi: Settlement and Foundation of a Mandinka State on the Gambia River*, Ohio University Center for International Studies, Africa Series, no. 32, Athens, Ohio, 1977, pp. 16-24.

   Kaabu was one of several polities in the Senegambia: "The whole of this area was deeply influenced by the Mande civilization; its social as well as its political structures ... These states were in existence before 1600 and apart from a few minor losses of territory and changes of boundary, changed little externally and internally till the end of the eighteenth century and in some cases well into the nineteenth. They all had a hierarchic social structure which operated a system of state control". Jean Suret-Canale, "The Western Atlantic Coast 1600-1800", in *History of West Africa*, 2 vols., eds. J.F.A. Ajayi and Michael Crowder, New York, Columbia University Press, 1972-73, 1, p. 392.

   Like Kaabu, the Jolof state and its vassals, Cayor, Baol, Walo, Sine and Saloum, as well as the Mandinka states along the Gambia River including Niumi, Baadibu, Niani, Wuli, and Kantora, fitted into this pattern.

3. António Carreira, *Mandingas da Guiné Portuguesa*, Centro de Estudos da Guiné Portuguesa, no. 4, Bissau, 1947, pp. 9-12. For information on trade see: Wright, *Early History*, pp. 16-24.

   For information on similar settlement patterns in northwestern Ivory Coast see: John Michael O'Sullivan, "Developments in the Social Stratification of Northwest Ivory Coast during the Eighteenth and

Nineteenth Centuries: From a Malinke Frontier Society to the Liberation of Slaves by the French-1907", Ph.D. dissertation, University of California, Los Angeles, 1976, p. 69.

4. A. Teixeira da Mota, Introduction to *Fulas do Gabú* by José Mendes Moreira, Centro de Estudos da Guiné Portuguesa, no. 6, Bissau, 1948, p. 6. Mamadou Mané's doctoral dissertation should clarify questions about Kaabu. Mané is using a combination of oral traditions collected in Senegal and the Gambia and European sources from French and Portuguese archives to reconstruct a history of Kaabu. See also Trevor Hall, "The Role of Cape Verde Islanders in Organizing and Operating Marinetime Trade between West Africa and the Iberian Territories, 1441-1616", Ph.D. dissertation, Johns Hopkins University, 1992.

5. B[akary] K. Sidibe, "The Story of Kaabu: Kaabu's Relationship with the Gambian States", paper presented to the Conference on Manding Studies, SOAS, London, 1972; B[akary] K. Sidibe, "The Story of Kaabu: The Fall of Kaabu", paper presented to the Conference on Manding Studies, SOAS, London, 1972; B[akary] K. Sidibe, "A Brief History of Kaabu and Fuladu, 1300-1930: A Narrative Based on Some Oral Traditions of the Senegambia", unpublished manuscript, 1974; and B.K. Sidibe, "Its Extent".
In recent years, Mandinka historians have begun collecting oral traditions about Kaabu. The main source of information on Kaabu is B.K. Sidibe's works. These are based on oral traditions collected in The Gambia, Senegal, Mali, and Guinea-Bissau.

6. B.K. Sidibe, "Its Extent", p. 16.

7. B.K. Sidibe, "Its Extent", pp. 8-11.

8. B[akary] K. Sidibe, "The Nyanchos of Kaabu", mimeograph, Gambian Cultural Archives, pp. 9-10.

9. B.K. Sidibe, "Nyanchos", pp. 9-10 and B.K. Sidibe, "Its Extent", p. 16.

10. B.K. Sidibe, "Its Extent", pp. 8-11.

11. B.K. Sidibe, "Nyanchos", pp. 10 and 12-3.

12. The term *soninke* referred to the people who practiced *soninkeyaa*. *Soninke* also refers to a specific group of people who speak a Mande dialect called Soninke. For more information on the Soninke people, who are also called Saracole or Serahuli see: Charles Monteil, "La légend du Ouagadou et l'origine des Soninké", in *Mélange Ethnologiques*, Mémoires de l'Institute Français d'Afrique Noire, no. 23, Dakar, IFAN, 1953, pp. 359-408. See also: Wright, *Early History*, pp. 29-30.

13. Wright, *Early History*, p. 31.

14. B.K. Sidibe's interview with Malang Nanki (GCA Ref. Nos. 354/55), 3 April 1975 (Badora-Brikama).

15. Wright, *Early History*, p. 31.

16. B.K. Sidibe, "Nyanchos", pp. 11-12; B.K. Sidibe, "Its Extent", pp. 11-12.

17. Quinn, *Mandingo Kingdoms*; B.K. Sidibe's interview with Malang Nanki (GCA Ref. Nos. 354/55), 3 April 1975 (Badora-Brikama); Gordon Innes, *Kaabu and Fuladu — Historical Narratives of the Gambian Mandinka*, London, School of Oriental and African Studies, University of London, 1976, pp. 72-115.

18. B.K. Sidibe, "Its Extent", pp. 17-18.

19. Even though Kaabu's states enjoyed a large measure of local autonomy, they looked to the central government for guidance and support. Similarly, in the fourteenth and fifteenth centuries, Kaabu also looked to Mali for inspiration. In fact, before Mali's decline, the *mansa*-elect of Kaabu as well as those of the chiefdoms within the kingdom went to Mali to receive the authority to rule. Thus, Mali played a significant role in the lives of the people and in their eyes they were part of the Malian Empire. See: B.K. Sidibe, "Its Extent", p. 9.

   For more information on the provinces within Kaabu see: Winifred Galloway, "A Working Map of Kaabu — with a shortlist of some Kaabu States and related areas", paper presented to the First International Kaabu Colloquium, Dakar, 1980.

20. The king was always a *nyancho* and the kingship rotated among the *nyancho* of the three leading provinces, depending upon where the oldest *nyancho* lived. "The elders always kept a very clear genealogy of the three houses and when an emperor died, the 'fetishes' [ancestral shrines] were consulted to confirm the memories of the elders, and the next eldest nyancho would be notified to appear at his family seat for installation ..." B.K. Sidibe, "Its Extent", p. 12.

   Even though everyone understood the succession system, the transition was not always smooth. Conflicts usually arose when the *nyancho* who was to be appointed king belonged to a different ruling house than the previous king. Naturally, the princely members of the king's immediate family did not want to relinquish power. And their persistence was often a source of internal problems.

   Eventually, the *jalang* started playing a more decisive role in the selection process. "Sometimes 2 or 3 nyanchos would contest for the throne. When this happened, gallantry, popularity and the choice of the gods determined who should succeed. It was not always the eldest who ruled then". B.K. Sidibe, "Its Extent", p. 13.

21. B.K. Sidibe's interview with Malang Nanki (GCA Ref. Nos. 354/55), 3 April 1975 (Badora-Brikama); Innes, *Kaabu and Fuladu*, pp. 72-115; Barry, *La Sénégambie*, pp. 238-45.

22. B.K. Sidibe, "Its Extent", p. 14.

23. Curtin, *Economic Change*, pp. 278-85; Roberts, *Warriors, Merchants*, pp. 58-63; Barry, *La Sénégambie*, pp. 112-27; and S.M. Cissoko, "L'empire de Kabou", p. 10.

24. S.M. Cissoko, "L'empire de Kabou", p. 10.

25. Wright, *Early History*, p. 30.

26. B.K. Sidibe's interview with Malang Nanki (GCA Ref. Nos. 354/55), 3 April 1975 (Badora-Brikama); Barry, *La Sénégambie*, pp. 187-208.

27. "... The *nyanchos* and *koringos* lived on the toils of their subjects ... There was no other way for them to live except by taxes and plunder". B.K. Sidibe, "Its Extent", p. 19.

28. B.K. Sidibe's interview with Malang Nanki (GCA Ref. Nos. 354/55), 3 April 1975 (Badora-Brikama); Miguel Fernandes, Bissau Series Tape 7 (Geba), 15 July 1977; Cherno Amadu Djaló, Bissau Series Tape 3 (Bafatá) 12 July 1977; Gregório Gomes Dias, Bissau Series Tape 4 (Bafatá) 10 July 1977; Mama Galade and Iaia Djaló, Bissau Series Tape 2 (Guelajau) 9 July 1977.

29. Galloway, "Working Map of Kaabu", pp. 34-5; Quinn, *Mandingo Kingdoms*, pp. 114-16; Robinson, *Holy War* pp. 179-81; B.K. Sidibe's interview with Malang Nanki (GCA Ref. Nos. 354/55), 3 April 1975 (Badora-Brikama); Innes, *Kaabu and Fuladu*, pp. 72-115.

30. Innes, *Kaabu and Fuladu*, pp. 72-115.

31. B.K. Sidibe's interview with Malang Nanki (GCA Ref. Nos. 354/55), 3 April 1975 (Badora-Brikama); Cherno Amadu Djaló, Bissau Series Tape 3 (Bafatá), 12 July 1977; Gregório Gomes Dias, Bissau Series Tape 4 (Bafatá), 10 July 1977.

32. The next to the last emperor of Kaabu was a Sane, named Mansa Siibo, who died in his capital of Saama. A year passed before the Sane family told the Mane family of his death. The Mane family was furious because their Jahnke Wali of Pachana was the legitimate heir to the throne. This deception created hostility between the two families, as well as between the two states, Saama and Pachana. See: B.K. Sidibe, "The Fall", p. 2.

33. B.K. Sidibe's interview with Malang Nanki (GCA Ref. Nos. 354/55), 3 April 1975 (Badora-Brikama).

34. Hyacinthe Hequard, *Voyage sur la côte et dans l'interieur de l'Afrique Occidentale*, Paris, Imprie. de Bernard et Cie., 1855, pp. 190-91; S.M. Cissoko, "L'empire de Kabou", p. 16; and Mamadou Mané, "Contribution à l'histoire du Kaabu des origines au XIX siècle", Memoire de Mâitrise Thèse, Université de Dakar 1974-75, p. 66.

35. The Mandinka believed that the masters of the land had "a special relationship with the *jinn*, or spirits of the region, which accorded to the family usufruct rights to the land and water with specified bounds". The

oldest family in any given area was entitled to rule at the village level, and the larger territorial level. When they arrived in new areas, the Mandinka strategy was to either marry into the founding family or, if that was impossible, defeat the family militarily. See: Wright, *Early History*, pp. 32-34.

According to Fulbe traditions, the original agreement between the Mandinka and Fulbe was that the Fulbe could use certain lands to graze their livestock and to cultivate some crops. In return, the Fulbe had to pay a tax of one bull per year per herd. Once they established hegemony in the area, the Mandinka began to alter this arrangement and they began to treat the Fulbe as their subjects. The Fulbe claimed that in some cases the Mandinka collected ten bulls per herd. Furthermore, they usually took the best bulls. According to the Fulbe, the Mandinka abused them in this and other ways. See: B.K. Sidibe, "The Fall", p. 1; B.K. Sidibe, "The Extent", p. 4; Bertrand Bocandé, "Notes sur la Guinée Portugaise en Sénégambie Meridonale", *Bulletin de la Société de Geographie* (Paris), 3d sér., no. 12, julliet-aôut 1849, p. 58; Alhaji Kawsu Sillah, Banjul Series Tape 16 (Brikama), 31 July 1978.

36. Alhaji Kawsu Sillah, Banjul Series Tape 16 (Brikama), 31 July 1978; Mamadou Falai Balde, Banjul Series Tapes 12-14 (Sankulikunda), 25 June 1978; B.K. Sidibe, "The Fall", pp. 1-2.

37. B.K. Sidibe, "The Fall", p. 2. For other references to Mandinka mistreatment of the Fulbe see: ANS, 1G91: Rapport. Loitard, "Mission dans le Fouladougou, le Niani, et le Kalonkadougou", 29 octobre 1888; ANS, 1G295, Doc. 208: H. de la Roncière, "Travail d'hivernage — Historique du Fouladou", 1903; Vasco de Sousa Calvet de Magalhaes, *Provincia da Guiné — Relatório apresentado pelo Administrador da Circumscrição Civil de Geba, 1914*, Porto, 1916, pp. 54-5.

38. From the Mandinka perspective, there were logical reasons for their policies towards the Fulbe. As mentioned, the *nyancho* and *koringo* populations lived off the taxes and tribute that their subjects provided. As their retinue grew and their responsibilities increased, the Mandinka tried to extract as much as possible from people living within their realm. Resentment of Mandinka oppression grew among the Fulbe during the construction and consolidation of Kaabu. Alhaji Kawsu Sillah, Banjul Series Tape 16 (Brikama), 31 July 1978; Mamadou Falai Balde, Banjul Series Tapes 12-14 (Sankulikunda), 25 June 1978.

39. Curtin, *Economic Change*, p. 46.

40. Daniel F. McCall and Norman R. Bennett, eds., *Aspects of West African Islam*, Boston University Papers on Africa, vol.5, Boston, African Studies Center, Boston University, 1971, p. vi.

41. Muhammad Zafrulla Khan, trans., *The Quran — The Eternal Revelation vouchsafed to Muhammad — The Seal of the Prophets*, 2d ed., rev., London, Curzon Press, 1975, p. 172; see also pp. 653, 328 and 353.

42. H.F.C. Smith, "A Neglected Theme of West African History: The Islamic Revolutions of the 19th Century", *Journal of the Historical Society of Nigeria*, 2, 1961, pp. 183-4. See also: M.G. Smith, "The *Jihad* of Shehu dan Fodio: Some Problems", in *Islam in Tropical Africa*, ed. I.M. Lewis, London, Oxford University Press, 1966, p. 414; John Willis, "*Jihad Fi-Sabil Allah*: Its Doctrinal Basis in Islam and Some Aspects of its Evolution in 19th Century West Africa", *JAH*, 8, 1967, p. 398.

43. Khan, *The Quran*, p. 30. See also: Murray Last, "Reform in West Africa: The Jihad Movements of the Nineteenth Century", in *History of West Africa*, 2 vols., eds. J.F.A. Ajayi and Michael Crowder, New York, Columbia University Press, 1972-73, 2, pp. 1-29; and Thomas Patrick Hughes, *A Dictionary of Islam*, London, W.H. Allen and Co., 1885, p. 243.

44. See: André Arcin, *La Guinée Française: races, religions, coutumes, production, commerce*, Paris, Challamel, 1907, p. 20.

45. A. Demougeot, *Notes sur l'organization politique et administrative du Labe avant et depuis l'occupation française*, Memoires de l'Institut Française d'Afrique Noire, no. 6, Paris, Librairie Larose, 1944, pp. 10-11.

46. Mamadou Samba Sow, "La Région de Labe (Fouta-Djallon) au XIXè et au debut du XXè siècle", Diplome d'Etudes Superieures, Université de Paris, n.d., pp. 15-16.

47. Sow, "Labe", pp. 16-17; and Suret-Canale, "Western Atlantic Coast", p. 419.

48. Walter Rodney, "Jihad and Social Revolution in Futa Djalon in the Eighteenth Century", *Journal of the Historical Society of Nigeria*, 4, June 1968, pp. 273-77.

49. Diallo, *Institutions*, p. 34.

50. Jean Suret-Canale, "The Fouta-Djalon Chieftaincy", in *West African Chiefs: Their Changing Status under Colonial Rule and Independence*, eds., Michael Crowder and O. Ikime, New York, Africana Pub. Corp., 1970, p. 79.

51. Suret-Canale, "Western Atlantic Coast", p. 421; and Willis, "Jihad", p. 398.

52. Barry, *La Sénégambie*, pp. 208-44; Philip D. Curtin, "The Abolition of the Slave Trade from Senegambia", in *The Abolition of the Atlantic Slave Trade: Origins and Effects in Europe, Africa and the Americas*, eds., David Eltis and James Walvin, Madison, University of Wisconsin Press, 1981, pp. 83-97. See also: Eltis, *Economic Growth*, pp. 164-8 and 182-4.

53. Robinson, *Holy War*, pp. 55-9.
54. Robinson, *Holy War*, pp. 55-9.
55. Robinson, *Holy War*, pp. 55-9.
56. Robinson, *Holy War*, pp. 55-9.
57. Demougeot, *Notes*, p. 14. The term Futa Jallon refers to the unification of Fulbe and Djalonké elements in society. See: Suret-Canale, "Western Atlantic Coast", p. 422.

     Kollade and Koin were originally excluded from the ruling group. But they petitioned the other seven for equal status and were granted it. See: Rodney, "Jihad", p. 278; William Derman, *Serfs, Peasants and Socialists: A Former Serf Village in the Republic of Guinea*, Berkeley, University of California Press, 1973, pp. 13-14.
58. Power at the local level resided with the *alfa* of the *diwal*. The *alfa* from all of the provinces, except the one from Timbo, were equal since they were the direct descendants of the original nine Fulbe territorial leaders. Each *alfa* had his own army, as well as independent sources of wealth. The *Alfa* of Labe was particularly successful in building a powerful army and manipulating the economy to serve his needs.
59. Winston Franklin McGowan, "The Development of European Relations with Futa Jalon and the Foundation of French Colonial Rule, 1794-1895", Ph.D. thesis, University of London, School of Oriental and African Studies, 1975.
60. McGowan, "Development", pp. 77-8 and Robinson, *Holy War*, pp. 49-57.
61. McGowan, "Development", pp. 75-9; Suret-Canale, "Western Atlantic Coast", pp. 423-5.
62. Rodney, "Jihad", p. 281. See also: Suret-Canale, "Western Atlantic Coast", p. 426. The gold came from Bouré, which was a client state of Futa Jallon.
63. As Diallo explains, "... the sovereigns (especially those of the Sorriya side) did not remain indifferent in front of the problem external commerce posed. Thus, they took an interest in relations with Bissau, Boke, Boffa ... and Freetown". (Diallo, *Institutions*, p. 220).
64. Alhaji Kawsu Sillah, Banjul Series Tape 16 (Brikama), 31 July 1978; and Eltis, *Economic Growth*, pp. 62-77.
65. Eltis, *Economic Growth*, pp. 62-77 and 164-8.
66. Alhaji Kawsu Sillah, Banjul Series Tape 16 (Brikama), 31 July 1978 and see also M.G. Smith, "The *Jihad*".
67. Barry, *La Sénégambie*, pp. 190-208; and Alhaji Kawsu Sillah, Banjul Series Tape 16 (Brikama), 31 July 1978. For more information on trade see: McGowan, "Development", pp. 133-43; 369-74; and 454-60.
68. Robinson, *Holy War*, pp. 53-9.

69.   J. Watt, *Journal of Mr. Watt in his Expedition to and from Teembo in the year 1794*, Ms. Africa, Rhodes House, Oxford, quoted in McGowan, "Development", pp. 57-8; pp. 89-91; and 108-110.

70.   Robinson, *Holy War*, pp. 56-9; Barry, *La Sénégambie*, pp. 208-20. For more information on the period between 1825 and 1840 see: Robinson, *Holy War*, pp. 93-112.

71.   Robinson, *Holy War*, pp. 116-21. Al-Hajj Umar was closely identified with the Alfaya house rather than the Soriya house. On one occasion, however, "He journeyed to Timbo, probably in 1844, and sought to bring the two sides together ... it would appear that he got the rival Almamies to listen and perhaps agree to a truce, but ... they soon fell to fighting again ..." (Robinson, *Holy War*, p. 119).

72.   Barry, *La Sénégambie*, pp. 238-45; Alhaji Kawsu Sillah, Banjul Series Tape 16 (Brikama), 31 July 1978.

73.   B.K. Sidibe, "The Fall", p. 3; Innes, *Kaabu and Fuladu*, pp. 72-115.

74.   Sow, "Labe", p. 30.

75.   Innes, *Kaabu and Fuladu*, pp.72-115.

76.   Mané, "Contribution", p. 77; Jorge Vellez Caroço, *Monjur: O Gabú e a sua História*, Centro de Estudos da Guiné Portuguesa, no. 8, Bissau, 1948, pp. 121-25. See also: B.K. Sidibe, "The Fall", p. 6.

77.   Jaime Walter, *Honório Pereira Barreto — Biografia-Documentos-"Memória sobre o estudo actual da Senegâmbia Portuguesa"*, Centro de Estudos da Guiné Portuguesa, no. 5, Bissau, 1947, pp. 14-5.

78.   R.J. Hammond, *Portugal and Africa 1815-1910: A Study in Uneconomic Imperialism*, Stanford, Stanford University Press, 1966, pp. 47-51; and Walter, *Barreto*, pp. 21-4.

79.   Walter, *Barreto*, pp. 20-1.

80.   Walter, *Barreto*, pp. 20-2.

81.   Hammond, *Portugal and Africa*, pp. 14-7; and Walter, *Barreto*, pp. 12-3. For more information on changes in Portugal during this period see: A.H. de Oliveira Marques, *History of Portugal*, 2 vols., New York, Columbia University Press, 1972, 2, pp. 1-75.

82.   Honório Pereira Barretto, *Memoria sôbre o estado actual de Senegambia portugueza, causas de sua decadência e meios de a fazer prosperar*, Lisbon, Typ. da Viuva Coelho & Co., 1843, pp. 3-4.

83.   Alhaji Irama Cissé, Bissau Series (Contuboel) Tapes 3 and 4, 13 July 1977.

84.   See Chapter 1.

85.   Robinson, *Holy War*, p. 95.

86.   Alhaji Salim Suwareh, Bissau Series Tape 1 (Bijini), 9 July 1977.

87.   Mamadu Soare, Bissau Series Tape 7 (Gabu), 20 July 1977.

88.   Alhaji Irama Cissé, Bissau Series Tapes 3 and 4 (Contuboel), 13 July 1977; Alhaji Salim Suwareh, Bissau Series Tape 1 (Bijini), 9 July 1977; Mamadu Soare, Bissau Series Tape 7 (Gabu), 20 July 1977.

89.   Cherno Amadu Djaló and Abdulai Sombili Djaló, Bissau Series Tape 3 (Bafatá), 12 July 1977.

90.   Alhaji Salim Suwareh, Bissau Series Tape 1 (Bijini), 9 July 1977; Alhaji Mamangari Djaló, Bissau Series Tapes 9 and 10 (Combore), 22 July 1977.

91.   Alhaji Salim Suwareh, Bissau Series Tape 1 (Bijini), 9 July 1977.

92.   According to B.K. Sidibe, it was always difficult for a stranger like Malal to win the confidence of his former masters. Even if he had distinguished himself, it is doubtful whether they would have given him one of their women. Thus, he looked for a "blemished" woman — someone who no one else wanted. This theme is common in the stories about heroes. (B.K. Sidibe, personal communication, July 1978).

    For more information on Molo Eggue's life see: Roche, *Conquête et resistance*, p. 126; Charlotte A. Quinn, "A Nineteenth Century Fulbe State", *JAH*, 12, 1971, pp. 427-40; and B[akary] K. Sidibe, "A Brief History of Kaabu and Fuladu, 1300-1930: A Narrative Based on some Oral Tradition of the Senegambia", unpublished manuscript, 1974. See also Mamadou Falai Baldeh, Banjul Series Tape 12 (Sankulikunda), 25 June 1978; INIC, Documentos Diversos de 1946: António Isidro de Campos Gramare, "Resposto ao Inquérito Ethnográfico: Fulas e Fula Forros da area do Posto Administrativo de Contubo-El", p. 3.

93.   Alhaji Kawsu Sillah, Banjul Series Tape 16 (Brikama), 31 July 1978; Mamadou Falai Baldeh, Banjul Series Tape 19 (Latridunda), 10 August 1978; Tasangkung Jabi, Banjul Series Tape 9 (Libras), 22 June 1978.

94.   Mamadou Falai Baldeh, Banjul Series Tape 13 (Sankulikunda), 25 June 1978.

95.   Mamadou Falai Baldeh, Banjul Series Tape 13 (Sankulikunda), 25 June 1978.

96.   Mamadou Falai Baldeh, Banjul Series Tape 13 (Sankulikunda), 25 June 1978; and Mamadou Falai Baldeh, Banjul Series Tape 20 (Latrikunda), 10 August 1978.

    When the marabout told Molo Eggue that a sheep would be the cause of his rise to kingship, the hunter did not understand the significance of this statement. Umar predicted that nine years would pass before any change would occur and near the end of that period the role of the sheep became clearer. Molo Eggue had two sheep that he nursed into large beautiful animals. One day while Molo Eggue was hunting, the nephews of Mofa Jenung, the Mandinka ruler in Kansonko, were traveling through Jalaba. When they saw Molo Eggue's sheep, they decided that they wanted to take them to their uncle. Kumba Wude, however, knew that she could not allow anything to happen to these sheep. Thus, she told these visitors that they could not take the sheep in Molo Eggue's absence. Her boldness surprised the Mandinka. They then threatened to take her, but in the end they seized one of the sheep. When Molo Eggue returned, he vowed that it was the last time that the Mandinka would get away with such an act. He also realized that this incident was part of Umar's prediction.

97. Alhaji Kawsu Sillah, Banjul Series Tape 1 (Banjul), 9 May 1978; and Mamadou Falai Baldeh, Banjul Series Tape 19 (Latrikunda), 10 August 1978.

It was quite normal to travel with a companion up to a river and then stop, while the one traveling continued on his way. (B.K. Sidibe, personal communication, July 1978).

98. Alhaji Kawsu Sillah, Banjul Series Tape 1 (Banjul), 9 May 1978.

99. Mamadou Falai Baldeh, Banjul Series Tape 20 (Latrikunda), 10 August 1978; Mamadou Falai Baldeh, Banjul Series Tape 12 (Sankulikunda), 25 June 1978.

100. Alhaji Salim Suwareh, Bissau Series Tape 1 (Bijini), 9 July 1977.

101. Cherno Amadu Djaló, Bissau Series Tape 3 (Bafatá), 12 July 1977.

102. Mama Galade, Bissau Series Tapes 2 and 3 (Quelejau), 9 July 1977; Robinson, *Holy War*, p. 180; Frances Anne Leary, "Islam, Politics and Colonialism: A Political History of Islam in the Casamance Region of Senegal (1850-1914)", Ph.D. dissertation, Northwestern University, 1970, p. 175.

103. The Baldeh family versions of Molo Eggue's story collected in The Gambia do not mention Futa Jallon as a source of support. Perhaps the family wants to portray Molo Eggue as a hero who did everything himself. It would be a mistake to claim that Molo Eggue acted independently, rather he was part of a larger process of reform and expansion which Futa Jallon led. See: Buli Galiça, Bissau Series Tapes 7 and 8 (Gabu), 20-21 July 1977.

104. Mane, "Contribution", p. 74.

105. Caroço, *Monjur*, p. 113.

106. Caroço, *Monjur*, pp. 114-15; B.K. Sidibe, "The Fall", p. 7. For more information on Alfa Yaya see: Paul Marty, *L'Islam en Guinée — Fouta-Diallon*, Paris, Éditions Ernest Leroux, 1921, pp. 40-49; M. Crespin, "Alpha Yaya et M. Frezouls", *Revue Indigène*, no. 2, 1906, pp. 45-46; G. Teullière, "Alfa Yaya et la politique indigène", *Revue Indigène*, no. 67, novembre 1911, pp. 615-20.

107. Buli Galiça, Bissau Series Tapes 7 and 8 (Gabu), 20-21 July 1977; Caroço, *Monjur*, pp. 113-5.

108. Boubacar Barry, "The Expansion of Futa Jallon towards the Coast and the Social and Political Crises in Southern Senegambia during the First Half of the Nineteenth Century", unpublished paper, 1983, pp. 1 and 14-15.

109. Robinson, *Holy War*, pp. 191-95.

110. Robinson, *Holy War*, pp. 197-98; Roberts, *Warriors, Merchants*, pp. 78-79.

111. Robinson, *Holy War*, p. 198; and Roberts, *Warriors, Merchants*, p. 79.

112. Roberts, *Warriors, Merchants*, p. 79; Robinson, *Holy War*, p. 116; and Buli Galiça, Bissau Series Tapes 7 and 8 (Gabu), 20-21 July 1977.

113. Quinn, *Mandingo Kingdoms*, p. 172.

114. Robinson, *Holy War*, p. 198; Roberts, *Warriors, Merchants*, p. 79.

115. António José Machado, "A Fraternidade Guiné e Cabo Verde — Folha Dedicada a Socorrer as Victimas da estiagem da Província Caboverdiana", *BOGP*, 31 October 1883; Buli Galiça, Bissau Series Tapes 7 and 8 (Gabu), 20-21 July 1977; ANS, 1G91: Rapport. Loitard, "Mission dans le Foulladougou, le Niani et le Kalondadougou", 28 octobre 1888; *BOGP*, 1890, Supplement to no. 48.

116. See: Robinson, *Holy War*; Buli Galiça, Bissau Series Tapes 7 and 8 (Gabu), 20-21 July 1977; Alhaji Salim Suwareh, Bissau Series Tape 1 (Bijini) 9 July 1977.

117. Buli Galiça, Bissau Series Tapes 7 and 8 (Gabu), 20-21 July 1977.

118. Innes, *Kaabu and Fuladu*, pp. 72-115; B.K. Sidibe's interview with Malang Nanki (GCA Ref. Nos., 354/55), 3 April 1975 (Badora-Brikama).

119. Buli Galiça, Bissau Series Tapes 7 and 8 (Gabu), 20-21 July 1977.

120. B.K. Sidibe, "The Fall", p. 12.

121. The *nyancho* believed that one could never be sure about paternity. They argued that a mother could have been unfaithful and therefore a son could be the product of another man. Jahnke Wali trusted his nephew's statement since he was his sister's child and thus definitely his own flesh and blood.

122. B.K. Sidibe, "The Fall", p. 13.

123. B.K. Sidibe, "The Fall", p. 15. The Battle of Kansala fits into the siege mentality of many West African states. According to Thierno Mouctar Bah, from the sixteenth century the *tata* became an important feature in the Sudan. Consequently, war strategies and tactics changed:

> "... [s]urprise, traitors or siege were the principal means of overcoming the strength of defense provided by the tata". (See: O'Sullivan, "Development", p. 173. Quote taken from: Thierno Mouctar Bah, "Architecture militaire traditionnelle et poliorcétique dans le Soudan Occidental (du XVIIè à la fin du XIXè siècle)", Thèse du doctorat du 3è cycle d'histoire, Paris, 1971, pp. 246-47)

The *tata* and the ruler of an area were intimately connected:

> The power of a sovereign was a function of that of his tata. The more that the latter was fortified, the more he was feared and obeyed. He established his *dominium* on the surrounding territory and could snap his fingers at the eminent sovereigns on whom he could depend. The surrounding population were at his mercy and tradition was the most often violated in these cruel times ... (Sékéné Mody Cissoko, "Traits fondamentaux des sociétés du Soudan Occidental du XVIIè au début du Xxè siècle", *BIFAN*, ser. B., 31, 1969, p. 7.)

124. Mane, "Contribution", p. 81.
125. Barry, *La Sénégambie*, pp. 331-8.
126. Tansangkung Jabi, Banjul Series Tape 9 (Libras), 22 June 1978; and Leary, "Islam, Politics", pp. 176-78. Much of the oral information on Futa Jallon's role in Alfa Molo's victory has been lost since the Baldeh family has a vested interest in portraying Alfa Molo as the person responsible for the Fulbe success in Fuladu.
127. ANS, 1G295, Doc. 208: H. de la Roncière, "Travail d'hivernage — Historique du Fouladou", 1903.
128. Leary, "Islam, Politics", p. 178.

3 The Rise of Fuladu

Fuladu's development under Alfa Molo

After the fall of Kansala, Alfa Molo took the central and northern remnants of dismembered Kaabu and formed Fuladu. He faced several political problems. Arguably the most difficult was forging a functional set of political institutions while dealing with the state's internal and external adversaries. It was a daunting task which was made all the more urgent by the potential political crisis in the Forria. Neither Alfa Molo nor his brother, Bakary Demba, nor his son, Musa Molo, would ever quite overcome it.

The Fulbe in Fuladu had no state building tradition. Their political system centered on the *galle* or compound, in which the eldest male provided leadership and served as a spokesman.[1] Consequently, Alfa Molo adopted the only model of a state that he knew — that of the Mandinka of Kaabu. In turn, Molo rewarded his former military subordinates by making them local officials in the new state.[2] In so doing, he resurrected Kaabu's system of military precincts but without the counterbalance of a civil administration. In this way he reduced the possibility of local rebellion but compromised the administrative capacities of the state.

Moreover, despite its importance during the war, Islam was not a sufficient ballast to the ambitions of the new military men once the war was over. Well after many Mandinka had in fact converted to Islam, the attempt to integrate communal and Koranic legal systems with the new state's apparent need for security and order grated against the inclinations of many Fulbe military leaders. These men were often more disposed to exact retribution from former enemies and those they deemed social inferiors than to administer the new provinces according to the canons of Islam. In short, Fulbe military leaders insisted on maintaining a monopoly on violence, while refusing to demilitarize the civil society of the new state. Molo's silence on such matters was taken as tacit consent by the military governors.[3]

This did not mean that the Fulbe military governors were more mean spirited than their predecessors, or that they were without an ideological slant on administrative matters. Rather they chose not to privilege religious ideology when dealing with the quotidian affairs of former enemies and dependents. For many of them genuinely believed that the Islamic millennium was at hand and that they were that millennium's immediate agency. By 1862, for example, such beliefs were widespread among many former *jihadists*. In 1864 the compelling nature of these beliefs was further enhanced by the death of Al-Hajj Umar.[4]

The problems Alfa Molo faced with Nbuku Nyapa, the provincial governor of Kanadu, for example, demonstrated the kinds of internal conflicts that existed in Fuladu and the inherent difficulties of integrating different groups into one state. Molo himself had come from rather humble origins. Nbuku Nyapa was a Fulbe aristocrat or *Fulbe-ribê* who, from the outset, had been contemptuous of Alfa Molo's achievements. The official history of Alfa Molo's reign — that is to say, the Baldeh family history — suggests that Alfa Molo began to increase the number of Fulbe aristocrats among his appointments around 1870, well after the heat of the resistance war had died down.[5] Molo's decision to appoint an occasional Fulbe aristocrat as provincial governor was apparently a deliberate attempt to increase the dependence of such aristocrats on his administration.[6] However, such officials were generally wealthier than many of the leaders who emerged during the war against Kaabu and for whom the war had often been a means of emancipation from domestic slavery. Moreover, because of their personal resources, aristocratic military commanders could provide their soldiers with provisions and ammunition at their own expense. Such was the case with Nbuku Nyapa.

Nbuku Nyapa grew dissatisfied with Alfa Molo's reign shortly after he was installed as governor of Kanadu in 1870. He and his people understood that their army and the wealth of their province were crucial to the continued existence of Fuladu. In fact, Nbuku Nyapa claimed his position was a result of his own bravery and influence rather than Alfa Molo's beneficence and executive ability. To prove his independence, Nbuku Nyapa refused to send a representative work force to Alfa Molo's capital at N'Dorna. Since each province had an obligation to provide labor for the king's fields, this refusal was an act of defiance that required Alfa Molo to censure Nbuku Nyapa.[7] Alfa

Molo and Nbuku Nyapa entered into open conflict, which did not resolve itself upon the death of Alfa Molo. In the 1880s, Nbuku Nyapa further complicated the relationship between his province and Fuladu's central government by making an explicit alliance with Portuguese merchants and officials at Geba. The test of wills between the central authority and the province of Kanadu was passed on to the next generation. After Nbuku Nyapa's death, his son Sambel Serandim refused to recognize the authority of Alfa Molo's son and successor, Musa.

Alfa Molo also faced competition from other Islamic religious leaders, such as Fode Kaba Dumbuya of Kerewan. Fode Kaba went to Alfa Molo's capital, N'Dorna, to inform him that he was bent on declaring *jihad* on all the remaining unbelievers in the Senegambia. Fode Kaba believed that Alfa Molo was in fact an unbeliever. He even suggested that the sovereign place himself under his spiritual authority, since Al-Hajj Umar was dead. Alfa Molo was greatly insulted by Fode Kaba's presumption. He and Fode Kaba, whose influence was greatest north of the Gambia River, entered into a series of conflicts. Neither leader was entirely victorious. Each of them was obliged to recognize the other's authority and sovereignty in their respective areas of influence.[8]

Alfa Molo's differences with Fode Kaba, like those between Molo and Nbuku Nyapa, underscored the persistent dilemma of Fuladu's legitimacy, particularly since the state had been established on an explicitly religious basis. It also posed the problem of the limits of the sovereign's personal power. Despite such inherent weaknesses Musa Molo chose to take the system that his father had developed at face value — so much so that it had become a caricature of itself by the turn of the century. Once Musa Molo assumed power in Fuladu, he found himself hemmed in by circumstances not unlike those that had constrained his father, but for radically different reasons.

The transfer of power

Before Alfa Molo died in 1881, he began to expand Fuladu's borders as a means of placating the more irascible military governors. But he had failed to work out a system of succession which could have insured a smooth transition after his death. According to tradition, Alfa Molo, in the manner of the former *Farim Cabos*, chose Bakary Demba, his brother born of the same mother, as his rightful heir. Before his death, however, Alfa Molo announced that he wanted his son Musa Molo to succeed him. Eventually Alfa Molo left his wives, property, and cattle to Bakary Demba, while leaving the throne to his son, Musa. Alfa Molo claimed that Fuladu had been the unique product of his own efforts, and that his own son Musa should succeed him rather than his brother Bakary Demba.[9]

Even though Musa Molo understood Alfa Molo's reasoning, he tried to work out an arrangement with Bakary Demba whereby his uncle would serve as king. However, in Musa Molo's mind, the king's position was to be ceremonial and without any real power. On balance the government was to remain intact, but the military governors, who conducted the day-to-day administration of the provinces, were to be directly responsible to Musa Molo. Musa himself was to serve as commander-in-chief of the army and was, under the circumstances, more powerful than the king himself.[10]

Initially, Bakary Demba accepted this plan. However, within a short period, he wanted to change some of Alfa Molo's policies. For example, Bakary Demba wanted the Fulbe in Fuladu to return to their forefather's religion and to eschew Islam. He expelled several important Muslim clerics and apostatized Islam. However, by the 1880s, Muslim clerics had begun to play a vital role in the religious life of Fuladu. They also had considerable political power. Consequently, by expelling the Muslim clerics, Bakary Demba cut himself off from a potentially important source of political support. Moreover, Musa Molo violently disagreed with his uncle's decision; for not only did it appear to vitiate an important segment of popular support within Fuladu, but it also threatened Fuladu's alliance with Futa Jallon's cleric sovereigns.[11]

Following his denunciation of Islam, Bakary Demba reintroduced the consumption of alcohol in Fuladu. Ostensibly Bakary Demba saw the use of alcohol as a means of distinguishing brave men from the cowards — in much the same way that its consumption had distinguished the princely aristocracy of Kaabu from the common people. Musa Molo opposed such a policy, in part because it violated Islamic law, but also because the widespread use of alcohol among his soldiers would have undermined the army's discipline.[12]

Perhaps the most fundamental difference between Bakary Demba and Musa Molo resided in their approach to the Europeans in the Senegambia. Bakary Demba was of the mind that the Europeans should be driven out of the region, even though he, on occasion, had enlisted the assistance of the Portuguese *provedors* or warrant officers at Geba and Bolama. He firmly believed that the Europeans were a menace, and that their commercial activities in the backland and coastal regions had to be curtailed, particularly since these initiatives were often underwritten by more forceful European military initiatives.[13] For example, Demba pointed to the network of plantations or *feitorias* established by French, Luso-African, and Portuguese merchants along the banks of the Rio Grande de Buba during the conflict between the Fulbe communities and Kaabu. By the middle of the 1870s — at the very moment that the Portuguese colonial budget ceased to register a deficit — these plantations began exporting tons of peanuts and other commercial crops to Europe.[14]

The immediate consequences of this new situation were not lost on the metropolitan Portuguese advocates of a more explicit colonial policy in

Portugal; for in 1878 José Corvo, the Portuguese Foreign Minister and Minister of the Colonies, detached Guinea from Cape Verde and made it a separate entity. Thousands of peasants and domestic slaves in Forria and Kanadu moved closer to the plantations and away from the direct jurisdiction of the Fulbe military governors. They traded their labor for plows, military protection and usufruct rights to the land. A minor economic revolution was effected in the process. Peasant men broke the soil of the rocky uplands with small plows and planted both millet and peanuts, while their women worked the mangrove laden lowlands or *bolanha* and planted rice and bulrush millet. The economic heartland of Fuladu, and the entire Guinea portion of the Senegambia, had begun to shift to those areas of the region where indigenous political authority was weakest. Musa Molo, at his capital of N'Dorna, was some distance away from this potentially unsettling situation.[15] On the other hand, Fulbe military strong men such as Bakary Demba governed areas that either abutted or included the expanding plantations.

Musa Molo simply failed to understand the long range implications of European initiatives. He was not alone in this regard, since few African rulers or European heads of state could have divined the political impact of the European penetration of Africa's hinterland in the 1860s and 1870s. Like his predecessors, Musa Molo attempted to play one set of Europeans off against another. However, Musa experienced only limited success with such an approach. For by the 1880s British, French and Portuguese interlopers were not content to control the external relations of the Senegambia under the rubric of Free Trade. Rather, they were determined to rule the region themselves, even at the cost of usurping the existing polities and imposing their own contingent version of law and order on the Senegambia's inhabitants. A gathering consensus in Europe abetted their aspirations in principle after the economic depression of the early 1880s and the 1884-85 Berlin Conference. On the other hand, the question of the appropriate stance toward the Europeans drove Musa and Bakary Demba even further apart. As we shall see, the power struggle between Musa Molo and Bakary Demba, which lasted from 1883 to 1892, accelerated the pace and widened the scope of French and Portuguese penetration. The dramatic increase in the output of the *feitorias* or plantations bore powerful witness to the enhanced European presence.

Musa Molo's relations with the French and the Portuguese

Mussá Moló, [is] the colossus who subjugated so many people in order to establish his power in the interior, between the Geba, Farim (S. Domingos) and Gambia rivers, [his prestige is such] that his name is heard with respect throughout Senegambia, whether in Portuguese, French or English possessions.

> Francisco Marques Geraldes, "Guiné Portuguesa — Communicação a Sociedade de Geografia sobre esta Provincia e suas condições actuaes", BSGL 7a serie, No. 1, 1887, p. 472

In that which concerns Firdou [Fuladu], the situation remains invariable. The iron hand of Moussa Moloh holds the country completely, the speed with which all the villages bring him taxes, the promptness with which his least important orders are executed prove this clearly.

> ANS, 13G482: Chef de Bataillon (Casamance) No. A11 to Governor General of French West Africa in St. Louis, 4 March 1896

After Alfa Molo's death, Musa Molo found it increasingly difficult to distinguish internal adversaries from external ones. Portuguese, French and British military officers and merchants readily intervened in Fuladu's local conflicts by supplying arms and, at times, troops. Of course, in their official correspondence to their home governments, Europeans on the spot vigorously denied involvement in local politics. But after the early 1880s they attempted to curry the favor of Musa Molo's rivals, including Bakary Demba, Dansa Demba and Dikory Kumba, with such enthusiasm that they often embarrassed their respective governments, which, prior to the Berlin Conference, were inclined to proceed in a more circumspect manner in the Senegambia. Musa Molo's ability to keep the Europeans at bay, then, reflected in part his success at manipulating their contradictory aspirations. Ironically, his eventual undoing was also a result of the fact that he acted on his own initiative; for Fuladu's formal alliance with Futa Jallon had begun to unravel at roughly the same time.[16]

On 3 November 1883 Musa Molo signed a treaty with French representatives, which, in effect, abrogated the series of treaties that his father had entered into with the Portuguese. The new treaty placed the lands that Musa Molo controlled and his subjects under French protection. According to the terms of the treaty, Musa Molo was also obliged to consult with the French government before ceding any portion of Fuladu's territory.[17] Finally, Musa Molo agreed not to interfere with French commercial companies operating in Fuladu and to protect the goods and persons of French merchants. In theory, this arrangement implied that Fuladu had become a French protectorate, and that all future relations between Musa Molo, his successors, and other Europeans were to be mediated by the prior interests of the French.[18]

Musa Molo entered into an alliance with the French to underscore his position as the legitimate ruler of Fuladu, and to isolate further his uncle Bakary Demba. Even though Bakary Demba chose not to uphold the terms of the treaties between Alfa Molo and the Portuguese, he was practically linked to the Portuguese *provedors* and plantation owners on Bolama. Musa believed that the French could help him eliminate Bakary Demba and other intransigent members of his official family and quell unrest in the provinces. From his vantage point, as well as that of other Muslim leaders in the Senegambia, the French appeared to be the most formidable Europeans in the region. For had not the French military campaigns of less than a generation before compelled the venerable Al-Hajj Umar and his successors to split the Umarian state into two parts in order to secure its survival?[19] Also, the French appeared to have more troops than either the Portuguese or the British. Moreover, according to local beliefs — beliefs that Musa Molo shared in part — the French leader, Faidherbe, had been born in Mecca and was, in fact, a Muslim. Consequently, the French presence in the Senegambia formed a part of the *baraka* or fate that Al-Hajj Umar had predicted. It was the will of Allah.

By contrast, Musa Molo was keenly aware of the relatively weak Portuguese position in the Senegambia. Portuguese troops were composed primarily of African auxiliary forces with divided loyalties. Consequently, the Portuguese could not always provide the residents of the areas they claimed to control with military protection. Portuguese residents and African peasants in the vicinity of Portuguese settlements at Geba, Buba, and Bolama were also inordinately dependent on French commercial firms and merchants. French merchants doubled as *feitoria* or plantation owners at Bolama, and African peasants farther inland had effected revolutionary changes in terms of the land's productivity and the work patterns of their households with the miniature plows that they purchased from French merchants. British influence in the Senegambia was confined to the northern banks of the Gambia River. And, British troops were rarely seen beyond the English settlements on the river. Even though British troops and their auxiliaries might have proved a formidable defensive bulwark within a prescribed area, particularly when backed up by British gunboats, they did not seem to want to enhance the scope of their influence in the Senegambia. Musa Molo, then, was obliged to respect the French position in the Senegambia from many interrelated vantage points.

For their part, the French claimed that they wanted to establish "peace" in the region — a peace which would have effectively excluded British and Portuguese commercial competition. The French believed that Musa Molo and Fuladu could assist them in this endeavor, which, in their minds, was the necessary first step in the conquest of the entire Senegambian region, including Futa Jallon. They also understood that Musa Molo could either be a useful ally — supplying troops, paying taxes, guaranteeing safe passage for caravans and insuring peace — or a formidable enemy that could disrupt commercial activity and plunge the entire region into a state of political uncertainty. For all these reasons the French wanted to establish control over Musa Molo and Fuladu as quickly as possible.

French traders also wanted control over the circulation of the products of Fuladu's domestic economy such as millet, maize, hides, ivory, beeswax, cotton and cloth.[20] Controlling the sale of hides was of particular importance to French merchants and also to American traders from the United States. By the 1870s, for example, American merchants were the principal purchasers of hides in Futa Jallon, offering twice the going rate in some instances; and toward the end of the 1870s American petroleum products and other lubricants had made their way to local markets in the Senegambia.[21] In 1883, on the eve of the Berlin Conference, a French military officer in Senegal reckoned the political dilemma in these terms:

> From a political point of view and from the point of view of the commercial future of the Casamance, we [the French] have an interest in reconciling with this chief; the country that he commands is vast ... [a treaty] with the chief [of Fuladu], will assure security along the railway that we are building ... in Haut-Senegal.[22]

The French colonial government in Senegal also believed that there had to be a general increase in agricultural output throughout the Senegambia in order to insure its survival, particularly since the Senegambia was being overshadowed by the increased commercial activity in the Niger Delta.[23] More cash crops such as peanuts and rubber were becoming increasingly important as sources of revenue for the colonial administrative infrastructure. This was particularly so after 1869, because of the buoyancy of the global market for peanuts and rubber and the increased production of both items in areas bordering Fuladu.[24] But with the slump of peanut prices on the world market in the 1880s, French colonial officials and merchants in the Senegambia feared that their efforts would be marginalized by British, German, and American competition, and by the indifference of African peasants in French spheres of influence to the prospect of collecting of wild rubber. And it was this fear that drove them to pin their hopes on stimulating rubber collection in Fuladu and the neighboring areas to the south.[25]

But without a working arrangement with Musa Molo, the French risked the possibility that Fuladu's monarch and his generals might in fact become even more hostile to French ambitions. According to a variety of French sources, the forays of Fuladu's army threatened the existence of French commercial posts all along the Casamance River, including those at Ziguinchor and Sedhiou. Moreover, caravans from Bundu in the south and the northern Sudanic regions began to avoid the French enclaves, preferring instead to go to the British enclave of Georgetown on McCarthy's Island and to Farim. The French also claimed that "Musa Molo's exacting policies of taxation, arbitrary judgement, or enforced conversion, forced (many entire villages) to emigrate into British Gambia or Portuguese Guinea, further weakening Fouladou's economy".[26]

The 1883 treaty between Musa Molo and the French exacerbated the tensions between Musa Molo and the Portuguese, and also those between the monarch and Fuladu's most disaffected provincial rulers.[27] These tensions came to a head once the Portuguese decided to assist Nbuku Nyapa's rebellion against Musa Molo's government. As we have mentioned earlier, the conflict between Fuladu and Kanadu was partly a result of the inherent shortcomings of Fuladu's political institutions. But Musa Molo further enhanced such weaknesses once he decided to oppose Portuguese ambitions in the Senegambia. The irony of the situation was that the growing peasant awareness of a commercial market for peanuts and other food products was accelerated by the activity of French merchants operating in the Portuguese spheres at Geba and Bolama.

Some time between January and March 1883 Musa Molo launched a series of small attacks on Kanadu's borders. Consequently, Nbuku Nyapa and his loyal retainers, some of whom had defected from Musa Molo's army, had to guard Kanadu's borders, leaving the more economically productive areas of the province to their own devices. Having drawn Nbuku Nyapa's soldiers to the borders, Musa Molo then attacked Kanadu's economic heartland with the bulk of his army.[28] His army raided the largest settlements and villages, carrying off women and children to use as slave labor in the fields further north in Fuladu — just at the moment that peasants were preparing for the peak period of the local trade, after having harvested the last of their fields of sesame, millet and peanuts.[29] Meanwhile the *feitors* or plantation owners along the Geba River and on Bolama Island eagerly awaited the arrival of the ships that would carry the peanuts, rubber, beeswax and palm products to European ports.

As we have mentioned earlier, the conflict between Fuladu and Kanadu was partly the result of the inherent shortcomings of Fuladu's political institutions. But Musa Molo further enhanced these weaknesses once he decided to oppose the Portuguese actions in the Senegambia. Musa Molo's campaigns against the plantations on the Geba River and against that segment of Kanadu's peasantry most actively involved in producing cash crops had a telling effect on Nbuku Nyapa's ability to prosecute the war and on the enthusiasm that Portuguese, French and Afro-European merchants and planters had for the rebellion.[30] Musa Molo's forces did in fact close many of the commercial routes from the interior to Geba and Bissau, which sped hides, ivory, gold, rubber, peanuts, and other oleaginous products on to Europe.[31] They also closed the Geba River to commercial vehicles, which meant that no imports from Europe could be received as well.[32] But Musa Molo's attacks were most destructive of the output and economic potential of the plantations.[33]

Between 1883 and 1887, peanut production on the plantations and nearby peasant farms in Kanadu went from 25 tons to less than 3 tons.[34] The rate of decline was steepest during the first two years of the rebellion, when peanut production fell by almost 20 tons. Even after the cessation of hostilities in 1887 commercial peanut production never achieved the sanguine features of the earlier period.[35] To be sure, there were a number of external factors that worked to undermine commercial peanut production in this particular region of the Senegambia — the competition of lard and petroleum based products from the United States, the reluctance of African peasants to plant peanuts on the most arable stretches of their own land, and the marginalization of peanuts by rubber in the 1880s and 1890s — but the impact of the war was immediate and palpable for contemporaries.[36] Consider the observations of an anonymous Portuguese official in 1886:

> The right bank of the river [Geba] is occupied by supporters of Mussá, our subject and terrible enemy, in spite of the light castigation which was given to one of the régulos who lived there, he continues to give serious worries to the traders and boats that travel on the river.

> In the interior, Mussá Moló threatens the frontiers of Ganadu, while his principal warriors attack with repeated raids [to] the flanks and the rearguard of our territory, already having raided a big settlement of ours two leagues from the fort.[37]

The Portuguese were anxious to end the war in Kanadu with their "terrible enemy". Geba was an important trading center and the Geba River was a key communication and transportation line through the region.[38] But, the Portuguese were relatively weak and could do very little to help Nbuku Nyapa. Even though Nbuku Nyapa claimed that the roads were open throughout his territory, by 1886, Musa Molo's forces were attacking Kanadu from all directions.[39]

Despite Musa Molo's victories and the control he exercised over Geba and the Geba River, he was still unable to crush the rebellion. On the other hand, peanut production on the plantations had plunged to less than sixteen percent of what it had been in 1878. Moreover, a minor famine was spreading inland, from the village communities at the headwaters of the Geba River. Predictably, the effects of the famine were more widespread on the plantations and among that portion of the peasantry that had participated enthusiastically in producing commercial crops for overseas markets. Doubtless such communities were particularly victimized by Musa Molo's reprisals. From the vantage point of the Europeans, especially the Portuguese, the local economy had all but collapsed. These circumstances were tragic and gave an ironic twist to the stipulation of the Berlin Convention that European powers had to demonstrate "effective occupation" of a given region of Africa before they could claim it as a colonial possession.[40]

Pressured by the ambitions of Britain and France in the area and its own substantial losses, the Portuguese government appointed Lieutenant Marques Geraldes commander at Geba and charged him with turning back Musa Molo's offensive. Toward the end of 1886, with the auxiliary assistance of Nbuku Nyapa's army, and after several confrontations, Marques Geraldes's army finally defeated the main force of Musa Molo's army. As a result, Molo was compelled to sign yet another treaty with the Portuguese. However, the language of the treaty and subsequent Portuguese commentary revealed the Portuguese dependence on Musa Molo's potential ability to revitalize the local economy. The treaty, in fact, charged Molo to make the region commercially viable once again. Given the implicit Portuguese recognition of Fuladu's claims to sovereignty over Kanadu, it is no wonder Musa Molo chose eventually to ignore the binding terms of the treaty. For in a very real sense, the Portuguese, by charging Musa Molo to restore the commercial prosperity of Kanadu, gave implicit support to his political claims.

... When the Secretary General of the government of this province, Augusto Cesar de Moura Cabral, found himself in charge of the government [he] accepted the solicitations of the king, Dembel [Bakary Demba], the master of Fuladú and from his chief of war, Mussa Molo, who asked him for a pardon for the hostilities practiced in Geba against the peaceful inhabitants of the same fort, with grave consequences for commerce, he signed a treaty in Farim pledging maximum obedient servitude to his majesty the King of Portugal and obliging them to divert all of the commerce from their dominions to Geba and Farim.[41]

On the other hand Nbuku Nyapa and the Portuguese garrison erroneously believed that this victory would end their problems with Musa Molo.[42] Portuguese traders and other European residents in Geba were not so naive and exhibited little confidence in the treaty. More or less disingenuously, in fact, they declared their lack of confidence in the new arrangement to the Portuguese Ministry of Colonies. The fears of the traders were echoed in the sentiments of the Ministry's chief secretary who, after a year, became concerned about the apparent inability of the treaty to erase the deficit in the Ministry's budget:

Mussá Moló never threatened nor will he ever threaten them in confident times, in light of his treacherous and disloyal character, demonstrated in various epochs by really savage acts and by his recognized disloyalty in fulfilling his promises. [The] conclusion [is] the complete expulsion of Mussá, with the annihilation of his forces and prestige in territories that are still considered ours [Portuguese] ...[43]

A year later the reservations of the traders and officials of the Ministry of Colonies appeared to be justified. For by mid 1887 Musa Molo's army launched a new series of offensives against Geba and Farim. Molo had perceived his defeat in early 1886 as a temporary setback and the subsequent treaty with the Portuguese as a means to gain enough time to replenish his army. He was determined to reassert his control over Kanadu. For in the previous decade it had become painfully obvious that whoever controlled Kanadu also controlled the southern Guinean portions of the Senegambia, which during the 1880s, had become the commercial hub of the entire region.

The rebellions in Kolla and Sankolla

Just prior to the 1886 defeat of Musa Molo's army, Nbuku Nyapa had begun to mobilize aristocratic Fulbe leaders in Fuladu's provinces of Kolla and Sankolla, both of which were in close proximity to the Portuguese settlement of Farim at the confluence of the Cacheu and Farim Rivers. A generation before the 1886 rebellion Kolla and Sankolla's governors had attempted to contest Alfa Molo's authority, and Nbuku Nyapa sought to capitalize on their smoldering discontent with the central government.[44] For at the outbreak of the 1886 rebellion the governors of these two provinces had not paid taxes to Musa Molo's government. They also refused to send levies of soldiers to the central army; nor did they send peasant work brigades to harvest Musa Molo's fields.[45] In so doing, they gave passive support to Nbuku Nyapa's rebellion. The implications of their actions did not elude Musa Molo; and after the signing of the 1886 treaty, he launched a vigorous military campaign against them.

With Kanadu, these provinces formed the core of the new agricultural heartland organized around producing food and other items for foreign and domestic markets. Like Geba, Farim received caravans from the interior and was a hub of overseas commercial activity. Musa Molo knew that if he could control Kolla and Sankolla, he could control indirectly the entire range of commercial activity in the Portuguese settlements, while simultaneously taxing foreign merchants and peasants who produced for the new markets. Similarly, Kolla and Sankolla's governors understood the new sources of commercial wealth to be the key to their putative independence from Fuladu.

In early 1887 Musa Molo's army attacked Panabó, the capital of Sankolla.[46] Once again the army's flanks engaged in a scorched earth campaign in the countryside before the main body of the army proceeded to the provincial capital. Thousands of peasants between Panabó and Farim fled to the French spheres of influence for protection. These attacks, which proved to be so destructive of the fruits of the peasantry's labor, instilled great fear in the local people — so much so, that peasants readily blamed the provincial rulers and the Portuguese merchants for the calamities that were visited upon them by Musa Molo's soldiers. However terrifying Musa Molo's campaign might have been to the province's inhabitants, it failed to unseat the provincial governors of Kolla and Sankolla, although it was not certain that this was, in fact, its objective. Nor did it compel the Portuguese to rule with the assistance of the rebel governors. In fact, Molo's campaign against the rebellious provinces, which came so soon after the dramatic intervention of Portuguese forces on behalf of Nbuku Nyapa, caught the Portuguese in the Senegambia off guard. For despite the nervousness displayed by the Ministry of Colonies and the colonial merchants, Portuguese officials on the spot genuinely believed that Musa Molo would abide by the terms of the 1886 treaty. Of course, the credulity of local Portuguese officials, most of whom were military officers, was predicated on the assumption that the main body of Musa Molo's army had collapsed during the course of Marques Geraldes and Nbuku Nyapa's counter offensive. Hence from the vantage point of the military men, there was no need to broaden Portugal's influence in the Senegambia by entering into a series of diplomatic arrangements on the order of the one they had arrive at with Nbuku Nyapa. Less than five years later they discovered how wrong they were.

In April 1887 Musa Molo signed yet another treaty with the Portuguese. The controversy surrounding the 1887 treaty was even greater than that associated with the previous one of 1886, particularly since the Portuguese Secretary General failed to consult either the local *Conselho do Governo* or Portugal's most important African ally in the region, Nbuku Nyapa.[47] However, taking sides in what appeared to be a conflict within Fuladu contradicted the official Portuguese policy on their relations with indigenous African states, which was "to always conserve friendship with all and in questions of wars between the different native tribes [to be] completely neutral, [desiring] to conserve peace and safety in the *presidio* [and] progress in agriculture and commerce".[48] Portuguese officials did in fact want to improve their relations with the more productive segments of Fuladu's peasantry. But their inability to protect peasants from Musa Molo's predations and repression severely damaged their prestige among the local people. By their own admission the Portuguese conceded that many residents of the Farim area left and settled in lands France controlled in order to elude the ravages of Musa Molo. Even though these reports appear to be contradictory, they were not. Ultimately local officials wanted to present their case against Musa Molo to their superiors as an excuse for the actions that they had already taken against him. At different times, depending upon Musa Molo's activities, the Portuguese, French and British in Farim, Geba, Sedhiou and Georgetown — that is, the principal nodal points of an expanding corridor of commercial agriculture — were adversely affected because of the disruption of economic activities and the out-migration of peasants.

The Portuguese colonial administration wanted to send a regular force of soldiers and African auxiliaries to the area to show Musa Molo that "it was time to stop his raids in Portuguese territories and to assure the people there that [Portuguese] protection is real".[49] They somehow believed that if they could send a gunboat up the Farim River for just one day that it would be enough of a threat to drive Musa Molo away. But the Portuguese were also fighting rebellious forces in Bissau and in Kanadu. A decisive military victory could not be had in any of the areas they claimed. Consequently, the Portuguese military had to rotate continuously their scant resources between these trouble spots. The Portuguese claimed that as soon as their forces arrived in Kanadu, for example, Musa Molo would move his troops to Kolla and Sankolla.[50] As a result, the Portuguese could not prevent the exodus of large numbers of peasants to areas under French control, nor could they definitively undermine Musa Molo's sovereignty. As late as the mid 1890s the Portuguese continued to underestimate Musa Molo.

The Portuguese had neither the manpower nor infrastructure to wage an all-out war against Musa Molo. Hence they formed weak, short-term alliances with disaffected Fulbe notables. While such alliances provided the context for the increased commercial activity in the Senegambia, Musa Molo's efforts to undo them or to tie them more directly to the central government became the source of terrifying instances of repression that compelled the most prolific strata of the peasantry to flee or to concentrate on subsistence production. Famine followed in the wake of Musa Molo's scorched earth campaigns. Musa Molo retained some measure of sovereignty — but at the expense of the most productive portions of the peasantry, many of whom found it less costly to abandon their villages by the thousands in the ensuing decade. The Portuguese remained — but only by allowing the military to vitiate the modest achievement of Portuguese merchants. Neither could generate an extensive or enthusiastic constituency for its policies.

Once Musa Molo's ties with the French became more explicit, his presence threatened the Portuguese even more. The Portuguese claimed that Musa Molo had become an agent of the French, and, together, they were bent on removing the Portuguese from the Senegambia. The Portuguese *chefe* in Farim believed that the French had encouraged Musa Molo to attack areas that the Portuguese claimed.[51] By 1891, the governor in Portuguese Guinea was calling Musa Molo an agent of French interests.[52] Although the French denied these charges, they never actively tried to stop Musa Molo from launching his attacks in Kanadu, Kolla or Sankolla — areas that the Portuguese claimed. The French wanted to gain control over these areas as well. They believed that if Musa Molo could destroy the little influence that the Portuguese had in the area and drain their coffers completely, that they would be a better position to acquire all of Senegambia.

Family rivalry

Musa Molo's relationship with the French was also the source of much confusion and enmity within his official family. Consequently, in addition to his difficulties with the rebellious provinces, Musa Molo also had to come to terms with the contumacious aspirations of his uncle, Bakary Demba, his cousin, Dansa Demba and his stepbrother, Dikory Kumba. In late 1891 Musa Molo broke off relations with Bakary Demba. He determined that Bakary Demba's ceremonial status as king was in fact a catalyst for the rebelliousness of Fuladu's most prosperous provinces. In early 1892, with substantial military support from the French, Musa Molo launched an attack against Bakary Demba and a core of handpicked bodyguards at Korop in Jimara. After a brief skirmish Bakary Demba fled and Musa Molo officially installed himself as king of Fuladu.[53] Bakary Demba and his followers escaped to the British territories in what later became the Gambia. Given the strong defensive positions of the British territories, Demba reasoned that he could live out the remaining years of his life there without fear of molestation from Musa Molo and his French allies.

After Bakary Demba's flight northward, Musa Molo turned his attention to the elimination of his other rivals — Dansa Demba and Dikory Kumba. Dansa Demba, Bakary Demba's son, was a popular figure in Fuladu well known for his courage and military prowess. Moreover, much of the peasantry believed that Dansa Demba had supernatural powers, and this, of course, contributed to his popular mystique.[54] Doubtless Musa Molo envied Dansa Demba's ostensible attributes, but he was more disturbed by the latter aristocrat's popular constituency. Consequently, he allowed the French to murder Dansa Demba before the news of the attack on his father's corp of bodyguards could reach him. Once again Musa Molo called on the French to assist him in dispersing his rivals and, in the process, enhanced his reputation as a tyrant.

By the beginning of 1893, one potential rival remained, Dikory Kumba. Although Dikory Kumba had no direct claims to the throne, given his reputation as the most formidable military tactician of his generation, Musa Molo saw his mere presence as a constant threat. In the late 1880s, Dikory Kumba attempted to join forces with Fode Kaba in order to defeat Musa Molo.[55] Although sympathetic to Dikory Kumba's goal of eliminating Musa Molo, Fode Kaba never threw his full support behind Dikory Kumba. In his correspondence with the French, Fode Kaba explained that he could not help Dikory Kumba fight Musa Molo without French approval because all three of them were theoretically allied to the French.[56] Toward the end of his struggle with Musa Molo, Dikory Kumba made a futile attempt to gain British protection for himself and his people. The British realized the possible repercussions of such actions and refused to take sides in the matter, thus strongly contributing to his further isolation.[57]   Once Dikory Kumba proved to be without any external support Musa Molo attacked his forces in late 1893, killed him, and silenced the last rival within his family.[58] Because of the smoldering rebellions in Kanadu, Kolla and Sankolla, Musa Molo became increasingly dependent upon French support to eliminate rivals. By the mid 1890s, Musa Molo's continued ability to rule very much depended upon French assistance.

Like his campaign against Kanadu, Musa Molo's war in the rebellious provinces near Farim in 1894 further undermined the regional economy. His soldiers burned and destroyed fields and crops which resulted in the paralysis of agricultural production. The constant threat of attack drove people to look for more peaceful areas in which to settle. People also fled because they feared that Musa Molo's army might enslave them and take them to the central region of Fuladu. These wars also prevented both local inhabitants and long distance traders from bringing their trade goods to Farim. Soldiers routinely attacked and robbed caravans travelling between Fuladu and Farim.[59]   Commercial activities from Geba to Farim declined rapidly from the late 1880s to the early 1890s. Goods that were not destroyed were diverted at times to the Casamance region, where the French provided better protection.

When Musa Molo attacked Kanadu, he claimed that he was avenging hostile actions taken against him, including raids against loyal villages and extortion of guns and gunpowder from his followers.[60] Sambel Seradim, Nbuku Nyapa's heir, continued the fight against Musa Molo throughout the early 1890s. Kanadu therefore remained in a state of upheaval.[61] Musa Molo's attacks against the rebellious provinces were intermittent rather than continuous.[62] Nevertheless, the attacks and counterattacks were immensely destructive. Numerous lives were lost on all sides and the productive capacity of the countryside in terms of both subsistence and commercial agriculture was in shambles. By early 1894, Musa Molo's army had isolated the largest portion of the north-south commercial corridor from the outside world.

By late 1894, even though Musa Molo retained his desire to establish control over the rebellious provinces, events farther south in Pachisse diverted his attention. The French, Musa Molo's erstwhile allies, had failed to occupy this province of Futa Jallon, after several months of fighting. Consequently, they requested his assistance in seizing Pachisse. Eventually, despite Musa Molo's longing to establish his uncontested rule in Kanadu, Kolla and Sankolla, and because of a contradictory set of obligations, he was compelled to redeploy his army southward.

French collaboration with Musa Molo in Pachisse

One might argue that the Pachisse campaign in 1894-95 was a perfect example of how the French used Musa Molo and his army to carry out their long-range objectives in the Senegambia. But more often than not, from the French vantage point, Musa Molo's collaboration did not have the desired effect. For example, Bamba Dalla, the local ruler in Pachessi, which had become a tributary state of Futa Jallon after the Fulbe siege of Kansala, had repulsed the French advance into his territory for several years. In 1894, a French officer, one Captain Baurès, decided to give Bamba Dalla an ultimatum to surrender or suffer the consequences. On 9 July 1894 Bamba Dalla gave his response: he launched a frontal attack on the French soldiers garrisoned at the town of Parumba, and on Musa Molo's auxiliary forces. The attack by Bamba Dalla's forces was so fierce that Musa Molo's soldiers deserted Captain Baurès and his battalion of sharpshooters or *tirailleurs*, leaving them to fend for themselves. As a result, the French soldiers were defeated and Baurès was recalled to France in disgrace.[63]

After this humiliating defeat, Musa Molo — for his own reasons and as a result of a rather disingenuous understanding of his obligations to the French — determined to conquer Pachessi and to incorporate it into Fuladu rather than hand it over to the French colonial government. Musa Molo requested assistance from the French, however. After considerable deliberation, the French did in fact send sixty *tirailleurs* under Lieutenant Moreau to support Musa Molo's troops.[64] On 21 January 1895, with his own force of about 3,000 soldiers and the French sharpshooters, Musa Molo attacked Pachessi's capital, Kankelifa. The town was sacked and burnt to the ground. Bamba Dalla fled, however, having received a prior warning about the attack. Even though Musa Molo's soldiers pursued him, Bamba Dalla managed to escape. But Pachessi was lost.[65] And, in a more protracted sense, so was the independence of Fuladu. For on the eve of the second offensive against Pachisse, Musa Molo had signed a treaty with the French in which he promised to give them half of the taxes he collected there.[66] The treaty also gave the French access to land within Fuladu itself in order to build a telegraph line.[67] Finally, it stipulated that the French were to be allowed to build a military post in the very heart of Fuladu at Hamdallai.[68] Upon the completion of the treaty the French resident sent an exuberant despatch to Paris: "We have gained absolute control over his [Musa Molo's] own acts and those of the chiefs of the region".[69]

Despite the outcome of the military contest, the degree of control that Musa Molo exercised over Pachessi declined precipitously. For as the terms of the above-mentioned treaty were implemented, Musa Molo's reliance upon the French increased more than even he had anticipated — so much so that he came to be perceived as a dependent of the French rather than a sovereign with whom the French collaborated. In fact, by 1895, Musa Molo had been effectively reduced to a relatively powerful mercenary, whose army was at the disposal of the French general staff and colonial administration. A French commandant assessed the French relationship with Musa Molo in blunt but insightful terms, while doing a tour of duty in the region a little more than a decade after the fall of Pachessi: "Each of these stages [various victories over his rivals] was marked with a new treaty so much more favorable to us [the French]".[70]

Musa Molo, the British and his exodus from French territory

By the mid 1890s, the Portuguese and the British knew that they had to meet the challenge of showing "effective occupation" if they wanted to prevent the French from taking over their enclaves in the Senegambia. Like the Portuguese, the British saw Musa Molo's destructive capacity in ominous terms. They too accused the French of encouraging Musa Molo's forays into their spheres of influence. In 1894, the British believed that the French were attempting to persuade Musa Molo to attack Kantora, a former Mandinka province on the south bank of the Gambia River over which both the British and Musa Molo claimed sovereignty. French military officers did in fact believe that Musa Molo's predations would eventually compel the British to withdraw from the northern regions of the Senegambia — leaving them for the French to exploit. Similarly, the British thought that the French wanted Musa Molo to attack the Jarra provinces, two prosperous Mandinka provinces that had sought British military protection during the course of Fuladu's establishment. Such an attack would have also forced Fode Kaba, the Mandinka warrior *imam* of northern Senegambia, to enter the fray. According to the British, "... the French wish in some way to depose Musah Moloh or get him under control. They do not care to attack him single handed but hope he will cause us to take the initiative, when they will probably offer cooperation with Fode Kaba ..."[71] These fears and suspicions contributed to an already tense situation in Fuladu. In many ways these problems were the natural result of the way that the Europeans sought to partition Fuladu. For Fuladu's boundaries sprawled across the artificial lines that Britain, France and Portugal had so cavalierly drawn on the wall maps at the Berlin Conference.[72]

As early as the 1880s, the British wanted to negotiate a treaty with Musa Molo in order to bring Fuladu under their control.[73] Like the French and Portuguese, the British recognized that Fuladu was a fairly rich agricultural region with resources that could be tapped and made to work for British interests. Resident British merchants were convinced that Fuladu's peasantry could produce commercial crops on the scale that they had in 1878 and, as a result, become reliable consumers of British manufactures. For example, in 1899, British officials estimated that Musa Molo had approximately eighty villages in areas claimed by their government. In turn, these villages contained 8,000 households — households that could be made to pay taxes and other revenues to the British colonial government.[74]

In 1901, Musa Molo met with the Governor of the British Protectorate to determine how his territories within British areas would be administered. They agreed that a British Commissioner would be present in Musa Molo's territory but that Musa Molo would hold Native Courts when the Commissioner was present. They also discussed the British desire to collect "hut taxes" and to pay Musa Molo an annual stipend. Given the potential wealth that could be generated by peasants and merchants, he was against their original offer of three hundred pounds sterling per annum. Musa Molo knew this offer would represent a net loss for his government. Finally, however, Musa Molo compromised and accepted a flat sum of five hundred pounds sterling per annum and relinquished his rights to collect taxes and revenue in these areas.[75]

Although Musa Molo signed no formal treaties with the British, these negotiations alarmed the French who still considered him to be under their "protection". Musa Molo reassured the French that his discussions with the British were only to regulate the organization of his people who had sought to place themselves under British military protection during the course of Musa Molo's campaigns against the rebellious provinces.[76] His agreement with the British meant:

> ... 1) that part of his kingdom within the British sphere of influence should become part of the Gambia Protectorate; 2) that a British officer should be put in charge there; 3) that all dealing in slaves would be outlawed; 4) that practices of punishment repugnant to the laws of humanity and civilization would be discontinued; 5) that the governor could impose and collect a hut tax there.[77]

At the same time that Musa Molo entered into this agreement, which was no more than a statement of intent, his relations with the French were becoming more and more difficult. By the end of the century, despite his statements to the contrary, Musa Molo's relationship with the French had begun to erode. In fact, as early as Fuladu's campaign against Pachisse in the mid 1890s, Musa Molo had begun to doubt the utility of his relationship with the French. As mentioned earlier, French arms shipments and military assistance became exceedingly unreliable at that point. Moreover, by 1901, the French had defeated Samori Touré, their most formidable enemy in West Africa. The French had also defeated Futa Jallon, the Islamic theocracy which had been vitally important in legitimating the existence of Fuladu. The French plan for building one huge colony in West Africa simply did not include Musa Molo. They could no longer allow him even the pretense of ruling Fuladu.

Between 1901 and 1903 the French accused Musa Molo of arbitrary policies that were underscored by enslavement, torture and other excesses.[78] To be sure, Fuladu's population did continue to flee. More than thirty villages moved to the British territories in this period, while several more fled to the contested border regions, where the authority of the French, Portuguese and Musa Molo was more or less ineffectual.[79] Toward the middle of 1903 the French colonial resident, H. de la Roncière, summoned Musa Molo to the newly constructed military post at Munini on the left bank of the Casamance River.[80] Allegedly Musa Molo was to be given the opportunity to respond to the charges levelled against him. But the implications of being summoned to a military post rather than a civilian center of French colonial administration such as Sedhiou was not lost on Musa Molo. Nor did the fact that the French were not entirely without blame for the violent excesses that had been visited on large segments of the peasantry elude Musa Molo. Consequently, rather than acceding to de la Roncière's request, Musa Molo fled north to the British enclave of the Gambia on 14 May 1903. Musa Molo's precipitous departure appeared to have been justified in part by the disingenuous motives of the French. But the fact remained that Musa Molo's forces no longer posed a threat to the French.

While the French did not disguise their pleasure at Musa Molo's departure, the nature of his exodus did not add to the legitimacy of their putative occupation of portions of Fuladu. Because Musa Molo departed with his entourage before de la Roncière could prepare Munini for what would have proved to be a military tribunal, the French actions took on an aura of studied duplicity:

> Moussa took with him several hundred women who compose his harem, around sixty horsemen who form his guard and ... a certain number of inhabitants following him. He burned his personal possessions in Hamdalahi and N'Dornan, and some villages located along his route, whose inhabitants consented to accompany him under the influence of his threat.[81]

Moreover, indigenous opposition to Musa Molo was quick to recognize that the French had abandoned him. Any notable or village that showed the slightest opposition to Musa Molo was assured that their opposition would experience no reprisals from Fuladu's beleaguered sovereign.[82] As the Governor General of French West Africa stated:

> ... From a political point of view, Moussa Moloh's departure has avoided us the trouble of stopping and deposing a chief who ruined his country and has proved to us the confidence that the population has in our French administration, we no longer have to be caught reckoning with his local

customs, [we] only have to proceed with a reorganization of the country which favors its exploitation.[83]

Hostility between France and Musa Molo continued after he left the Casamance. Musa Molo accused the French of harassing and threatening his subjects who followed him into British territory. He claimed that the French sent messengers across the border to tell his followers that the British would force Musa Molo to return within a short time and that if they did not return immediately, they would face stiff penalties upon extradition.[84] But despite the French desire to have Musa Molo extradited, the British refused to comply with their requests.

The British allowed Musa Molo to remain in the Gambia as long as he obeyed their rules and refrained from performing any hostile acts against the French.[85] He also had to abide by the provisions outlined in the agreement he made with the British in 1901. Moreover, he could not interfere with the governance of former subjects of Fuladu who had taken up residence in the Gambia before or after his arrival.[86] Consequently, the British offer was not entirely an act of charity; for British colonial officials believed that Musa Molo's followers, as well as subsequent refugees from Fuladu, would dramatically increase the revenue at their disposal by increasing agricultural production. A year after their initial arrival, refugees from Fuladu planted some food crops as well as peanuts, but their contribution to the state's coffers was minimal. However, in the years that followed, they produced cash and food crops with alacrity, thus markedly increasing their contribution to the colonial government's revenue.[87]

Meanwhile the establishment of French and Portuguese administrations in portions of Fuladu did not stanch the out-migration of numerous African peasants. Many villages and provinces within Fuladu had celebrated Musa Molo's departure. But, by the turn of the century, French and Portuguese rule proved to be just as, if not more, egregious. By 1910 peasants from those areas of Fuladu controlled by the French were turning up in the Gambia by the thousands. These peasants, who were called "strange farmers" preferred to cultivate peanuts in the British territory because taxes were considerably lower there. The "strange farmers" paid farm rents to the British colonial government and then returned to French territory as soon as they had sold their crop of peanuts. After the revenues they received from "hut" taxes, farm rents were the next largest source of income for the British in the Upper River District of Gambia, all of which had once been a part of Fuladu.[88] The British colonial government in the Gambia not only profited from the efforts of the migrants, but it also increased its political currency among the African population at the expense of the French and Portuguese.

Musa Molo's story was similar to those of other African leaders in the last quarter of the twentieth century. He, like his counterparts elsewhere, lived in the tumultuous times when the motivations of Europeans changed very quickly — for reasons that neither Europeans nor Africans could have predicted a generation before. Rather than trade *per se*, the Europeans now aggressively pursued what one contemporary historian has succinctly termed an "investment in law and order", in an attempt to establish their political control over potential peasant consumers of the by-products of periodic European overproduction. Tragically, in the short run, the quintessential expression of the European advantage was the ability of the industrial nations to produce devastating weapons on a mass scale. Insofar as Musa Molo understood these circumstances and the new, more contingent nature of European objectives in the Senegambia, he tried to use the Europeans, particularly the French, to assist him in extending Fuladu's boundaries and extending his own power. However, the Europeans were also determined to exploit Musa Molo for their own ends. Because of conflicting interests, many problems ensued and Musa Molo and his subjects came out on the losing end.

Musa Molo had turned to the French for a variety of reasons. He was plagued by rivalries within his official family as well as rebellion in several key provinces. He believed the French to be strongest and the most capable party of Europeans in the Senegambia; and that French arms and military assistance would enable him to eliminate aristocratic rivals, crush internal dissent and expand Fuladu's borders. In the end, however, he found himself and Fuladu swallowed up by forces that neither he nor the French sufficiently understood. Musa Molo also suffered because Fuladu traversed the artificial boundaries that the British, French and Portuguese had drawn in the Senegambia. Consequently, all three powers, in their own way, wanted to form alliances with Musa Molo in order to secure a portion of Fuladu in the future.[89]

In his efforts to make Fuladu a regional power, Musa Molo engaged Futa Jallon, client states, family members, and finally, the Europeans. The French and Portuguese in particular were often drawn into Fuladu's internal conflicts in spite of their immediate interests. In general they entered into Fuladu's domestic crisis with an eye toward making potential African opposition less formidable. On the other hand, Musa Molo entered into diplomatic agreements with the Portuguese, French and British that obliged them to accept Fuladu's sovereignty, if only in a contingent fashion. But until the mid 1890s, for their own reasons, both Musa Molo and the Europeans determined to leave the matter of Fuladu's borders in a decidedly ambiguous state. Between 1881 and 1894 Musa Molo was remarkably successful at pitting the Europeans against one another, but after the latter date, for internal and external reasons, he lost momentum and Fuladu was divided among the colonial powers in question.

In many ways Musa Molo was a victim of his times, who complicated his own existence through the use of excessive force and terror. His actions were very destructive of the indigenous assumption that a ruler should be well-bred, discreet and imminently dignified. His subjects came to see his destructive capacity in much the same way that they viewed forces of nature such as drought or locusts. His scorched earth campaigns did much to embellish this popular analogy. Instead of loyalty, they instilled a disquieting passivity among the peasantry. Part of Musa Molo's undoing was that, after 1894, he appeared uniquely handicapped in discerning these two very different qualities in his own subjects. Finally, Musa Molo was an opportunist who tried to manipulate both the French and Islam to his advantage. He realized too late though that the French had used him for their own purposes. Like his father, Musa Molo used Islam as a unifying force within Fuladu. But although Islam contributed to cohesion within Fuladu, it could neither shore up the institutions of the state nor save it from the onslaught of the European advance in Senegambia during the last two decades of the nineteenth century. Moreover, by the turn of the century much of the Senegambia had become a study in desolation and its people terrorized into languorous resignation about the future.

Notes

1. See Chapter One for more information.
2. Mamadou Falai Baldeh, Banjul Series Tape 21 (Latrikunda), 21 August 1978.
3. Alhaji Kawasu Sillah, Banjul Series Tape 16 (Brikama), 31 July 1978; and António José Machado, "A Fraternidade Guiné e Cabo Verde — Folha Dedicada a Socorrer as Victimas da estiagem da Província Caboverdiana", *BOGP*, 31 October 1883.
4. For more on Al-Hajj Umar see: Robinson, *Holy War*.
5. The Molos were pawn members of the Baldeh family.
6. Alhaji Kawsu Sillah, Banjul Series Tape 16 (Brikama), 31 July 1978.
7. Mamadou Falai Baldeh, Banjul Series Tape 12 (Sankulikunda), 25 June 1978.
8. Leary, "Islam, Politics", p. 178.
9. Mamadou Falai Baldeh, Banjul Series Tape 22 (Latrikunda), 12 August 1978; and PRO, CO 87/141: Manager of McCarthy Island to Llewelyn, Administrator of the Gambia, 3 March 1892.
10. Leary, "Islam, Politics", pp. 183-84.
11. Mamadou Falai Baldeh, Banjul Series Tapes 22 and 23 (Latrikunda), 12-13 August 1978; and Alhaji Kawsu Sillah, Banjul Series Tape 16 (Brikama), 31 July 1978.
    Fuladu never became a theocratic state like other states in West Africa.

Neither Alfa Molo nor Musa Molo were Islamic scholars, but they both recognized that this religion could help them to develop a sense of unity among recently conquered groups.

12. Jali Sanejang Kuyateh, Banjul Series Tape 10 (Bansang), 25 June 1978.
13. Roche, *Conquête et resistance*, pp. 242-44.
14. Hammond, *Portugal and Africa*, pp. 36-76.
15. PRO, CO 87/141: Manager of McCarthy Island to Llewelyn, Administrator of The Gambia, 3 March 1892. See also: B.K. Sidibe, "Brief History" and Roche, *Conquête et resistance*, pp. 237-63.
16. PRO, CO 87/141: Musa Molloh to Governor in Bathurst, 13 April 1892; and AHU, Guiné Pasta 411: ; Governor in Bolama to Ministro e Secretário d'Estado dos Negócios da Marinha e Ultramar, 22 March 1888; AHU, Guiné, Pasta 414: Eduardo Augusto Perfelin, Chefe em Farim to Secretaria Geral do Governo, 8 June 1890; and ANSOM, Sénégal IV, Dossier 131: Governor General of A.O.F. to Ministre des Colonies, 23 June 1903.
17. Christian Roche pointed out that this clause was important because Musa Molo claimed some areas located in Portuguese and British claimed territories. See: Roche, *Conquête et resistance*, p. 238.
18. ANS, 13G4: Traité avec les chefs indigènes. A copy of the text of this treaty is in Roche, *Conquête et resistance*, pp. 238-9.
19. ANS, 1G295, Doc. 208: H. de la Roncière, "Travail d' hivernage — Historique du Fouladou", 1903; see also: Robinson, *Holy War*.
20. ANS, Sénégal 4B74: Cleret, "Rapport du Gouvernement", 7 June 1883; PRO, CO 87/129: E.A.M. Smith, Manager of McCarthy Island, to G.T. Carter, Administrator of The Gambia, 12 October 1886; BOGP, 1886, No. 17, p. 73; and BOGP, 1885, No. 35, p. 166.
21. Goerg, *Commerce et colonization*, p. 80.
22. ANS, Sénégal 4B74: Cleret, "Rapport du Gouvernement", 7 June 1883.
23. Goerg, *Commerce et colonization*, p. 82; and James F. Searing, *West African Slavery and Atlantic Commerce: The Senegal River Valley, 1700-1860*, Cambridge, Cambridge University Press, 1993. For information on the Niger Delta see: K.O. Dike, *Trade and Politics in the Niger Delta*, Oxford, Oxford University Press, 1957. For more details on other regions of West Africa see: Robin Law, ed., *From Slave Trade to "Legitimate Commerce": The commercial transition in nineteenth century West Africa*, Cambridge, Cambridge University Press, 1995.
24. Goerg, *Commerce et colonization*, pp. 76-7.
25. Goerg, *Commerce et colonization*, pp. 339-40; ANSOM, Sénégal IV, Dossier 106 (b): Governor to Ministre de la Marine et des Colonies, December 1883; and ANS, 4B74: Correspondence of Lt. Governor Cleret

to Governor, 7 June 1883.

26. ANSOM, Sénégal IV: H. de la Mothe, Governor to Governor of Guinée Française, 22 January 1894; ANS, 13G327: "Sénégal et Dépendances, Mission du Fouladou, Rapport du Capitaine Baurès, 1894"; and Leary, "Islam, Politics", p. 192.

27. *BOGP*, 1883, No. 31, pp. 143-44; *BOGP*, 1883, No. 49, pp. 217-18; *BOGP*, 1886, No. 31, p. 129; and AHU, Guiné, Pasta 410: Francisco de Paula Gomes Barbosa, Governor to Ministro e Secretário d'Estado dos Negócios da Marinha e Ultramar, 28 July 1886.

28. AHU, Guiné, Pasta 402: Report of the *Conselho do Governo*, 22 April 1887.

29. AHU, Guiné, Pasta 402: Report of the *Conselho do Governo*, 22 April 1887.

30. *BOGP*, 1886, No. 41, p. 172.

31. *BOGP*, 1886, No. 17, p. 73; and AHU, Guiné, Pasta 402: Residents and Traders of Geba to Governor of the Province, 18 March 1887.

32. AHU, Guiné, Pasta 402: Report of the *Conselho do Governo*, 22 April 1887.

33. Marques Geraldes, "Guiné Portugueza", pp. 487-91.

34. AHU, Guiné, Pasta 402: Governo da Provincia to Ministro e Secretário d'Estado dos Negócios da Marinha e Ultramar, 24 April 1887.

35. *BOGP*, 1886, No. 41, p. 172; and AHU, Guiné, Pasta 411: Governor Francisco de Paula Gomes Barbosa to Ministro e Secretário d'Estado dos Negócios da Marinha e Ultramar, 26 August 1886.

36. Goerg, *Commerce et colonization*, pp. 104-5; and, AHU, Guiné, Pasta 402: Governo da Provincia to Ministro e Secretário d'Estado dos Negócios da Marinha e Ultramar, 24 April 1887.

37. *BOGP*, 1886, No. 41, p. 172.

38. *BOGP*, 1883, No. 17, p. 84; and *BOGP*, 1883, No. 31, pp. 143-45.

39. *BOGP*, 1886, No. 23, p. 97.

40. Marques Geraldes, "Guiné Portugueza", pp. 487-91.

41. AHU, Guiné, Pasta 402: Governo da Provincia to Ministro e Secretário d'Estado dos Negócios da Marinha e Ultramar, 24 April 1887.

42. *BOGP*, 1886, No. 41, p. 172; and AHU, Guiné, Pasta 411: Governor Francisco de Paula Gomes Barbosa to Ministro e Secretário d'Estado dos Negócios da Marinha e Ultramar, 26 August 1886.

43. AHU, Guiné, Pasta 402: Governo da Provincia to Ministro e Secretário d'Estado dos Negócios da Marinha e Ultramar, 24 April 1887.

44. ANS, 1G91: Rapport. Loitard, "Mission dans le Fouladougou, le Niani et le Kalondadougou", 28 October 1888.

45. ANS, 1G295, Doc. 208: H. de la Roncière, "Travail d'hivernage — Historique du Fouladou", 1903.

46. AHU, Guiné, Pasta 402: Francisco António Marques Geraldes to Secretaria Geral, 18 March 1887.

47. AHU, Guiné, Pasta 402: Governor da provincia to Ministro e Secretário d'Estado dos Negócios da Marinha e Ultramar, 22 April 1887.

48. AHU, Guiné: Eduardo Augusto Perfelin, Chefe em Farim to Secretário Geral do Governo, 8 June 1890; AHU, Guiné, Pasta 414: Governor Santos to Ministro e Secretário d'Estado dos Negócios da Marinha e Ultramar, 21 July 1890; and AHU, Guiné, Pasta 415: Governo do distrito da Guiné to Ministro e Secretário d'Estado dos Negócios da Marinha e Ultramar, 24 May 1893.

49. AHU, Guiné, Pasta 414: Governor Santos to Ministro e Secretário d'Estado dos Negócios da Marinha e Ultramar, 20 January 1891.

50. AHU, Guiné, Pasta 414: Governor da provincia em Bolama to Ministro e Secretário d'Estado dos Negócios da Marinha e Ultramar, 22 Jun 1891.

51. AHU, Guiné, Pasta 415: Presídio de Farim to Secretaria do Governo do Distrito, 7 June 1893.

52. AHU, Guiné, Pasta 414: Governor Santos to Ministro e Secretário d'Estado dos Negócios da Marinha e Ultramar, 25 March 1891.

53. ANS, 1G295, Doc. 208: H. de la Ronciére, "Travail d'hivernage — Historique du Fouladou", 1903; and ANSOM, Sénégal IV, Dossier 108 (d): Capitaine Laumonnier, Sedhiou to Governor of Senegal, 2 March 1892.

54. Mamadou Falai Baldeh, Banjul Series Tape 13 (Sankulikunda), 25 June 1978; Mansajang Banja, Banjul Series Tape 7 (Bansang), 21 June 1978; and Alhaji Kawsu Sillah, Banjul Series Tape 16 (Brikama), 31 July 1978.

55. PRO, CO 87/136: Mittford, Acting Administrator of The Gambia to Knusford, Secretary of State for the Colonies, 10 October 1889.

56. ANSOM, Sénégal IV, Dossier 108 (b): Fodé Kaba to Commandante of Carabane, 9 February 1894.

57. PRO, CO 87/144: Decore of Sukuta to Governor of Bathurst, 27 July 1893; PRO, CO 87/144: Acting Administrator of Bathurst to Decori Cumba, 28 July 1893.
The British avoided the issue by demanding that Dikory Kumba come in person to Bathurst. Dikory Kumba explained to the British that he refused to go to Bathurst when they initially called him, because Musa Molo had taken most of his men and he was alone and subject to attack. When the British repeated their demand that Dikory Kumba make his request in person, they were in effect avoiding taking sides in the conflict.

58. Although Musa Molo's forces attacked Dikory Kumba's headquarters in Nioro in early 1892, Dikory Kumba's death came sometime between October and December of 1893. See: AHU, Guiné, Pasta 415: Governor in Bolama to Ministro e Secretário d'Estado dos Negócios da Marinha e Ultramar, 23 December 1893; Mansajang Banja, Banjul Series Tape 7 (Bansang), 21 June 1978; Arafang Tombong Tambajang, Banjul Series Tape 9 (Bansang), 21 June 1978; and Alhaji Kawsu Sillah, Banjul Series Tape 16 (Brikama), 31 July 1978.

59. AHU, Guiné, Pasta 414: Governor Santos to Ministro e Secretário d'Estado dos Negócios da Marinha e Ultramar, 25 March 1891; and AHU, Guiné, Pasta 413: Act No.7, 26 September 1890.

60. AHU, Guiné, Pasta 411: Governo da Provincia em Bolama to Ministro e Secretário d'Estado dos Negócios da Marinha e Ultramar, 22 March 1888; and ANSOM, Sénégal IV, Dossier 27 (a): Moussa Molo to Administrator of Sedhiou, March/April 1888.

61. *BOGP*, 1890, Supplement to No. 48.

62. ANSOM, Sénégal VI, Dossier 27 (a): Moussa Molo to Governor, translated 28 April 1893; and ANS, 2B209: Minister of the Colonies to Governor of Senegal and its Dependencies, 11 August 1894.

63. ANSOM, Sénégal IV, Dossier 128 (d): "Rapport d'ensemble du Colonel de Trentian" to Ministre des Colonies, 7 May 1895; and Mansajang Banja, Banjul Series Tape 7 (Bansang), 21 June 1978.
    Musa Molo also provided support in the French wars against Mamadou Lamine in 1886.

64. AMNE, Maço 7: H. de la Mothe, Governor of Senegal to Governor of Guiné Portugueza, 8 January 1895; and Alhaji Kawsu Sillah, Banjul Series Tape 1 (Banjul), 9 May 1978.

65. INIC, Documentos Diversos de 1895: Commando Militar de Geba to Secretária do Governo, 11 March 1895; ANSOM, Sénégal IV, Dossier 128 (d): "Rapport d'ensemble du colonel de Trentian" to Ministre des Colonies, 7 May 1895.

66. ANS, 13G473 (1): "Rapport Semetriel (1894)" from Administrator Adam (Haute Casamance).

67. Leary, "Islam, Politics", p. 188.

68. ANS, 13G473 (1): "Rapport Semestriel (1894)" from Administrator Adam (Haute Casamance).

69. ANS, 13G482: "Traité entre la France et le Firdu", 25 January 1896.

70. ANS, 13G67: Administrateur-Adjoint Commandant du Cercle de la Haute Gambie to Lt. Governor of Senegal, 9 August 1910.

71. PRO, CO 87/146: Administrator Llewelyn to Secretary of State for the Colonies, 8 May 1894.

72. The British and the Portuguese both blamed the French for this dilemma because they said that the French drew the lines.

73. PRO, CO 87/128: Rowe, Governor-in-chief in Sierra Leone to the Earl of Granville, 15 May 1886.

74. PRO, CO 87/158: Administrator Llewelyn to Chamberlain, 15 June 1899.

75. PRO, CO 87/163: Governor in Bathurst to Secretary of State for the Colonies, 7 June 1901.

76. ANSOM, Sénégal VI, Dossier 128 (d): Governor-General of A.F.O. to Ministre des Colonies, 3 October 1901.

77. Leary, "Islam, Politics", p. 188; ANS, 1F9 (3): "Report for 1901 to both Houses of Parliament by Command of his Majesty, July 1902", Colonial Reports, Annual no. 355-Gambia.

78. For more specific information on Musa Molo's activities see: ANSOM, Sénégal IV, Dossier 131: Governor-General of A.O.F. to Ministre des Colonies, 22 June 1903.

79. ANSOM, Sénégal IV, Dossier 131: Governor-General of A.O.F. to Ministre des Colonies, 22 June 1903.

80. Roche, *Conquête et resistance*, pp. 258-9.

81. ANSOM, Sénégal IV, Dossier 131: Governor-General of A.O.F. to Ministre des Colonies, 22 June 1903.

82. ANSOM, Sénégal IV, Dossier 131: Governor-General of A.O.F. to Ministre des Colonies, 22 June 1903.

83. ANSOM, Sénégal IV, Dossier 131: Governor-General of A.O.F. to Ministre des Colonies, 22 June 1903.

84. PRO, CO 87/169: Moussa Moloh to Governor Denton, 30 July 1903.

85. PRO, CO 87/170: Governor Denton to Governor-General of Senegal, 13 October 1903.

86. PRO, CO 87/170: Governor Denton to Secretary of State for the Colonies, 7 November 1903.

Musa Molo stayed in the Gambia until his death in 1931. The British deported him to Sierra Leone during World War I, but he never received permission to return to his former territories in either Senegal or Portuguese Guinea. He made numerous requests to both the French and the Portuguese for permission to enter these territories but they were always denied. The French were concerned that Musa Molo might go to Portuguese Guinea and try to form an alliance with Abdul Njai who, by 1917, was operating independently in the regions near the border with Senegal. See: Chapter Six; ANS, 13G67: Lt. Governor of Senegal, No. 171 to Governor-General of A.O.F., W. Ponty, 17 August 1914; ANS, 13G67: Governor-General of A.O.F., W. Ponty to Lt. Governor of Senegal, 8 September 1914; ANS, 13G67: Governor-General of A.O.F.

to Lt. Governor of Senegal, January 1915; and Joye L. Bowman, "Abdul Njai: Ally and Enemy of the Portuguese in Guinea-Bissau, 1895-1919", *JAH*, 27, 1986, pp. 463-79.

87. PRO, CO 87/171: Governor to Secretary of State for Colonies, 13 May 1904; PRO, CO 87/169: Lt. Stanley, Travelling Commissioner to Colonial Secretary, 2 July 1903; and PRO, CO 87/171: Governor to Secretary of State for the Colonies, 13 May 1904.

88. PRO, CO 87/170: Governor Denton to Secretary of State for the Colonies, 7 November 1903; and PRO, CO 87/169: Lt. Stanley, Travelling Commissioner to Colonial Secretary, 2 July 1903. See also: Ken Swindell, "Serawoolies, tillibunkas and 'Strange Farmers': The Development of Migrant Groundnut Farming along the Gambia River, 1848-95", *JAH*, 21, 1980, pp. 93-104.

89. The problems these arbitrary division created did not end with the destruction of the colonial regimes. Rather, boundary disputes are still common and continue to plague independent African nations today. For example, some of the tensions between Senegal and The Gambia, Guinea-Bissau and Guinea (Conakry), Kenya and Uganda, and Togo and Ghana reflect the artificial nature of these international lines.

4 The Internal Crisis in Senegambia and Guinea, 1880-1903

The struggle for the Forria

> In 1856 the fullas [Fulbe] rebelled against their legitimate masters, and this rebellion continues until today. It is a war of life and death. It is the cause of the continuous wars to which the government troops are subjected.
>
> António José Machado, "A Fraternidade Guiné e Cabo Verde — Folha Dedicada a Socorrer as Victimas da estiagem da Província Caboverdiana", *BOGP*, 31 October 1883

Well before 1867 Fulbe communities began streaming into the Forria, as a result of Al-Hajj Umar's call for *heshira* as well as Mandinka repression and terror. The notables of the Biafada and Nalu, the autochthonous inhabitants of the Forria, granted Fulbe refugees permission to settle on their lands.[1] On the other hand, Biafada generosity was seconded by the growing number of armed bands of Fulbe irregulars or *yelle mansa* from Futa Jallon that had begun to use the Forria as a staging area for their raids into Kaabu's outlying provinces such as Badora and Kanadu. Also, toward the end of the 1850s, a number of Biafada chiefs, in their capacity as landlords or "protectors" of Portuguese *feitors* or planters, were steering a large number of Fulbe peasants toward the burgeoning plantations on the northern edge of the Forria, along the banks of the Rio Grande. Soon the Forria, which had previously been a buffer zone between

Kaabu and Futa Jallon, was drawn into the escalating hostilities. Yet the flow of Fulbe refugees from Kaabu continued to increase.

The Biafada in the Forria required that each Fulbe family pay an annual tax of one male calf or sixty bands of cotton cloth. Initially the Fulbe readily complied with the Biafada demand. Fulbe, in turn, received "pastures for their cattle and salt for their food" from the Biafada.[2] Because many Fulbe settlers, particularly those from Kanadu and Badora, had chosen to become farmers with cattle rather than pastoralists *per se* in the previous generation, they adapted well to Forria's fertile plains. Moreover, their cattle became a source of fertilizer and residual revenue for them and their Biafada patrons. On balance, the new Fulbe settlement in the Forria appeared to be mutually beneficial to the migrants and the original inhabitants.[3]

But once the Forria was transformed into a series of armed camps, this relatively peaceful arrangement evaporated. As they swept westward, Fulbe settlers began to encroach upon the communal lands of the Biafada. As a result, the Biafada increased their demands on the Fulbe — so much so, in fact, that the Fulbe came to perceive themselves as the "object of innumerable extortions and acts of violence, actually living a servile life".[4] But the Fulbe were unwilling to be reduced once again to a servile position. For many of the Fulbe that poured into the Forria were former slaves or *Fulbe-djiábê* who had become farmers in order to underscore their emancipation.[5] However, their enthusiasm for farming was both a blessing and a curse; for it had caught the attention of the increasingly predatory Mandinka aristocracy in Kaabu — and, subsequently, that of the Biafada chiefs in the Forria. On the other hand, the increasing rate of settlement and the presence of armed irregulars from Futa Jallon militated strongly in favor of an aggressive reaction to escalating Biafada exactions from Fulbe migrants.

Predictably, communal struggles among the Biafada, which had been exacerbated by Fulbe settlement in the eastern portions of the Forria such as Dandum-Gussara, further undermined Biafada authority.[6] Eastern Biafada notables chafed at the prospect of becoming clients and subordinates themselves. But after the fall of Kansala, the number of Fulbe in the Forria increased once again. Ironically, Biafada notables whose communities were not in the path of Fulbe expansion were obliged to suppress the complaints of displaced Biafada with the armed force of nominal Fulbe clients. In return for Fulbe armed assistance, Biafada notables would often relieve them of paying taxes.[7] Consequently, by the close of the 1860s, the Fulbe were entering the Forria as potential soldiers rather than as refugees and supplicants.

Chica Embaló was one of the more illustrious Fulbe communal leaders who shook off his obligations to his Biafada patron by becoming an armed retainer. The communal conflict among the Biafada had given him a better appreciation of the strength of the Fulbe position in the Forria. After the fall of Kansala he converted to Islam, changed his name to Bakary Quidali, and placed himself and his supporters at the disposal of Alfa Ibrahima of Labe. At the outset of the 1870s, with the tacit consent of the *Almamy* of Futa Jallon, Alfa Ibrahima made Bakary Quidali military governor of the Forria. Of course, given Ibrahima's anxiety about Alfa Molo's growing influence in Fuladu, his motives for the appointment were not entirely straightforward. But Bakary Quidali enthusiastically pursued his charge. Once ensconced in his new position, he vigorously suppressed the most powerful Biafada notables, including his former patron, and initiated what amounted to a small scale holy war or *jihad* in the Forria.

Fulbe groups from Bolola, Contabani and Buba — in short, from the south and east — joined with Bakary Quidali to storm the last Biafada strongholds in the west.[8] Many of the new recruits furnished their own arms; for a number of them had previously sworn allegiance to Alfa Molo and readily served as Molo's spies, keeping him informed of the tenor of relations between Bakary Quidali and Alfa Ibrahima. By the mid 1870s, some five years after the destruction of Kaabu, it became apparent that Bakary Quidali could not suppress the Biafada resistance with the forces at his disposal. Consequently, Alfa Ibrahima despatched several thousand soldiers from Futa Jallon into the Forria. Afterwards the Fulbe forces smashed the last vestiges of opposition. However, the intervention of troops from Futa Jallon raised difficult questions of military protocol and of how the Forria was to be governed.[9]

The protracted nature of the conflict in the Forria was in part a consequence of the disputes between aristocratic Fulbe military commanders and men of the moment such as Bakary Quidali and Alfa Molo.[10] For example, Bakary Quidali had not requested the regular troops from Alfa Ibrahima. Rather, the request was made by an aristocratic military leader, one Bakar Demba, who was a Fulbe military leader in the Forria but ostensibly subordinate to Bakary Quidali in the chain of command.[11] Once the Biafada and Mandinka were defeated, the real struggle over the future of much of the Senegambia was between former Fulbe masters and former Fulbe slaves — all of whom had presumably been made equal by Islam.[12] The French and Portuguese advance and the consequent growth of commercial plantations on the estuaries and banks of the southern waterways was largely a function of how the Europeans intervened in this preexisting struggle.

Slaves against masters in the Forria

The received wisdom of tradition tells us that for nearly two generations — from Al-Hajj Umar's call to *heshira* in the 1850s to the death of Alfa Molo in 1881 — *Fulbe-djiábê* and *Fulbe-ribê* in the Senegambia set aside their differences and joined with the Fulbe warrior-cleric rulers of Futa Jallon against the Mandinka aristocracy of Kaabu and unbelievers in general throughout the region. This "traditional" gloss was also echoed in the contemporary observations of French and Portuguese officials and merchants residing in the Senegambia. Consider, for instance, Joaquim da Graça Correia e Lança:

> [The] Fula-forros [*Fulbe-ribê*] and the Fula-pretos [*Fulbe-djiábê*] united by the same idea of liberty, although despising one another at heart, joined together in common cause ... Once the Fula-forros were on the verge of achieving power, however, and of submitting the Fula-pretos once again to an odious servitude, they shed the appearance of camaraderie. Internal dissension within the Fula ranks resurfaced and was further exacerbated by the intervention of soldiers from Futa Jallon that had been sent into the Forria, for Almamy Sory claimed the region as part of his dominions. In exchange for the assistance of his troops in the military campaigns near Corrubal between 1870 and 1872, he wanted nothing less than complete submission to his authority.[13]

By 1878, and perhaps as early as 1873, the apparently amicable relations between *Fulbe-ribê* and *Fulbe-djiábê* had once again been transformed into a class struggle. *Fulbe-djiábê* perceived the Forria as a "land of redemption".[14] *Fulbe-ribê*, particularly the military and religious leaders of Futa Jallon, perceived the Forria and its burgeoning population as a new province and a potentially important source of revenue. Consequently, despite the apparent position of Bakary Quidali's forces, the ambitions of Futa Jallon threatened to reimpose servile dependence upon *Fulbe-djiábê* in the Forria.[15]

As mentioned earlier, the transition from the slave trade to "legitimate commerce" had adversely affected Futa Jallon's economy. Once European merchants and traders began to demand new raw materials such as peanuts, palm products and rubber rather than hides, Futa Jallon's inland location undermined its ability to compete with the coastal enclaves. Consequently, some years after the corrosive operations of the *yelle mansa*, the rulers of Futa Jallon determined to incorporate the fertile alluvial plains of the Forria. Therefore, between the 1850s and the 1890s, Futa Jallon's military campaigns became the catalyst for the creation of three new Fulbe spheres of influence — Fuladu, Forria and Gabu.[16]

The situation in Forria was further complicated by Alfa Ibrahima's belief that the region possessed a special relationship with his province of Labe, as well as a more general tributary one with Futa Jallon as a whole. For Alfa Ibrahima held the position of "the protector and principal master of Forria". As a province of Futa Jallon and more immediately as a precinct of Labe, Forria had an obligation to pay annual taxes to the *Alfa mo Labe* in the form of cattle, cloth and amber. The new economic order that the abolition of the Atlantic slave trade had compelled also forced Futa Jallon to look in the direction of commercial agriculture for alternative sources of revenue. Annexing the Forria would have enabled Futa Jallon to collect new taxes and tribute to make up for the economic losses that the state had sustained from the 1840s onward. And, of course, Futa Jallon also claimed that it wanted to convert unbelievers to Islam. Yet by the late 1870s the influence of the call to *jihad* was waning in Futa Jallon. Moreover, the death of Al-Hajj Umar had deprived the Fulbe Islamic *jihad* west of the Niger River of its moral center of gravity.

As Futa Jallon's designs on the Forria became more explicit, Bakary Quidali concentrated his energies on consolidating his power in Gabu, a northern sub-region of the Forria, and in the northwestern fringes of Forria proper. Meanwhile Bakar Demba became the nominal ruler of the Forria's heartland instead of Bakary Quidali. But the political situation in the Forria remained riven by factional disputes and political intrigue; for the officers of the soldiers from Futa Jallon continued to take their orders from Alfa Ibrahima who, in turn, often dealt with Bakar Demba through Bakary Quidali, in order to underscore the point that Bakar Demba's position was due to Alfa Ibrahima's patronage and intervention.[17] In fact the rulers of Futa Jallon, including *Almamy* Sory, would have preferred the more capable Bakary Quidali as the titular authority in the Forria and Gabu; but their preferences and practical decisions were limited by the strictures of Futa Jallon's political and social order, particularly in a period when that order appeared to be challenged from so many quarters.[18]

Meanwhile Bakary Quidali proceeded to act in a more independent fashion in Gabu — appointing chiefs and notables, assigning Islamic clerics and judges to particular areas, and entering into protracted discussions with the Portuguese at Buba about the limits of their jurisdiction. He, like Alfa Molo in Fuladu, solicited the approval of *Almamy* Sory and Alfa Ibrahima in Futa Jallon but only as a courtesy. Once he was ensconced in Gabu, however, Bakary Quidali determined to assume what he considered his "rightful" position as ruler of both Forria and Gabu. But Bakar Demba was not inclined to relinquish his authority over Forria. A struggle for power ensued — one in which all the unresolved enmity between former masters and former slaves came to the surface.[19]

Disputes also emerged among the former lieutenants of Al-Hajj Umar east of Futa Jallon and Fuladu after they had been dealt a number of humiliating military defeats by the French expeditionary army.[20] In 1877, for instance, Bakar Sado of Bundu enjoined Alfa Ibrahima to assist him in making war on their former comrades-in-arms at Cussalam. In turn, Alfa Ibrahima called upon Bakar Demba and Bakary Quidali to provide troops for the campaign. Bakar Demba made it known that he considered Alfa Ibrahima's orders an imposition. He entered into a series of public disagreements with Alfa Ibrahima that dragged on for two years. Toward the end of the conflict in Cussalam, Bakar Demba was assassinated. Doubtless Bakary Quidali had something to do with

Demba's assassination; for toward the end of 1879, Alfa Ibrahima formally installed him as governor of Forria and Gabu. Some time after his installation, Quidali made his lieutenant and long-time collaborator, Mamadu Pate Coiada, the military strong man in Gabu and entered into a closer relationship with Alfa Molo in order to contain the ambitions of Futa Jallon and the Portuguese at Buba and Geba.[21]

However, given the manner in which the lines of power had been redrawn in the Forria and Gabu, Bakary Quidali became more vulnerable to the demands of Futa Jallon's rulers. In late 1879, for example, Alfa Ibrahima demanded that Bakary Quidali send all unbelievers in the Forria southward to Futa Jallon, along with so many head of cattle.[22] This was a particularly egregious policy, in as much as *Fulbe-djiábé* and "unbelievers" were one in the same for Alfa Ibrahima. As a result, the largest portion of the Fulbe population in the Forria and Gabu now saw their former liberator transformed into an instrument of a new version of the policies that had subjugated them prior to the war with the Mandinka aristocracy of Kaabu.

Some Fulbe peasants sought refuge in the shadow of the Portuguese fort at Buba, while others decided to defend themselves. Those who chose to prepare for a confrontation began to build walled villages or *tabancas*. Bakary Quidali feared that these acts of defiance would spread. He ordered his soldiers to destroy those fortified villages that were already built and placed a ban on their further construction. At Combijan and a few other localities peasants actually turned back the first assault by Bakary Quidali's soldiers. Afterwards, fearing reinforced detachments of soldiers, peasant rebels sought refuge at the Portuguese fort at Buba. Enraged over this new turn of events, Bakary Quidali did, in fact, send more troops to these areas. The repression intensified.

Portuguese intervention

In 1881, the year of the death of Alfa Molo of Fuladu, the most formidable Fulbe military leader in the Senegambia, the Portuguese intervened in the Forria. A detachment of Portuguese troops from Buba attacked a detachment of Bakary Quidali's soldiers at Gam-Suoma. The Portuguese were soundly defeated, but mounted another attack on Fulbe positions the following year in September 1882. The defending troops were under the command of Mamadu Bolola, another close confederate of Bakary Quidali. Toward the end of the month Bolola and his soldiers were overwhelmed. The Portuguese took a number of prisoners — many of whom, no doubt, were spirited away to plantations on Bolama and to those along the banks of the Rio Grande — and demanded an indemnity in the form of several hundred head of cattle. Bakary Quidali was also compelled to sign a treaty with the Portuguese governor at

Buba, one Pedro Inácio de Gouveia, which effectively shifted his economic clientage from Futa Jallon to the Portuguese at Buba:

> ... He [Bakary Quidali] assumes the obligation himself and for individuals of his race — fula-forros [*Fulbe-ribê*], to spread the commercial preference of Buba over any other point of the province, employing his influence with that of Futa, for this end; for which he will police the roads, if necessary, to guarantee peace for the caravans coming to Buba.[23]

The Portuguese allowed Mamadu Paté Bolola to rebuild his village, but he and Bakary Quidali had to pay the Portuguese an indemnity of two hundred head of cattle. Bakary Quidali was also obliged to offer the Portuguese military assistance.[24] But like so many other treaties the Portuguese negotiated with local rulers, this one lasted only a short while. The dearth of Portuguese firepower and a local administrative infrastructure made the enforcement of such treaties a moot issue.

Meanwhile Bakary Quidali became increasingly unpopular as he sought to comply with the demands and policies of the *Almamy* and *Alfa mo Labe*. Moreover, in 1879, Alfa Ibrahima in Labe was succeeded by Alfa Yaya, Ibrahima's son by a *nyancho* Mandinka princess. That his mother had been a Mandinka aristocrat made Alfa Yaya's demands for labor and cattle even more distasteful to the Fulbe of Forria. Villages were raided with impunity and women and cattle were sent south in ever greater numbers.[25] On the other hand, precisely because of his compliance with the wishes of Alfa Yaya and the *Almamy*, Bakary Quidali prohibited caravans from Futa Jallon from passing through the Forria on their way to Buba.[26] In fact, Bakary Quidali's decision was merely one of several factors that disrupted overland commercial traffic between the Guinean or southern regions of the Senegambia and points farther north. The continuing slump in global prices, the depression of the early 1880s, and the more or less permanent state of belligerency between Fuladu, the strongest of the new Fulbe states, and every other power in the Senegambia all contributed strongly to the deceleration of local commerce. Portuguese planters and officials in particular were eager to attribute the economic stagnation to apparent circumstances. For example, some seven years after the fact, Teixeira de Barros, a Portuguese military officer stationed in Buba, implied that Bakary Quidali's activities had caused the destruction of the "commercial flowering in Buba and all of the Forria".[27] The peasants of Futa Jallon and Forria felt the loss of the caravan trade as keenly as the Portuguese planters, if not more so. Caravans provided the peasantry with an outlet for their surplus grain as well as hides, beeswax, shea butter, gold, ivory, and export crops such as coffee and peanuts. Caravans also gave peasants access to items that were unavailable in their own region. And as late as the turn of the century items produced in other regions of Africa, as well as commodities of

European provenance, still continued to matter in this long distance trade. For example, kola, which the long-distance caravans brought from the forest zones of West Africa, was particularly lucrative, since Muslims could not consume alcohol or tobacco.[28] Combined with the growth of European plantations, peasant participation in commercial agriculture laid the groundwork for the revolutionary impact of peanut production throughout the Senegambia during the halcyon days of the period from the 1830s to the late 1870s.[29] Peasant initiatives translated into a marked increase in the production of millet, rice, certain kinds of wood, leather, wax, and what contemporary European observers in the British and French enclaves described as a "farming mania".[30] In turn, the general increase in agricultural production, particularly on the estuaries and along the river banks of the southernmost rivers of the Senegambia, and the African and European networks of distribution, served to improve the quality of urban and commercial life from Gorée to the Portuguese settlement at Buba.[31]

After 1882 many of the Fulbe peasant communities in the Forria continued to contest Bakary Quidali's authority. A number of Bakar Demba's former soldiers, who blamed Bakary Quidali for their leader's death, attempted to exploit popular discontent for their own purposes. In 1886 Demba's former officers sent a delegation to Alfa Yaya to ask for support against Quidali. The Alfa agreed to support them since he was interested in reestablishing Futa Jallon's control in the Forria. The local strength of the coalition, however, turned on the defection of Bakary Quidali's principal subordinate Mamadu Paté Bolola. Bolola went over to the disaffected group shortly after their visit to Alfa Yaya. Toward the end of the year a detachment of Alfa Yaya's troops marched into the Forria — some four years after Bakary Quidali's banning of caravans from Futa Jallon in the Forria. Bakary Quidali's forces, and those of Mamadu Paté Coiada of Gabu, withstood the advance of the Alfa Yaya's troops for three days. Eventually Coiada of Gabu attempted to convince Bakary Quidali to flee into Corubal. But he chose instead to seek protection from the Portuguese at Buba. Shortly after his retreat, according to Portuguese sources, Quidali committed suicide, "preferring death to exile".[32] After Bakary Quidali's death, Mamadu Paté Coiada fled to Gabu.

On 3 December 1886, some four years after the signing of the 1882 treaty with Bakary Quidali, the Portuguese drew up a new treaty with representatives of Alfa Yaya at Buba. The new treaty stipulated that Alfa Yaya rather than the Almamy of Timbo was the *régulo* of the Forria. Alfa Yaya and his supporters agreed to:

protect commerce from the territories [under their control] and to make [all commerce] converge on Buba, [and] to insist on the same end with his neighboring chiefs, and promote whenever possible the security of traders especially on the roads that they have to travel to this fort [Buba].[33]

Writing ten days after this treaty was signed, the Secretary General of the Portuguese government expressed his hopes for an improvement in the economic situation in Forria. For not only did Alfa Yaya promise to send all of the commerce from his territories to Buba, but he also agreed to protect and maintain security for the properties and the products along the banks of the Rio Grande. The Secretary General genuinely believed that Buba could attain the prosperity it had prior to 1879.[34] But Portuguese officials in the Ministry of Colonies failed to take into account that they had not resolved their differences with Alfa Molo's successor in Fuladu, Musa Molo, and that their weakened position in the Senegambia was largely a consequence of Portugal's marginal position in the global economy. In fact, peace only lasted for a short time: The Portuguese were drawn into a much more extensive but protracted conflict with Musa Molo in Fuladu; Alfa Yaya's condominium over local Fulbe leaders in the Forria fell apart; and because of the strength and persistence of peasant discontent Mamadu Paté Bolola became a kind of military strong man in the Forria.

The Portuguese in the Forria

Mamadu Paté Bolola's relationship with the Portuguese was tenuous at best. The temperaments and political shortcomings of both the local Fulbe leadership and the Portuguese did much to undermine their respective positions. For example, within the three year period between 1885 and 1888, the Portuguese posted five governors to Guinea. Meanwhile, Mamadu Paté Bolola's ability to readily exploit the Portuguese lack of political acumen became legendary in this period — even among the Portuguese themselves. Consider the observations of Correia e Lança:

> Mamadi-Pate was more daring, more insolent and above all more tolerant of the abuses of his subordinates.

> He is intelligent and treacherous, ambitiously striving to be elevated to *régulo* of Forria ... knowing that the support of the Almamy of Futa-Djallon is more valuable than that of the present Portuguese government, ... [he] did not hesitate to distinguish himself in the open hostilities against our authority, and against the traders and agriculturalists placed under our [Portuguese] protection. The phrase, to cook one's dinner in Buba with the Portuguese flagpole, is notoriously famous in Forria and is echoed as far away as Futa-Djallon.[35]

But in marked contrast to his contemporary Musa Molo of Fuladu, Bolola did not want to expel the Portuguese from the Senegambia. Rather he wanted them to cease what he perceived as a disingenuous tack of paying a *daxa* or ground rent to a weakened but intractable core of Biafada chiefs along the southern banks of the Rio Grande de Buba.[36] Although fearful of the repressive power concentrated in the hands of Fulbe strong men after the 1870s, the few remaining influential Biafada chiefs did, on occasion, double as labor contractors and forcefully nudge inhabitants of the more vulnerable Fulbe communities, as well as their own people, onto the European and Luso-African plantations along the river.[37] Bolola wanted the planters and Portuguese officials to deal directly with him. Instead of rekindling the fervor that had led to the *jihad* of a generation before, he chose to launch a series of small-scale attacks on the strongholds of the intransigent Biafada chiefs and, occasionally, on the plantations themselves.

Francisco Teixeira da Silva, the recently installed Portuguese governor, tried desperately to take the political edge off of these events in his dispatches to the Ministry of Colonies: "Small isolated groups robbed one or two beafadas a day, who [then] became slaves of Mamadi Paté or who were sent to Futa Djallon. [At] other times an isolated place would suffer from an attack of fulas".[38] But even as Teixeira da Silva sent his bland dispatches to Lisbon, more mobile Portuguese officials and magistrates were acquiring a very different picture of the situation in the Forria from the testimony and tax complaints of planters and African peasants: At the outset of 1885, for example, a planter from the vicinity of Buba, one Christiano Marques de Barros, told a rather different story to a magistrate in Bolama:

On 8 October 1884 at 9:00 am I arrived from a trip to Buba in my boat and in the company of a trader, José Monteiro de Macedo, and found 60 beafada on my estate. I asked them what they wanted and they responded that they had come to wait for a boat of fulas that was to pass by there. I warned them off my property by setting a fire that made them flee to the river. Since they had no boat, they had to take one of mine. Initially I denied their request, but they threatened me, and I relented. They killed nine fula and took two to their villages. When they returned my boat, it had four bullet holes in it. Yet they deigned to ask me for two barrels of gunpowder, *aguardente* [a spirit], and tobacco, all of which I gave to them since I had no other recourse.

This is the third time that I have suffered at their hands. Since I have no means to prevent them from molesting my property and since nothing has been resolved, I cannot risk another attack. I am going to abandon my property and go to Bolama.[39]

Perhaps the greatest irony of the situation in the Forria was that by April 1885 — just as the rainy season began and the peanut crop was to be harvested —

Mamadu Paté Bolola sought to enlist Portuguese support for his repressive campaign.[40]

The Portuguese were most anxious about Bolola's connection to French merchants in the area, who supplied him with gunpowder and munitions. As long as he could act independently, the Portuguese administrators and the plantation owners were at a decided disadvantage, particularly since the Portuguese were, by this time, faring so badly in the war with Musa Molo's forces in Fuladu. European planters in general, but particularly the Portuguese, claimed that Mamadu Paté Bolola's soldiers readily attacked their estates, stealing their goods and kidnapping many of their workers in the process. The few planters and Portuguese officials who remained beyond Buba were very nearly resigned to being overrun. Consider the observations of one of the travelling magistrates in the mid 1880s:

> In view of such facts which continue to undermine our [Portuguese] authority and prestige in which already no one believes, judging it fictitious since the massacre of Bolor [1879] ... it is necessary that the superior powers take energetic steps if they do not want to see the province reduced to the island of Bolama, the forts of Bissau, Cacheu and Buba; and I say forts because it is only in these small enclosures that one knows our [Portuguese] authority, and all that lies outside of the range of our artillery is only Portuguese territory in official documents.[41]

Bolstered by French support, and the apparent disarray of the Portuguese, Mamadu Paté Bolola finally determined to seize the Portuguese fort at Buba in 1890. However, in the attempt to seize the fort, Bolola was killed. His expeditionary force quickly withdrew after his death. Predictably, the Portuguese readily overestimated the significance of their victory:

> Mamadi Paté Bolola had planned to assassinate the officials in order to surprise the sentries afterwards and to take the fort [Buba] by assault ... [Mamadu Paté Bolola] merely had a human form, but his manner of acting was perfectly one of a barbaric savage, a complete monster and his death was a real benefit for all the Forrea and especially for Buba.[42]

Following Mamadu Paté Bolola's death, the Portuguese officials in Buba and Bolama were quite aware of the potential for reprisals. They were not to be disappointed.[43] The report of the governing council, which was issued the following year, claimed that there had been no peace in the area since Bolola's death, and that people refused to go to Buba to talk with the Portuguese.[44] Even though the segment of the Fulbe military elite that opposed Bolola was gratified over his death, they still held grave misgivings about the Portuguese. Consequently, the Portuguese could not turn the political situation in the Forria decisively to their advantage with their own resources. Ironically, Mamadu

Paté Bolola's successor, Cherno Cali was forced to seek Portuguese assistance, once Alfa Yaya on the one hand and the former confederate of Bakary Guidali, Mamadu Paté Coiada, on the other forcefully sought to intervene in the Forria and bring the political impasse to a close. However, the ongoing conflict between Coiada and Alfa Yaya served to enhance further the political anxiety of the Forria's population.

By 1889, Futa Jallon's regular army and Alfa Yaya's provincial forces had pushed Coiada's forces out of the Forria's southeastern borderlands and the tributary province of Pachisse. Many of Coiada's soldiers were killed on the open savanna as they retreated southward in an attempt to reach the protective cover of swamp and forest along the banks of the tributaries of the Geba and the Rio Grande. Coiada's losses were so great in fact that he could not raise another expeditionary army and risked the threat of mutiny; for while his troops were not averse to defending their home region against the more powerful army of Futa Jallon, they were most reluctant to initiate a military offensive against a demonstrably more powerful foe.[45] Coiada was obliged to stifle his dream of achieving a degree of independence from Futa Jallon's influence on the order of Musa Molo's in Fuladu.[46] Nor could he enter into a full-fledged military alliance with Fuladu, once Musa Molo succeeded his father and embarked upon a policy of internal repression that provoked an extensive war with the Portuguese. By 1890 Mamadu Paté Coiada's army was bottled up in Gabu.[47]

By 1892 Coiada's position had become desperate as a result of Futa Jallon's military pressure. But he recognized that the ambitions of Futa Jallon's rulers were fueled in part by their increasing dependence upon the French commercial and military presence in the Senegambia. He also understood that the Portuguese wanted to restore the profitability of commercial agriculture in the Forria and Gabu, and that such a condition could not be had without a cessation of hostilities. However, the Portuguese vied with the French in supplying Coiada's army with gunpowder and iron bars to make weapons, shoring up, in turn, some of the more ironic and perverse aspects of Portugal's simultaneous commitment to free trade and "effective occupation". French merchants and administrators were also concerned about the conflict's negative effects on commerce. But the French looked more to the possibilities associated with a more extensive collection of wild rubber in the Senegambia rather than to the restoration of the profitability of the plantations and commercial agriculture in general. By the 1880s, for example, Pachisse and the margins of the Forria and Gabu had become important rubber producing centers for the representatives of French commercial houses based on the rivers of the south. French officials believed that if they could build a fort at Kandifara and garrison it with a column of soldiers, they could shield the areas of rubber collection from the consequences of the hostilities and guarantee the safety of the commercial routes to the south.[48] F. Milanini, the French official at Rio Nunez, was echoing this belief as late as 1895:

> ... the traders of the Rio Nunez, particularly of the Cie. Française, ... add that it is indispensable to create a post in Kandiafara where they want to establish factories [trading stations] that will be administered by Europeans. The Portuguese government is unable to keep the routes free and to stop the plundering of all the traffic that passes today in Buba and above all on both sides of the Rio Grande ...[49]

The French were also concerned to monopolize the trade in hides, cattle, gold, and ivory as well. Moreover, between January and May 1893, both Coiada and Futa Jallon's rulers began to tire of the war, because of the way that it had sapped resources needed to maintain the long range administrative and military capacities of both states.[50]

As the war wound down, local opposition to Coiada's rule in Gabu and Forria became more virulent. Taxes rose and the coffles of "unbelievers" sent southward to Futa Jallon increased. By 1894 a large number of notables and chiefs in the Forria and Gabu had been won over to the opposition. As with Bakary Quidali more than a decade earlier, peasant dissenters and their leaders either appealed to the Portuguese garrison at Buba for protection or armed themselves as well as they could and fortified their villages with stockades.

Notes

1. Alberto Xavier Teixeira de Barros, *Breves Apontamentos sobre a História do Forria*, Lisbon, Imprensa Nacional, 1896, p. 5.

2. Joaquim da Graça Correia e Lança, *Relatório da Provincia da Guiné Portugueza — Referido ao anno económico de 1888-89*, Lisbon, Imprensa Nacional, 1890, p. 52; Abdulai Djaló, Bissau Series Tape 3 (Bafata), 12 July 1977.

3. Vasco de Sousa Calvet de Magalhaes, *Provincia da Guiné — Relatório apresentado pelo administrador da Circumscrição Civil de Geba, 1914*, Porto, 1916, p. 51.

4. Frederico Pinheiro Chagas, "Povos da Guiné Portugueza", *Annaes do Club Militar Naval*, 41, 2, p. 88; AHU, Guiné, Pasta 365: Pedro Inácio de Gouveia, Governor to Ministro e Secretário d'Estado dos Negócios da Marinha e Ultramar, 7 November 1884; AHU, Guiné, Pasta 409: Pedro Inácio de Gouveia, Governor to Ministro e Secretário d'Estado dos Negócios da Marinha e Ultramar, 6 October 1884; Abdulai Djaló, Bissau Series Tape 3 (Bafata), 12 July 1977

5. Rodney, "Jihad", pp. 273-77.

6.   See: Carreira, "Aspectos históricos", p. 419.

In 1868, a year after the fall of Kansala, Doiam, a Biafada notable in Abi allowed communities of Biafada from Dandum-Gussara to settle at Quidali. Doiam expected these new groups to supply him with palm wine as evidence of their clientage. They complied with the requests for a short time; but after they had established themselves, they stopped sending palm wine to Doiam. Doiam perceived the cessation as an act of hostility. Consequently, he enlisted the aid of his Fulbe client, Cuntam Embaló, and his son, Chica Embaló, in suppressing the contumacious Biafada refugees.

7.   Teixeira de Barros, *Breves apontamentos*, p. 6.

8.   AHU, Guiné, Pasta 365: Pedro Inácio de Gouveia, Governor to Ministro e Secretário d'Estado dos Negócios da Marinha e Ultramar, 7 November 1884; AHU, Guiné, Pasta 409: Pedro Inácio de Gouveia, Governor to Ministro e Secretário d'Estado dos Negócios da Marinha e Ultramar, 6 October 1884; Abdulai Djaló, Bissau Series Tape 3 (Bafata), 12 July 1977; Buli Galiça, Bissau Series Tape 8 (Gabu), 20 July 1977.

9.   Madrolle, *Notes d'un voyage*, p.22.

Many of the Biafada were driven to the Rio Nunez region. The Biafada felt safe in this area because they believed that the Fulbe would not cross the banks of the rivers to pursue them. They thought that the Fulbe feared the water and the muddy swamps. In fact, the Fulbe probably wanted to avoid this area because of the tsetse flies and the potential damage they could cause to their cattle.

10.   Ibrahima Koba Casama, Bissau Series Tape 1 (Bijini), 10 July 1977; and Buli Galiça, Bissau Series Tape 8 (Gabu), 20 July 1977.

11.   Correia e Lança, *Relatório*, p. 53; Buli Galiça, Bissau Series Tape 8 (Gabu), 20 July 1977; and Ibrahima Koba Casama, Bissau Series Tape 1 (Bijini), 10 July 1977.

12.   AHU, Guiné, Pasta 409: Secretaria do Governo da Guiné Portugueza to Ministro e Secretário d'Estado dos Negócios da Marinha e Ultramar, 17 July 1879.

13.   Correia e Lança, *Relatório*, p. 53; Buli Galiça, Bissau Series Tape 8 (Gabu), 20 July 1977; and Ibrahima Koba Casama, Bissau Series Tape 1 (Bijini), 10 July 1977.

14.   For information on similar struggles elsewhere in Senegambia see: Barry, *La Sénégambie*.

15.   Carreira, "Aspectos históricos", p. 423. See also: AHU, Guiné, Pasta 409: Pedro Inácio de Gouveia, Governor to Ministro e Secretário d'Estado dos Negócios da Marinha e Ultramar, 6 October 1884; AHU, Guiné, Pasta 409: Pedro Inácio de Gouveia, Governor to Ministro e Secretário d'Estado dos Negócios da Marinha e Ultramar, 7 November

1884; *BOGP*, 1911, Annex No. 2, p. 8.

16. Teixeira de Barros, *Breves apontamentos*, p. 5; and Carreira, "Aspectos históricos", p. 416.

17. Ibrahima Koba Casama, Bissau Series Tape 1 (Bijini), 10 July 1977; and Buli Galiça, Bissau Series Tape 8 (Gabu), 20 July 1977.

18. See: Roberts, *Warriors, Merchants*.

19. Jorge Vellez Caroço, *Monjur — O Gabú e a sua História*, Centro de Estudos da Guiné Portuguesa, no. 8, Bissau, 1948, pp. 136-37 and 140-44.

20. See: Roche, *Conquête et resistance*.

21. Teixeira de Barros, *Breves apontamentos*, p. 10; *BOGP*, 12 December 1885, No. 50, p. 228.

22. Teixeira de Barros, *Breves apontamentos*, p. 10.

23. *BOGP*, 1882, No. 40, p. 170.

24. In 1883, for example, Bakary Quidali offered to send *Fulbe-ribê* auxiliaries to help the Portuguese fight against the Balanta, but his offer arrived too late. See: AHU, Guiné, Pasta 409: Governor, No. 146 to Ministro e Secretário d'Estado dos Negócios da Marinha e Ultramar, 27 June 1883.

25. Teixeira de Barros, *Breves apontamentos*, p. 10.

26. Teixeira de Barros, *Breves apontamentos*, p. 11.

27. Teixeira de Barros, *Breves apontamentos*, p. 11.

28. Carreira, "Aspectos históricos", p. 425. See: Paul E. Lovejoy, "Kola in the History of West Africa", *Cahiers d'Etudes Africaines*, 20, No. 77-78, 1980, pp. 97-134.

29. Bernard Schnapper, *La Politique et le Commerce Française dans le Golfe de Guinée de 1838 à 1871*, Paris, Mouton & Co., 1961, pp. 230-40.

30. Swindell, "Serawoolies, Tilibunkas", pp. 82-4; Schnapper, *La Politique et le Commerce*, pp. 25 and 231.

31. Carreira, "Aspectos históricos", p. 425.
    The caravans preferred the route that passed through Gabu and went south to Buba, in part because the coastal people in the Rivières du Sud region of French Guinea made it difficult for them to cross their lands. This route to Buba was also easier because there were fewer *bolanhas* (rice fields) and *lalas* (swamps). Furthermore, this route was well-established and thus preferred. But the problems in Forria forced the caravans to go south to the Rio Nunez region. This rerouting affected European and Luso-African traders in Forria because the caravans represented a ready market for imported European goods and a source for hides, beeswax, gold, ivory, and shea butter.

32. One Portuguese report mistakenly claimed that Bakar Quidali died from an illness in the fort. AHU, Guiné, Pasta 410: 27 September 1886.

33. *BOGP*, 1886, No. 49, p. 202.

34. AHU, Guiné, Pasta 411: Secretária Geral do Governo da Província em Bolama, No. 265 to Ministro e Secretário d'Estado dos Negócios da Marinha e Ultramar, 13 December 1886 and *BOGP*, 1886, No. 50, p. 207.

35. Correia e Lança, *Relatório*, p. 58.

36. AHU, Guiné, Pasta 387: "Declaração de Durême", 6 February 1885.

37. AHU, Guiné, Pasta 411: Francisco Teixeira da Silva, Governor, No. 101 to Ministro e Secretário d'Estado dos Negócios da Marinha e Ultramar, 22 March 1888. See also: AHU, Guiné, 6413, Process 13: Military Commander in Buba, No. 26 to Secretário Geral do Governo da Província, 3 March 1887; and Caroço, *Monjur*, pp. 146-48.

38. AHU, Guiné, Pasta 411: Francisco Teixeira da Silva, Governo, No. 121 to Ministro e Secretário d'Estado dos Negócios da Marinha e Ultramar, 14 April 1888. See also: Correia e Lança, *Relatório*, p. 58.

39. AHU, Guiné, Pasta 387: "Declaração de Christiano Marques de Barros", (early 1885).

40. An agreement, signed on 4 December 1885, existed between the *Fulbe-ribê*, Biafada and Portuguese. It stated that the Fulbe would "submit all of the conflicts that might follow...between the [*Fulbe-ribê*] people and the Beafada, to the analysis of a tribunal." Consequently, declaring war would have violated the terms of this agreement and upset the Portuguese. Rather than declaring an all out war against the Biafada, Mamadu Paté Bolola chose to launch small attacks. See: AHU, Guiné, Pasta 411: Francisco Teixeira da Silva, Governor, No. 101 to Ministro e Secretário d'Estado dos Negócios da Marinha e Ultramar, 22 March 1888. See also: AHU, Guiné, 6413, Processo 13: Military Commander in Buba, No. 26 to Secretário Geral do Governo da Provincia, 3 March 1887; and Caroço, *Monjur*, pp. 146-48.

41. AHU, Guiné, Pasta 414: Governor Santos, No. 174 to Ministro e Secretário d'Estado dos Negócios da Marinha e Ultramar, 21 June 1890.

42. AHU, Guiné, Pasta 414: Governor to Ministro e Secretário d'Estado dos Negócios da Marinha e Ultramar, 20 August 1890.

43. *BOGP*, 1891, No. 28, p. 122. See also: AHU, Guiné, Pasta 413: Acta No. 7, Sessão de 26 September 1890.

44. *BOGP*, 1890, No. 40, p. 233; and AHU, Guiné, 6434, Processo 25, Doc. 2, 10 February 1892.

45. *BOGP*, 1889, No. 17, p. 68.

46. AHU, Guiné, Pasta 412: Military Commander in Buba, Manoel José da Piedade Alvares, No. 3 to Secretária Geral, 17 March 1889.

47. AHU, Guiné, Pasta 412: Governor, No. 68 to Ministro e Secretário d'Estado dos Negócios da Marinha e Ultramar, 20 March 1889; *BOGP*, 1889, No. 17, p. 68.

48. ANSOM, Guinée IV, Dossier 1 (a): Baillat in Boké "Rapport Politique", 10 October 1892.

49. ANSOM, Guinée IV, Dossier 1 (a): F. Milanini, Administrator of Rio Nunez to Governor of French Guinea in Conakry, 12 August 1895.

50. AHU, Guiné, Pasta 415: Governor, No. 150 to Ministro e Secretário d'Estado dos Negócios da Marinha e Ultramar, 24 May 1893.

5 "Legitimate Commerce" and the Investment in Law and Order

The future prosperity of the country that today constitutes the province of Portuguese Guinea is principally dependent on the development of its agriculture and the transformation of its actual products [for foreign and national markets] ...

BOGP, 1881, No. 9, p. 34.

... the production of peanuts, the principal source of wealth for the country, has been sufficiently diminished lately and the agriculturalists have been forced by necessity to sell almost all of their products, without leaving a suitable reserve, as they customarily did, to sow the lands this year ...

AHU, Guiné, Pasta 387: Francisco Paula Gomes Barbosa, Governor to Ministro e Secretário d'Estado dos Negócios da Marinha e Ultramar, 30 June 1885.

Portuguese slave traders introduced peanuts from the Americas to West Africa as early as the sixteenth century. By the late eighteenth century, European observers like Philip Beaver were discussing the potential of peanut production in the region. Beaver, who established an agricultural colony on Bolama Island in 1792, cultivated the peanut seeds he received from Nalu people on the mainland, as early as 1793.[1] But the upsurge in production came later, after the

119

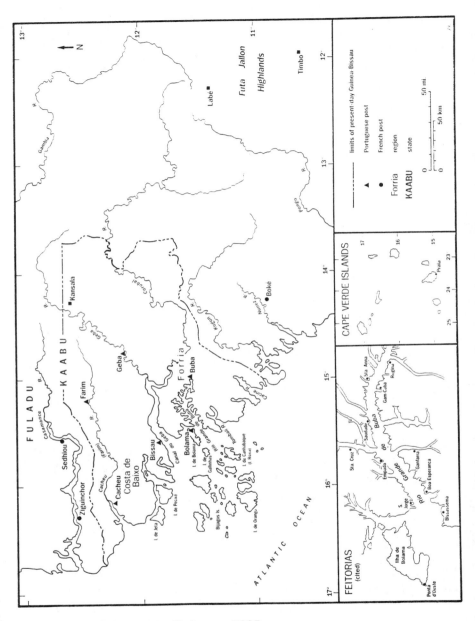

Figure 5.1 Portuguese Guinea c. 1885

120

traders most actively involved in the slave trade understood the meaning of abolition.[2]

In the first quarter of the nineteenth century,

> ... peanut cultivation on the Upper Guinea Coast was of negligible importance, but that cultivation was spreading. Peanuts came to be grown in the drier areas of the Senegambia as a safeguard against failure of the millet harvest, and along the coast to the southward as a subsidiary food crop of marginal, though increasing, consequence.[3]

By the late 1840s and early 1850s changing market conditions in Europe and the abolition of the Brazilian slave trade dramatically altered this situation and local traders and producers began to take advantage of the new economic opportunities.

The Senegambian region became the major peanut producing zone of West Africa. The Gambia shipped the first recorded exports to the West Indies in 1829 and 1830. By the mid 1830s the volume was remarkably higher, indicating that earlier exports went unrecorded. By the end of the decade, traders in the Rivières du Sud and Sierra Leone, were exporting peanuts and in the early 1840s, merchants in Senegal and Portuguese Guinea began sending peanuts to Europe.[4]

Peanut cultivation for export in Portuguese Guinea started on an island in the Bijagós archipelago, Ilha das Gallinhas, and from there spread to Bolama Island and the Rio Grande region.[5] The earliest exports from Gallinhas and Bolama were relatively small and went unrecorded. However, by 1845-46 records show *feitoria* owners on Bolama were shipping substantial amounts of peanuts.

Two famous individuals to emerge on Bolama were the *Nhara* Mãe Aurélia Correia and her husband Caetano José Nozolini.[6] Like many *feitoria* owners, they owed much of their success and notoriety to their active involvement in the slave trade. Mãe Aurélia was an African woman, perhaps of Papel origin, who was captured and raised on Orango Island in the Bijagós archipelago. She and her sister Mãe Julia

> manifestly took advantage of rights, privileges, and opportunities afforded by their ties with Bijagó and Papel to achieve positions of considerable wealth and influence. Together with Caetano Nozolini they dominated the commerce of the Geba-Grande area and the Bissagos archipelago.[7]

Nozolini's father was Italian and his mother was Cape Verdian. He joined the Portuguese army and rose through the ranks very quickly. Like other military men and traders on the West African coast, Nozolini recognized the benefits of building alliances with local women. Mãe Aurélia, and other African and Afro-European women, provided Nozolini and his counterparts with invaluable information about local politics, languages, mores and commerce. These women developed relationships with men like Nozolini and his competitor Joaquim António de Mattos, to improve their own economic and social standing. Some were more successful than others. Mae Aurélia and Nozolini, unlike many other trading partners, actually married one another, and maintained commercial dominance in Portuguese Guinea between 1826 and 1840.[8]

The 1830s and 1840s were critical decades in the transition from the slave trade to "legitimate commerce". Mãe Aurélia, Nozolini and their competitors continued to sell slaves illegally to slavers dodging British antislavery patrols. But they also expanded agricultural holdings and used slaves that could not be sold into the Atlantic network to produce cash crops like rice, and eventually peanuts, for sale to European traders. From the 1830s through the 1850s, the British squadron attempted to stop slave traffic in the Senegambia by raiding prominent traders including Nozolini and Mãe Aurélia. Raids in December 1838 and April 1839 resulted in substantial losses for them. These attacks outraged Nozolini. In the first raid, British soldiers capture 212 slaves from Ponta d'Oeste, Nozolini and Mãe Aurélia's *feitoria* on Bolama. Nozolini felt particularly violated because the British waited to launch the attack while he was on business in the Rio Nunez region. Nozolini explained:

> ... I had an immense loss in the capture of my stolen slaves who made up a large portion of my property because of the crops that will be lost in the ground for lack of work hands to harvest [them] ...[9]

British soldiers directed the final insult, according to Nozolini, when, after taking his slaves, they asked his family for food and drink. In the second attack British damage to Mãe Aurélia and Nozolini's holdings compelled them to halt temporarily their commercial activities.[10] These raids continued unabated through the 1850s.[11]

The troubles faced by local merchants such as Nozolini and Mãe Aurélia were a reflection of British efforts to abolish the slave trade and free slaves. Although Bissau and Cacheu were still commercial centers, with abolition and the new economic opportunities "legitimate commerce" afforded, Bolama became increasingly important. The British believed that they had a right to this island. Their claims to the island stemmed from the agricultural settlement that Philip Beaver established on Bolama in the 1790s, and from a number of treaties signed with the indigenous rulers on Bolama. Thus, when the British squadron raided properties looking for slaves, they felt justified.[12] Beaver's settlement was short lived, however, lasting only from May 1792 through November 1793. Once the settlers left, the Portuguese renewed their claim on Bolama. The Portuguese argued that the treaties that the British signed were invalid since they signed them with rulers who did not have jurisdiction over the Island. The Biafada ruler on the mainland signed papers with the British giving away land that the King of Canhabaque Island actually controlled.[13] The persistence of the slave trade from Bolama intensified British desires for the Island. Furthermore, the British blamed the continuation of slave trading activities further south in the Rio Nunez on traders from Portuguese Guinea, and claimed that many slaves were fleeing their masters and taking refuge with them on Bolama.[14]

The battle between Portugal and Great Britain over Bolama continued until 1870, when Ulysses S. Grant, then President of the United States, acted as an arbitrator in the case. Portugal received the rights to Bolama.[15] Even though Britain lost the case, the external slave trade finally died out, albeit gradually. Merchants had already decided it made better economic sense to hold slaves and put them to work cultivating peanuts on Bolama and in new areas opening up in Forria, along the Rio Grande.[16]

Portuguese Guinea's peanut economy

> The banks of the Rio Grande, Bissasseme, Tombali, Bolama and the Ilha das Galinhas, offer us [the Portuguese] great wealth and a good fortune. [Portuguese] Guinea could be another Brazil.[17]

For several decades during the nineteenth century after Brazil declared its independence in 1822 until the collapse of the peanut economy in the 1880s, some Portuguese and Luso-African traders in Guinea believed it had the potential to become a thriving agricultural colony. These merchants were often alone in this belief as Brazil continued to dominate Portuguese trading relations. As G. Clarence-Smith notes in his work on the third Portuguese empire, the commercial connections between Portugal and Brazil actually grew stronger after their formal break: "... a leading historian and intellectual, Alexandre Herculano, wryly declared in 1873 that 'our [Portugal's] best colony is Brazil, after it ceased to be our colony'".[18] Even so, in Guinea a desire to encourage development existed and took the form of proposals to establish a mercantile and agricultural company, Companhia Mercantil e Agrícola, that would have encouraged and developed trading relations between Portugal and Guinea. Supporters of this company believed that without an institution to monitor trade, foreigners would dominate it. In the 1830s, merchants believed gold, tortoise shell, palm oil, rice, coffee, ivory, hides, and wax would be the most profitable exports — only later did they realize the potential of peanuts.[19] Because of the region's potential wealth, the Associação Mercantil Lisbonese, individual local traders like Nozolini, and the Governor General, supported the creation of such a company.

Once it became clear that even with Brazilian independence Portugal could still benefit from her "former" colony, the metropolitan government showed little interest in developing the Companhia Mercantil e Agrícola.[20] It was only with the real abolition of the Brazilian slave trade in 1850 "that Africa suddenly appeared as an attractive possibility once again".[21] Brazilian abolition coincided with an increase in the European, primarily French, demands for vegetable oils. Consequently, Luso-African and Portuguese traders were in an excellent position to take advantage of new trading opportunities.

By the mid-1840s, even before the official abolition of the Brazilian slave trade, Mãe Aurélia and Nozolini were exporting peanuts from Ponta d'Oeste. Similarly, another infamous slave trader on Bolama, João Marques de Barros, had begun cultivating peanuts for export on his *feitoria*, Casa Nova. These traders and other Luso-Africans realized the potential gins from the peanut trade and thereupon extended cultivation to Forria, along the banks of the Rio Grande.[22] This area was particularly well-suited for peanut production because the soils along the river were fertile and the river itself was navigable for most vessels about fifty leagues inland.[23] During the next thirty years, traders from Bolama and Bissau often set up other family members in Forria. For example, at least two of Mãe Aurélia and Nozolini's children, Eugenia and Leopoldina, cultivated peanuts on their own *feitorias* along the Rio Grande. As the world market demand for peanuts increased, French, Portuguese and Afro-European traders alike descended on the Rio Grande to set up *feitorias*.[24]

These traders tried to gain access to the land on Bolama and along the Rio Grande however they could. The only records available indicate the Portuguese authorities signed treaties with local rulers on occasion; and some individuals actually bought land from indigenous rulers. In the 1850s for example, Honório Pereira Barreto, a mixed blood who became Governor of Cacheu and subsequently Governor of the district of Guinea, bought land from indigenous rulers and then gave the land to his "mother country", Portugal. He also signed treaties with rulers in Forria which gave Portugal rights to certain lands and waterways, including the Rio Grande.[25] As in other parts of Africa, rulers placed their "Xs" on these pieces of papers. How well they understood what they were signing remains a subject of speculation. Although the Portuguese and their representatives probably discussed some of the treaties' clauses, many issues were left unexplained. These indigenous rulers and their subjects were not literate in Portuguese, thus they depended on unreliable translations.[26] These treaties allowed European and Afro-European traders to establish themselves and begin building their commercial empires.

The land deals resulted in a rapid increase in the area available for peanut cultivation. Reconstructing production figures for peanuts prior to the formal separation of Cape Verde and Guinea in 1879 is difficult. By the late 1850s there were thirty *feitorias* and by the end of the 1870s the number had tripled. European travellers visiting West Africa commented on the growth in the peanut trade. E. Bouet-Williaumez (1848) and F. Travassos-Valdez (1852) noted that peanut exports and the number of commercial ships had grown dramatically.[27] One hundred thousand bushels of peanuts were exported in 1852 and by 1858 that number had doubled with 40,000 bushels exported from Bissau to Lisbon and another 160,000 bushels to Marseille, Rouen and Envers.[28] Six years later, in 1864, the volume had doubled again with between 400,000 and 500,000 bushels being shipped to Europe. By the 1870s, the figure was much higher — exports from the Rio Grande doubled again between 1873 and 1878 when over 1,120,000 bushels were exported.[29]

The organization of work on the *feitorias* in the Rio Grande

The *feitorias* along the banks of the Rio Grande and on Bolama were agricultural properties as well as commercial posts. The proprietors or *feitorias* of these holdings often were successful traders who made the transition from the slave trade to "legitimate commerce". Their ability to develop profitable agricultural enterprises based on peanut exports depended upon their capacity to find cheap African labor. The *feitors* used a combination of contract labor and slave labor. The primary difference between contract labor and slave labor was that the workers on contracts were migrants who had some limited rights of person. These laborers worked in conditions that resembled slavery but they were not chattel slaves. The slaves, on the other hand, were considered property. Although migrant workers made up about two-thirds of the labor force on the *feitorias*, the owners needed the chattel slaves as a dependable source of labor. Even after the 1875 decision to abolish slavery by 1878, proprietors continued using slave labor.

Feitoria owners had little success attracting Forria residents to work for them. When the Biafada and Fulbe groups present in the region refused to provide agricultural labor, the owners were forced to look elsewhere for work hands. They turned to Manjaco workers from the Costa de Baixo region and the islands of Jeta and Pecixe to meet their labor needs. The Manjaco became migrant laborers, much like the "strange farmers" in the Gambia and the *navetanes* in Senegal.[30] The concept of hiring out one's labor was not new to the Manjaco. During the Atlantic slave trade, many Manjaco sold their labor to Luso-African, other Afro-European and European traders in the port cities of the Senegambia and the Upper Guinea Coast.[31] The abolition of the slave trade meant unemployment for many Manjaco who worked for the slavers in various capacities. Unemployment created problems for Manjaco men because they were expected to pay several kinds of taxes to their rulers at the local and regional levels and also to the "King of Kings" at the national level.[32] Young men also had to pay for presents to give to their bride's family. Abolition of the slave trade forced these young men to look elsewhere for work. The *feitorias* along the Rio Grande provided an alternative for them.

Feitoria owners sent hired agents to the Manjaco homeland to recruit migrant laborers needed in Forria. The owners furnished the food and transportation for the workers' trip south. When they arrived on the *feitorias*, they were expected to cultivate a certain amount of land. The owners supplied them with seeds, utensils and provisions for a prearranged price which they paid at the end of the harvest season.[33] If anything remained after the debt was paid off, the workers could buy cloth and other commodities they wanted to take back home. More often than not, however, the workers had very little of their peanut harvest left after clearing their debt. In this respect these laborers resembled sharecroppers rather than migrant laborers. As Jeffery Paige notes about sharecropping,

> ... It is impossible to accumulate property in such systems, and any property which is accumulated usually must be mortgaged to pay off debts. Whatever the sharecropper produces in addition to his normal crop will be taken by the landlord ...[34]

Unlike sharecroppers, however, these migrant laborers maintained their ties to their homelands.

The system of credit worked against the laborers on the *feitorias*. They had no say in the prices they received for their peanuts. Instead of receiving a percentage of the crop's value, the workers had to sell their crop at whatever price the proprietor wanted to pay.[35] Contracts bound the workers to a particular *feitoria* and therefore, they were unable to sell their peanuts to other owners, even if they could have obtained a higher price. If their owners had a small stock of merchandise, the laborers were constricted further because they could not take their produce to other *feitoria* owners with larger stocks.[36]

Although Manjaco workers did accept contracts to cultivate peanuts in Forria, these laborers never developed strong ties to the region. Most workers travelled to Forria by themselves and worked long enough to generate capital needed to pay their tribute, buy cloth or other imported commodities and/or buy gifts for their bride's family. Given the nature of the contract system, workers often ended up staying longer than they anticipated. Even if they worked for several seasons on the same *feitoria*, however, these migrant laborers never thought of the Forria as "home" or of the land as "theirs".

Chattel slaves on *feitorias* worked under similar conditions, but had no choice about who they worked for, or the length of their stay. They also had no prospect for amassing capital of their own. Most importantly they had no rights over their own person. From the outset of peanut cultivation, proprietors used slave labor to work their fields. Mãe Aurélia, Caetano Nozolini, João Marques de Barros, David Lawrence and other *feitoria* owners held slaves. As peanuts increased in value it was more profitable for these entrepreneurs to hold their slaves rather than run the risk of having the British patrols capture them.[37]

French commercial domination along the Rio Grande

The growth of the peanut economy led to the development of a new commercial system in Forria. Existing African and European commercial networks provided a foundation for this system. The area was a part of the South Atlantic system from its inception. European and eventually Afro-European coastal traders in part depended upon long-distance caravans that brought slaves, gum, ivory, kola, hides, beeswax and other goods from Futa Jallon to the coast.[38] Initially, as peanut cultivation expanded, caravans continued supplying Buba and in turn European markets with these commodities. The caravans collected European goods as well as indigenous products unavailable in the interior. One of these commodities, salt, was particularly valuable since it was used to cure hides in Futa Jallon.

Although the Portuguese presence in the region dated to the fifteenth century, by the 1840s their economic and political influence in Portuguese Guinea was limited. Once peanuts became the "king" of commerce, French rather than Portuguese merchants began to dominate the export business. Between the 1840s and 1880s, individual Portuguese traders benefitted from increased peanut production, but it did little to bolster the Portuguese economy. French nationals were primarily responsible for marketing and shipping the peanuts to Europe, especially to the oil factories in France. Some French traders claimed that they took the initiative in developing the peanut enterprises along the Rio Grande, but, as we have seen Luso-African traders played an even more significant role in the rapid spread of peanut cultivation.[39]

Access to French ships enabled the *feitoria* owners and traders to expand their properties. These traders shipped their peanuts in the shell, meaning larger, heavier boats were needed to transport this bulky cash crop.[40] The industrial base in Portugal was not sufficiently developed to take advantage of peanuts being produced in Portuguese Guinea. French industries created the demand for peanut oil and they could handle the large volume of peanuts produced in Senegambia. By the 1880s French firms dominated the trade on the Rio Grande, as well as on the Senegal, Gambia, Casamance, Nunez and Pongo Rivers.[41] French firms with representatives in Bolama and along the Rio Grande included Gaspard-Devês & Co., Arine Olivier, Durême, Maurel & H. Prom, and Blanchard & Co. In addition to exporting peanuts, these firms also bought local products from the interior such as hides, beeswax, rubber and small amounts of ivory and gold. The imports they sold included textiles, *aguardente* (a spirit), tobacco, gunpowder and firearms.[42]

In the first five years of Guinea's existence as a separate entity from Cape Verde (1879-1884), the economic situation was so "desperate" for the Portuguese, one Governor declared that commerce was almost completely in French hands.[43] He believed that Guinea was in reality a colony of the French commercial houses, rather than of Portugal or her few representatives there. In fact, the Portuguese traders active in the area relied heavily upon imported goods and credit from the French firms. Portuguese traders passed these costs on to the local people and *feitoria* workers. Because of the higher prices Portuguese traders charged for their merchandise, African workers and merchants preferred to buy directly from French merchants at lower prices. Furthermore, because of their commercial dominance, French traders could usually keep their warehouses better stocked than their Portuguese counterparts who had to wait for sporadic deliveries from the metropole.[44] "The fabulous prices, augmented still with duties and transportation costs [placed] the [price of] the goods at such a point that the local people go looking for other more favorable markets ..."[45] The markets in the Rio Cacine and Rio Nunez areas offered an attractive alternative.

Traders along the Rio Grande, regardless of their nationality, had grievances with the Portuguese government. Portuguese traders complained that the government did very little to help them and this lack of support made it more difficult to establish themselves, especially in the face of French competition. They believed that with both financial and military support from the metropole they could have changed the trading patterns in the region. In making this argument Portuguese nationals ignored the fact that Portugal, unlike France, lacked industries that could have utilized the peanuts and their oil. They also failed to understand that "Lisbon merchants, with their old-fashioned sailing ships and cumbersome system of indirect trade, were ill-equipped to compete ..."[46] As we shall see, from the 1870s, French traders also disagreed with new restrictions that the Portuguese government imposed on them.

The decline of peanut production in Portuguese Guinea

At the peak of peanut production in the early 1870s, there were approximately one hundred *feitorias* along the banks of the Rio Grande and its branches. *Feitorias* began closing in 1876, however, and by 1885 more than fifty had closed. In two years at least another forty had shut down. Less than twelve were still operational in 1887 and their lives were short-lived.[47] Because peanut exports accounted for a large portion of commercial activity, the rapid decline in production meant economic disaster for the colony (see Table 5.1).

Contemporary observers often commented about the importance of a good peanut harvest for the colony's economic survival.[48]

> Among all the other export products, this product [peanuts] attracts most of the shipping traffic to our [Portuguese] ports; and [with] the exchange of this oilseed annually, ships come with goods from the European markets, opening up a valuable foundation of revenue for the public coffers and gives work to a part of the population.[49]

No single factor can account for the decline in peanut production and the closure of *feitorias* in the 1880s. One particularly sensitive governor blamed Guinea's economic crisis on a combination of international and local problems:

> ... the decline of commerce due to the decay of agriculture, the contraction of agricultural production because of successive bad harvests, the depreciation of peanuts on the European market, the lack of security for individuals and property on the agricultural holdings, the difficulty if not impossibility of guaranteeing either [kind of security] without steamboats, [the problems of repressing] contraband, [and] the incomplete definition of our [Portuguese] boundaries relative to the neighboring colonies ...[50]

On the international level, the economic recession in Europe between 1873 and 1896 adversely affected cash crop production in Guinea. Because of Portugal's small industrial base, this recession disrupted the country's economy. Clarence-Smith points out that in Portugal:

> Agriculture was faced with a flood of cheap foodstuffs on both foreign markets and on the home market, infant industries wavered in the face of cut-throat competition, and the merchant navy was on the point of being swept off the high seas altogether. Public revenue fell, the deficit on the balance of payments grew alarmingly, gold reserves dwindled, and the country could no longer service its foreign debt ... Portugal reacted like the other states of Western Europe, first protecting the home market and then seeking to extend protected markets by colonial expansion.[51]

In addition to the economic recession, the demand for peanuts in Europe fell as cheaper oil-seeds from both America and India began entering the market. Cotton seeds from the United States were more readily available after 1865 and with the opening of the Suez Canal in 1869 sesame seeds from India were a viable alternative to peanuts from Guinea.[52] As the economic crisis in Europe deepened, prices for raw materials fell, and less capital was available to buy these commodities. Consequently, the cheaper oil seeds were very attractive.

On the local level, the recession pushed Portugal to try to eliminate French competition in Guinea. Transportation laws as well as higher duties on imports and exports were the immediate response. For example, Portugal tried to

129

prevent French vessels from sailing on the Rio Grande. Neither Portuguese merchants nor the government, however, could provide enough vessels for traders to ship their goods to Bolama.[53] Because of Portugal's weak administrative presence and her unwillingness to invest the manpower or military force necessary to protect the various rivers and their branches, laws restricting French merchants were difficult to enforce.

Table 5.1
Peanuts exported between 1878 and 1897 (in bushels)

Year	Bushels	
1878	1,120,828	
1879	898,070	
1880	840,506	
1881	716,019	
1882	610,386	
1883	723,936	
1884	563,646	
1885	164,375	
1886	196,214	
1887	70,788	
1888	136,113	
1889	209,217	
1890	288,242	
1891	290,318	
1892	206,366	(Jan.-June)
1892	354,250	(July-Dec.)
1893	460,450	
1894	238,947	
1895	101,280	
1896	18,753	
1897	16,455	

Source: AHU, Guiné, Pasta 398: Alfandega da Guiné em Bolama to Secretaria Geral do Governo em Bolama, 24 January 1898.

These economic problems of the 1870s and early 1880s contributed to an already tense political situation and created labor problems for the *feitoria* owners. The power struggles between local polities, which began even before the flowering of the *feitoria* system took on new dimensions with the decline in peanut production. Conflicts between the original inhabitants of the region, the Biafada, and recent Fulbe immigrants intensified during the late 1860s and early 1870s. This warfare, and subsequent battles between rival Fulbe groups in the late 1870s and 1880s, forced migrant workers to reconsider their positions. Many migrant laborers, like their counterparts elsewhere, maintained ties with their homelands and often with subsistence production. Thus, they could and did return "home" when things went awry.[54] They chose to leave since staying meant risking their lives and becoming victims of wars they were not a part of. Some workers fled even in the middle of the cultivation season:

> [Workers] ... at times abandoned the cultivation of land already begun, others spread out the seeds and let the products rot in the soil which [if harvested] would have compensated the owners for the large expenditures made, thus causing a general bad state of affairs in commerce, the main source of wealth for this important province.[55]

Slaves responded in a similar fashion. They also wanted to protect their lives and avoid being trapped in the crossfire. One option slaves on the *feitorias*, as well as slaves held by the Fulbe, had, was escape. They often fled to the Portuguese *praça* in Buba. According to Portuguese sources, these slaves were then allowed to proceed to Bolama or other parts of Portuguese Guinea.[56] Many of the slaves mentioned were women and children — how successful they were in reestablishing themselves elsewhere remains unclear.

The loss of profits and the increasingly dangerous environment also drove the *feitoria* proprietors away. Furthermore, the number of trading companies operating in the Rio Grande fell drastically in the 1880s. These proprietors and trading company representatives wrote letters to the Portuguese government about their situation. The proprietors of Saudade and Ganfarra, two *feitorias*, complained that attackers killed some of their workers and stole their cattle, chicken, goats, *aguardent* and foodstuffs.[57] Other owners, like Durême on the *feitoria* Regina, said their workers were taken as slaves — meaning they were left without the labor needed to produce the peanut crop.[58] By 1886 Blanchard & Co. had closed its estates including Gam-Caba, Gorée, São Jorge, Santa Cruz and Boa Esperança. Similarly, Maurel & H. Prom closed down its warehouses and properties — Saudade, Empada and Bissau.[59] These companies and individual traders turned their attention to the Casamance and Rio Nunez areas where they could depend upon military support from French gunboats. In addition to this physical support, France also protected its nationals through tariffs placed on imported goods shipped to France on foreign ships.

These proprietors blamed their trouble on what they believed was an "ethnic conflict". In their minds, the animosity the Biafada felt towards the Fulbe and the divisions between the different Fulbe groups represented the root of the problem in Forria.[60] Although ethnic rivalry played a role in the wars fought from the late 1860s through the 1880s, several other factors were more important sources of tensions. During the first phase of the warfare between 1868 and 1878, the Fulbe, with support from their brethren in Futa Jallon, replaced the indigenous Biafada rulers. In part, these united Fulbe groups wanted to spread their religion, Islam, and so these wars had elements of *jihad* in them.[61] But the Fulbe were also interested in the region for its economic potential. The abolition of the slave trade and the new emphasis on "legitimate commerce" forced Futa Jallon and its clients in Forria to look for new sources of revenue. The Fulbe believed that by eliminating the Biafada rulers, and establishing political control, they could reap the economic benefits of the peanut trade — especially access to firearms and in turn, slaves.

By 1878, the Fulbe controlled the Forria, but the peanut industry was entering a period of decline. Consequently, the new Fulbe rulers' source of firearms and other European goods began drying up as the *feitorias* shut down. The resulting economic pressures on the Fulbe exacerbated existing conflicts between the *Fulbe-ribê* and their slaves, the *Fulbe-djiábê*. Furthermore, the economic crisis meant that masters placed more pressure on their slaves. From 1878 the *Fulbe-djiábê* rose in revolt against their masters. Throughout the 1880s, the slaves fought for freedom, as well as control of the region's dwindling economic resources. They turned to the Portuguese for help and some sought refuge in the Portuguese fort in Buba.[62] In return for Portuguese support, the *Fulbe-djiábê* served as auxiliaries in the Portuguese army in their wars against the *Fulbe-ribê*.

The Portuguese, however, were in a weak position. They had never established economic control. In fact, the ten years between 1879 and 1889 were chaotic ones for them. Seven different Portuguese governors and five secretary generals served during this period. This administrative instability prevented the Portuguese administration from developing economic strategies to improve conditions in Guinea.[63] The administrative revolving door reflected the economic and political problems Portugal faced at home and in her colonies. Portuguese decisions were often short-sighted — hoping only to improve the current economic situation. The Crown's representatives on the spot made and broke alliances with Fulbe groups in Forria — supporting the *Fulbe-djiábê* at first, then the *Fulbe-ribê* — all the while proclaiming their neutrality when it came to local politics.[64]

As a result of these international and local factors, commercial activities in Portuguese Guinea slowed down during the 1880s. Peanut exports from Bolama dropped from about 1,120,000 bushels in 1878 to 136,000 bushels in 1888. Fewer ships frequented the ports, imported consumer goods disappeared, and the market for European goods dried up. Similarly, the caravans from Futa Jallon stopped going to the Rio Grande area because their routes were totally unprotected and caravans became the targets of attack for those groups embroiled in war. Like *feitoria* owners and trading companies, the caravans went to markets in the Rio Nunez and Rio Cacine regions.[65] This diversion south also reflected Portugal's inability to control the areas she claimed — a situation that continued to plague Portuguese administrators well into the twentieth century.[66]

Notes

1. Beaver, *African Memoranda*, pp. 347 and 483-84.
2. For information on peanut production elsewhere in West Africa see: Yves Pehaut, *Les Oléagineaux dans les Pays d'Afrique Occidentale Associés au Marché Commun: La production, le commerce et la transformation des produits*, 2 vols., Paris, Edition Honoré Champion, 1976; Martin Klein, "Social and Economic Factors in the Muslim Revolution in Senegambia", *JAH*, 13, 1972, pp. 419-41; Martin A. Klein, *Islam and Imperialism in Senegal: Sine-Saloum, 1847-1914*, Stanford, Stanford University Press, 1969; George E. Brooks, "Peanuts and Colonialism: Consequences of the Commercialization of Peanuts in West Africa, 1830-1870", *JAH*, 16, 1975, pp. 29-54; Goerg, *Commerce et colonization*; Searing, *West African Slavery*; Peter M. Weil, "Slavery, groundnuts and European capitalism in the Walé Kingdom of Senegambia, 1820-1930", *Research in Economic Anthropology*, 6, 1984, pp. 77-119.
3. Brooks, "Peanuts", p. 32.
4. Brooks, "Peanuts", pp. 29 and 31-32.
5. A. Teixeira da Mota, "A agricultura de Brames e Balantas vista através de fotografia aéres", *BCGP*, 5, April 1950, p. 147.
6. The term *Nhara*, like *sinare* and *senora*, is "derived from the Portuguese *senhora* and signified women of wealth and influence. The most successful of these women possessed trading craft, numerous domestic slaves including seamen and skilled artisans, European-style dwellings and storehouses, and quantities of gold and silver jewelry, splendid cloths, and other wearing apparel". George E. Brooks, "A Nhara of the Guinea-Bissau Region: Mãe Aurélia Correia", in *Women and Slavery in Africa*, eds. Claire C. Robertson and Martin A. Klein, Madison, University of Wisconsin Press, 1983, p. 295. For more information on *Nharas* in the Senegambia see: George E. Brooks, "The Signares of Saint Louis and Gorée: Women Entrepreneurs in Eighteenth-Century Senegal", in *Women in Africa: Studies in Social and Economic Change*, eds. Nancy J. Hafkin and Edna G. Bay, Stanford, Stanford University Press, 1976; and George

E. Brooks, "Artists' Depictions of Senegalese Signares: Insights Concerning French Racist and Sexist Attitudes in the Nineteenth Century", *Geneve-Afrique*, 18 1980, pp. 75-89.

7. Brooks, "A Nhara", p. 301.

8. Brooks, "A Nhara", pp. 301-02 and 312-14. For more information on a similar situation further south see: Bruce L. Mouser, "Women Slavers of Guinea-Conakry", in *Women and Slavery in Africa*, eds. Claire C. Robertson and Martin A. Klein, Madison, University of Wisconsin Press, 1983, pp. 320-39; Bruce L. Mouser, "Landlords-Strangers: A Process of Accommodation and Assimilation", *IJAHS*, 8, pp. 425-40; and Bruce L. Mouser, "Trade and Politics in the Nunez and Pongo Rivers, 1790-1865", Ph.D. dissertation, Indiana University, 1971.

9. AHU, Cabo Verde and Guiné, Maço 782: Caetano Nozolini to Governor Honório P. Barreto, 20 January 1839. See also: Brooks, "A Nhara", p. 314; and José Cristiano de Senna Barcellos, *Subsidios para a história de Cabo Verde e Guiné*, 7 vols., Lisbon, 1899-1912, 4, pp. 253-58. For information on other British attacks against Mãe Aurélia and her counterparts see: AHU, Cabo Verde, Pasta 62: Governor General to Ministro e Secretário d'Estado dos Negócios da Marinha e Ultramar, 27 January 1848; AHU, Cabo Verde, Pasta 64A: "Memoria sobre o Estabelecimento de Bissau remettida com officio de Dezembargados Juiz de Direito da Comarca de Sotavento da Provincia de Cabo Verde", 9 June 1852.

10. Brooks, "A Nhara", p. 314.

11. AHU, Cabo Verde, Pasta 62: Governor General to Ministro e Secretário d'Estado dos Negócios da Marinha e Ultramar, 27 January 1848; AHU, Cabo Verde and Guiné, Maço 782: Nozolini Junior and Company to Governor of Guiné, 30 August 1858; AHU, Cabo Verde e Guiné, Maço 782: João Marques Barros to Governor of Guiné, 31 August 1858; AHU, Cabo Verde e Guiné, Maço 782: Honório Pereira Barreto, Governor of Guiné, No. 85 to Governor General of Cabo Verde and Guiné, 13 September 1858; AHU, Cabo Verde e Guiné, Maço 781: British Officer in Cape Verde to Her Majesty the Queen, 14 March 1843.

12. AHU, Cabo Verde e Guiné, Maço 782: Governor General to Ministro e Secretário d'Estado dos Negócios da Marinha e Ultramar, 4 September 1852; AHU, Cabo Verde, Pasta 64A: "Alguns apontamentos sobre Bissau", 8 April 1851; AHU, Cabo Verde, Pasta 62: Governor General to Ministro e Secretário d'Estado dos Negócios da Marinha e Ultramar, 27 January 1848.

13. AHU, Cabo Verde e Guiné, Maço 782: Secretaria da Camara dos Deputados, No. 173 to Ministro e Secretário d'Estado dos Negócios da

Marinha e Ultramar, 6 February 1861; AHU, Cabo Verde e Guiné, Maço 782: António Candido Zagato, Governor of Guiné, No. 11 to Governor General of Cabo Verde e Guiné, 9 January 1861. See also: George E. Brooks, "Bolama as a prospective site for American colonization in the 1820s and 1830s", *BCGP*, 28, April 1973, pp. 5-21; and Beaver, *African Memorandum.*

14. AHU, Cabo Verde e Guiné, Pasta 775: Howard Walden to Le Conseiller Rodrigo de Fonseca Magalhães, 11 May 1841; AHU, Cabo Verde e Guiné, Maço 782: Governor General of Cabo Verde e Guiné, No. 137A to Ministro e Secretário d'Estado dos Negócios da Marinha e Ultramar, 14 June 1859.

15. For more information on the struggle for control of Bolama see: Richard Adeboye Olanigan, "The Anglo-Portuguese Dispute over Bulama: A Study in British Colonial Policy, 1860-1870", Ph.D. dissertation, Georgetown University, 1969; and Brooks, "Bolama".

16. AHU, Cabo Verde, Pasta 66: António Maria Barreiros Arrobas, Governor General of Cabo Verde and Guiné, No. 2339 to Ministro e Secretário d'Estado dos Negócios da Marinha e Ultramar, 4 September 1856.

17. AHU, Cabo Verde, Pasta 66: António Maria Barreiros Arrobas, Governor General of Cabo Verde e Guiné, No. 2339 to Ministro e Secretário d'Estado dos Negócios da Marinha e Ultramar, 4 September 1856.

18. Gervase Clarence-Smith, *The Third Portuguese Empire 1825-1975: A Study in Economic Imperialism*, Manchester, Manchester University Press, 1985, p. 7.

19. AHU, Cabo Verde e Guiné, Maço 774: Manoel António Martins to João d'Oliveira, Ministro e Secretário d'Estado dos Negócios da Fazenda e Presidente do Tesouro Publico, 17 January 1838.

20. For more information on the efforts to establish the Companhia Mercantil e Agrícola see: AHU, Cabo Verde e Guiné, Maço 774: "Memoria assignada por Manoel António Martin, Jeronimo d'Almeida Brandão, José Ignácio de Seixas e João Gomes da Costa", February 1838; AHU, Cabo Verde e Guiné, Maço 774: Associação Mercantil Lisbonense to Ministro e Secretária d'Estado da Fazenda e do Tesouro Publico, 16 May 1838; AHU, Cabo Verde e Guiné, Maço 774: Sala das Conferências da Commissão na Secretaria d'Estado dos Negócios da Marinha e do Ultramar, 14 March 1839; AHU, Cabo Verde e Guiné, Maço 774: Francisco de Paulo Bastos, Governor General, No. 353 to Ministro e Secretário d'Estado dos Negócios da Marinha e Ultramar, 30 October 1842; AHU, Cabo Verde e Guiné, Maço 774: Francisco de Paula Bastos, Governor General, No. 364 to Ministro e Secretário d'Estado dos Negócios da Marinha e Ultramar, 19 November 1842; AHU, Cabo Verde

e Guiné, Maço 774: Manuel José Maria da Costa e Sá, João da Costa Carvalho, João de Mattos Pinto, Pedro Alexandrino de Cunha, José Angelo de Barros to King, 27 February 1843.

21. Clarence-Smith, *Third Portuguese Empire*, p. 56; see also, pp. 22-55.

22. Brooks, "Peanuts", p. 47; Joaquim Machado da Fonseca, "Amendoim na Guiné Portuguesa", *Revista Agronomica*, 2d. ser., 11th year, Vol. 2, 13-16, 1915, p. 31; and AHU, Cabo Verde, Pasta 64A: "Memoria sobre o Estabelecimento de Bissau remettida com oficio de Dezembargados Juiz de Direito da Comarca de Sotavento da Província de Cabo Verde", 9 June 1852.

23. AHU, Cabo Verde, Pasta 66: Governor General to Ministro e Secretário d'Estado dos Negócios da Marinha e Ultramar, 4 September 1856; AHU, Cabo Verde, Pasta 88: Governor General to Ministro e Secretário d'Estado dos Negócios da Marinha e Ultramar, 12 April 1878.

24. "Provincia da Guiné Portuguesza (Abandono)", p. 138; AHU, Cabo Verde, Pasta 88: Governor General to Ministro e Secretário d'Estado dos Negócios da Marinha e Ultramar, 12 April 1878.

25. AHU, Guiné 6390, Processo 6: "Tratado feito por H.P. Barreto, Governador da Guiné Portugueza com os régulos de Bolola e Buba no rio de Bolola", 13 June 1856; AHU, Cabo Verde e Guiné, Maço 781: "Tratado celebrado entre H.P. Barreto, Governador da Guiné Portugueza e o régulo e chefes biafadas do Guinala no Rio Grande na aldeia de Umbaná pertencent a povoação de Guinala", 16 June 1856. See also: J.D. Silva and A. Teixeira da Mota, *Honório Barreto, Português da Guiné*, Lisbon, 1973 and Jaime Walter, *Honório Pereira Barreto*, Centro de Estudos da Guiné Portuguesa, No. 5, Bissau, 1947.

    Until 1879, Portuguese Guinea was actually a part of Cape Verde. The Governor General served over the two provinces. However, because of the distances involved, the delay in communications and the lack of resources, the local governor in Bissau had a fairly free hand to conduct business in the name of the King.

26. For an interesting discussion of the problems African rulers faced signing treaties see: Stanlake Samkange, *On Trial for My Country*, London, Heinemann, 1966. Although this account is fictional, it is based on an historical situation and shows how treaties were used to achieve European goals.

27. E. Bouet-Williaumez, *Commerce et traite des noires aux côtés occidentales d'Afrique*, Paris, 1848, pp. 67-70; Francisco Travassos-Valdez, *Six Years of a Traveller's Life in Western Africa*, 2 Vols., London, 1861, 1, p. 260; and AHU, Cabo Verde e Guiné, Maço 782: António Candido Zagato, Governor in Bissau, No. 11 to Governor General of Cabo

Verde and Guiné, 9 January 1861.

28. AHU, Cabo Verde, Pasta 64A: "Memoria sobre o Estabelecimento de Bissau remettida com officio de Dezembargador Juiz de Direito da Comarca de Sotavento da Província de Cabo Verde", 9 June 1852; and AHU, Cabo Verde e Guiné, Maço 782: Governor General to Ministro e Secretário d'Estado dos Negócios da Marinha e Ultramar, 23 April 1858.

29. PRO, CO 87/79: D'Arcy, Governor of Gambia to Duke of New Castle, 23 April 1864.

30. See: Swindell, "Serawoolies, Tillibunkas", pp. 93-104.

31. For more information on the Manjaco generally see: Carreira, *Vida Social*; and Gable, "Modern Manjaco".

32. Bocandé, "Notes sur la Guinée Portugaise", p. 340; and Gable, "Modern Manjaco", pp. 89-103.

33. AHU, Cabo Verde, Pasta 85: Quartel Geral do Governo na Praia to Ministro e Secretário d'Estado dos Negócios da Marinha e Ultramar, 15 December 1873; and *BOGP*, 1883, No. 23, p. 111.

34. Jeffery M. Paige, *Agrarian Revolution: Social Movements and Export Agriculture in the Underdeveloped World*, New York, The Free Press, 1975, p. 60; AHU, Guiné, Pasts 363: "Indemnisação de Pedro Luciano Durême", no date; AHU, Guiné, Pasts 409: Pedro Inácio de Gouveia, Governor to Ministro e Secretário d'Estado dos Negócios da Marinha e Ultramar, 8 January 1882.

35. AHU, Cabo Verde, Pasta 85: Quartel Geral do Governo na Praia to Ministro e Secretário d'Estado dos Negócios da Marinha e Ultramar, 15 December 1873; AHU, Guiné, Pasta 363: "Indemnisação de Pedro Luciano Durême", no date; AHU, Guiné, Pasta 409: Pedro Inácio de Gouveia, Governor to Ministro e Secretário d'Estado dos Negócios da Marinha e Ultramar, 8 January 1882; AHU, Guiné, Pasta 387: Governo em Bolama to Ministro e Secretário d'Estado dos Negócios da Marinha e Ultramar, 1 August 1883.

36. AHU, Guiné, Pasta 365: Pedro Inácio de Gouveia, Governor to Ministro e Secretário d'Estado dos Negócios da Marinha e Ultramar, 7 November 1884. See also: Correia e Lança, *Relatório*.
   These workers' counterparts further north, the 'strange farmers' along the Gambia River, worked under better conditions, since they were only responsible for giving ten percent of their harvest and two days of work per week to the owners of the land. See Swindell, "Serawoolies, Tillibunkas", p. 99.

37. For more information on this phenomenon elsewhere see for example: Pehaut, *Les Oléagineaux*, 1, pp. 332-33; Klein, "Social and Economic Factors", pp. 419-41; Klein, *Islam and Imperialism*. See also: AHU, Cabo

Verde e Guiné, Maço 782: Caetano Nozolini, No. 3 to Honório Pereira Barreto, Governor, 20 January 1839.

38. "Relatório de 1882 — Governador Pedro Inácio de Gouveia", *BCGP*, 7, April 1952, p. 446; Correia e Lança, *Relatório*, p. 29; AHU, Guiné, Pasta 387: Rio Grande traders to the King, 12 February 1885; AHU, Guiné, Pasta 413: Governor to Ministro e Secretário d'Estado dos Negócios da Marinha e Ultramar, 20 June 1890; and *BOGP*, 1883, No. 48, p. 215.

39. ANSOM, Sénégal XIII, Dossier 11 (c): Marseille traders to the President of the Chamber of Commerce, 30 June 1877. For more information on the role of Luso-Africans in commerce see: George E. Brooks, *Luso-African Commerce and Settlement in the Gambia and Guinea-Bissau Region*, Boston University African Studies Center Working Papers, no. 24, Brookline, MA, 1980; and Brooks, *Landlords and Strangers*, pp. 167-196.

40. See: Goerg, "Exchanges, Réseaux", p. 39.

41. João Bentes Castel-Branco, *Guia do Colono para a Africa Portugueza*, Porto, Typ. da Empreza Literária e Typographica, 1891, pp. 91-2; and "Relatório de 1882", pp. 441, 445 and 447.

42. de Barros, "A praça", p. 52.

43. "Relatório de 1882", pp. 445-47.

44. AHU, Cabo Verde, Pasta 88: Governor General to Ministro e Secretário d'Estado dos Negócios da Marinha e Ultramar, 12 April 1878.

45. AHU, Cabo Verde, Pasta 85: Quartel Général do Governo to Ministro e Secretário d'Estado dos Negócios da Marinha e Ultramar, 15 December 1873.

46. Clarence-Smith, *Third Portuguese Empire*, p. 70.

47. "Provincia da Guiné Portugueza (Abandono)", p. 138 and *BOGP*, 1886, No. 45, p. 186. The precise figures vary. For example, António Carreira's figures are slightly different — he states that sixty-nine *feitorias* closed by 1885 and another forty-three closed between 1886 and 1887. All of the figures show a dramatic reduction in the number of *feitorias* and consequently in peanut production. See: António Carreira, *Documentos para a História das Ilhas de Cabo Verde e "Rios de Guiné" (Séculos XVII e XVIII)*, Lisbon, 1983, pp. 32-3.

48. AHU, Guiné, Pasta 387: Governo da Província em Bolama to Ministro e Secretário d'Estado dos Negócios da Marinha e Ultramar, 30 June 1885; AHU, Guiné, Pasta 411: Governo da Provincia to Ministro e Secretário d'Estado dos Negócios da Marinha e Ultramar, 13 December 1886; and AHU, Guiné, Pasta 387: Junta da Fazenda em Bolama to Ministro e Secretário d'Estado dos Negócios da Marinha e Ultramar, 28 April 1885.

49. AHU, Guiné, Pasta 387: Traders and Property owners in Guinea to His majesty, 12 February 1885.

50. AHU, Guiné, Pasta 409: Francisco de Paula Gomes Barboza, Governor to Ministro e Secretário d'Estado dos Negócios da Marinha e Ultramar, 28 October 1885.

51. Clarence-Smith, *Third Portuguese Empire*, p. 81.

52. Pehaut, *Les Oléagineaux*, 1, pp. 344-46; Goerg, "Exchanges, Réseaux", p. 119; AHU, Guiné, Pasta 409: Pedro Inácio de Gouveia, Governor to Ministro e Secretário d'Estado dos Negócios da Marinha e Ultramar, 8 January 1882; AHU, Guiné, Pasta 410: Governo da Província em Bolama to Ministro e Secretário d'Estado dos Negócios da Marinha e Ultramar, 13 June 1887; and Alfredo Loureiro da Fonseca, *Guiné: Finanças e Economia*, Lisbon, Typographia da Cooperativa Militar, 1910, p. 28.

53. ANSOM, Sénégal XIII, Dossier 11 (c): Marseille traders to President of the Chamber of Commerce, 30 June 1877; and ANSOM, Sénégal XIII, Dossier 11 (c): Marseille traders to Commander in Gorée, 9 August 1877.

54. Paige, *Agrarian Revolution*, pp. 66-68; AHU, Guiné, Pasta 409: Pedro Inácio de Gouveia, Governor to Ministro e Secretário d'Estado dos Negócios da Marinha e Ultramar, 8 January 1882; AHU, Guiné, Pasta 409: Francisco de Paulo Gomes Barboza, Governor to Ministro e Secretário d'Estado dos Negócios da Marinha e Ultramar, 30 May 1885; AHU, Guiné, Pasta 387: Governor to Ministro e Secretário d'Estado dos Negócios da Marinha e Ultramar, 30 June 1885; "Relatório de 1882", p. 446; and Castel-Branco, *Guia do Colono*, p. 91.

55. *BOGP*, 1882, No. 43, p. 182.

56. de Barros, "A praça", pp. 51-2.

57. AHU, Guiné, Pasta 387: "Declaração de Christiano Marques de Barros", (early 1885); AHU, Guiné, Pasta 387: "Declaração de Domingos Maria Gomes Buré", 12 January 1885.

58. AHU, Guiné, Pasta 387: "Declaração de Durême", 6 February 1885; see also: AMNE, Guiné, Caixa 1101, No. 73: Durême to Le Consul de France à Lisbonne, 25 May 1883.

59. *BOGP*, 1886, 6 February, p. 26; *BOGP*, 1889, No. 27, p. 103; and de Barros, "A praça porto", p. 52.

60. AHU, Guiné, Pasta 387: "Declaração de Joaquim Thiago e Vasto", 14 January 1885; AHU, Guiné, Pasta 387: "Rapport de Messieurs Maurel & H. Prom", 26 January 1885; AHU, Guiné, Pasta 387: "Declaração des Messieurs Maurel & H. Prom", 30 January 1885.

61. Correia e Lança, *Relatório*, p. 52; Abdulai Djaló, Bissau Series Tape 3 (Bafatá), 12 July 1977; Vasco de Sousa Calvet de Magalhaes, *Província da Guiné — Relatório apresentado pelo administrador da Circumscrição Civil de Geba, 1914*, Porto, 1916, p. 51; de Barros, *Breves apontamentos*; Frederico Pinheiro Chagas, "Povos da Guiné Portuguesa", *Annaes do Club*

Militar Naval, 41, 2, p. 88; AHU, Guiné, Pasta 365: Pedro Inácio de Gouveia, Governor to Ministro e Secretário d'Estado dos Negócios da Marinha e Ultramar, 6 October 1884.

For more specific information on Futa Jallon see: McGowan, "The Development of European Relations", and Barry, *La Sénégambie*.

62. Teixeira de Barros, *Breves apontamentos*, p. 10; Carreira, "Aspectos históricos", pp. 405-56; BOGP, 1911, Annex No. 2, p. 8; AHU, Guiné, Pasta 409: Pedro Inácio de Gouveia, Governor to Ministro e Secretário d'Estado dos Negócio da Marinha e Ultramar, 6 October 1884; AHU, Guiné, Pasta 409: Pedro Inácio de Gouveia, Governor to Ministro e Secretário d'Estado dos Negócio da Marinha e Ultramar, 7 November 1884.

63. Correia e Lança, *Relatório*, p. 7. The unstable political situation continued well into the colonial period. For more information on administrative changes in the early twentieth century see: Bowman, "Abdul Njai", pp. 463-79.

64. Portugal and France both claimed to be neutral about local politics, but they actively supported groups against their enemies in return for favors. See: AHU, Guiné, Pasta 410: Francisco Teixeira da Silva, Governor, No. 178 to Ministro e Secretário d'Estado dos Negócios da Marinha e Ultramar, 13 July 1887.

65. "Relatório de 1882", p. 446; AHU, Guiné, Pasta 387: Palácio do Governo to Ministro e Secretário d'Estado dos Negócios da Marinha e Ultramar, 29 November 1883; *BOGP*, No. 32, p. 124; and AHU, Guiné, Pasta 410: Governo da Província em Bolama to Ministro e Secretário d'Estado dos Negócios da Marinha e Ultramar, 13 July 1887.

66. ANSOM, Guinée IV, Dossier 1 (a): Administrator of Rio Nunez to Governor General of Guinée Française, 12 August 1895; AHU, Guiné, Pasta 393: Governor to Ministro e Secretário d'Estado dos Negócios da Marinha e Ultramar, 24 January 1892.

6 Portuguese Colonialism and its Discontents: Abdul Njai and the Investment in Law and Order on the Ground, 1903-1919

Abdul [in the] Oio region has been the most harmful to our "native" affairs, the wealth of the region and above all our prestige in the [eyes] of the indigenous people. He achieved a rule of personal domination through terror, attempting to convince the indigenous people that only he conquered them. His authority and prestige are enormous because since Oio's submission he has done whatever he wanted, practicing major crimes and abuses, always winning impunity. [These actions and this impunity] convince not only the people of Oio but those of other regions that he is the absolute master ...

Administrador de Farim to Governador 18 November 1915 [1]

The political situation in the neighboring Portuguese colony where two administrators, one in Cacheu and one in Mansoa, have been assassinated ... is totally at the mercy of the Wolof chief Abdou N'Diaye who for several years recruited numerous partisans and profited from the perpetual troubles of Guinea by creating a royalty for himself ...

Lt. Gouvernuer de Sénégal to W. Ponty, Gouverneur-Général de l'Afrique Occidentale Française, 17 August 1914 [2]

Between 1895 and 1915, the Portuguese in Guinea, like their European counterparts elsewhere in Africa, embarked on campaigns to consolidate their

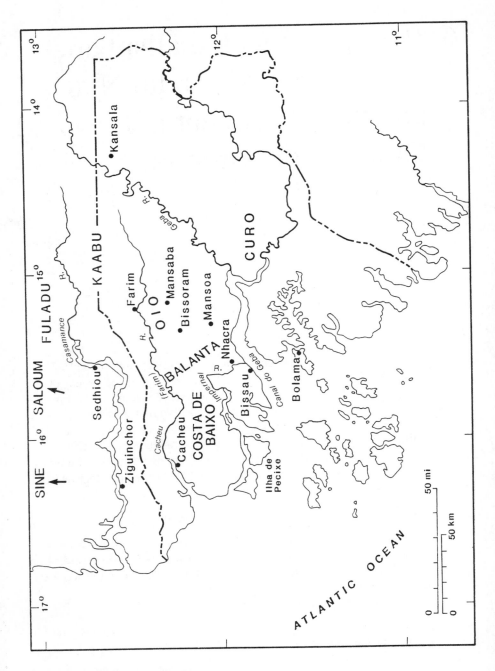

Figure 6.1   Portuguese Guinea c. 1915

142

hold on the region and attempted to establish the framework for a colonial state. French pressure from adjoining territories forced the Portuguese to show "effective occupation" of the area claimed in accordance with the conventions reached at the Berlin Conference in 1884-85. As we have demonstrated, proving "effective occupation" of southern Senegambia or Guinea became a protracted and ambiguous struggle for the Portuguese. Its difficulties reflected the weakness of both the state and the economy in Portugal, and the determination of the Africans of the region to maintain their sovereignty. Although some parts of the region entered the Portuguese sphere of influence before 1900, most remained outside Portuguese control until the second decade of the twentieth century. Some areas of the Bijagós archipelago, for example, did not come under effective Portuguese influence until the 1930s; the final campaign on Canhabaque was completed only in 1936.[3]

Abdul Njai's early career as a Portuguese ally

Perhaps one of Portugal's most problematic ally in its quest for control of the southern portions of Senegambia was Abdul Njai. Born between 1860 and 1865 in Sine-Saloum (Senegal), Njai launched his initial career as an itinerant trader at an early age.[4] Basing himself at Ziguinchor in the Casamance (Senegal), he traded a variety of commodities including dried fish, rubber, beads, kola nuts and slaves. By the early 1890s Njai had established close ties to communities in the southern Senegambia at Cacheu and Costa de Baixo. In 1894, while in search of greater commercial opportunities, Njai moved to Bissau island and became an employee of the French trading house of Blanchard.[5]

One of Njai's contemporaries claimed that even before he left for Bissau people considered Njai an adventurous and courageous person with gifts of leadership. According to this colleague, Njai believed he needed something more than just trading in his life and so he consulted a *marabout* about his future.[6] Other oral accounts say the *marabout* told Njai he would become a "king" and rule over a territory of his own.[7] Thus Njai's move to Bissau was in part the result of his *marabout's* advice. On the other hand, Njai knew that the Portuguese were much weaker than the French. Once in Bissau, however, he moved speedily to enhance his own power.

At the very outset of his stay on the island, Njai was recruited by the Portuguese military officer, Sousa Lage, for the campaign against the Papel, the indigenous people of the island.[8] This particular campaign ended in a Portuguese defeat. However, the defeat demonstrated that money was the sole inducement of the African irregulars fighting on the Portuguese side. Njai, for instance, sold his entire stock of merchandise and abandoned his career as a trader in order to enter into the Portuguese military service.[9]

Njai continued as an African irregular for the Portuguese during most of their military campaigns in Guinea. Even though the Portuguese recruited numerous Africans to fight their campaigns in Guinea during the 1890s, they were incapable of formulating an effective long-term strategy. In 1900, after six years of fighting on behalf of the Portuguese, Njai asked Governor A. Herculano da Cunha's permission to recruit his own levy of African soldiers for subsequent campaigns in Guinea. Njai simply wanted the Portuguese to supply the arms and ammunition necessary to carry out the offensive and the boats needed to transport his soldiers. Njai's skills as a military leader had previously come to the attention of Portuguese officialdom, so the Governor readily consented to Njai's request. Njai's own account of these circumstances claimed:

> ... after my [Njai's] men disembarked in Portuguese Guinea, the first operation carried out was against Samoge [a village on the Cacheu River between Cacheu and Farim] ... where I entered with a powerful force of eight hundred men. [This force] fought a terrible and bloody battle but this time, after being defeated for six years, God wanted me to leave there proud of having defeated the savages ...[10]

Njai and his forces fought other campaigns in 1900, 1902, 1903, 1906 and 1908. They succeeded in disarming local forces and compelled them to pay the Portuguese "hut" tax. In 1908 the Portuguese offered Abdul Njai the governorship of the Curo region after the defeat of its former ruler, Infaly Sonco. Njai saw the offer as reasonable compensation for his services. As he defended himself against charges of treason some eleven years later, Njai looked back on this turn of events and claimed,

> I have always aided the government of that province valorously in the tremendous combats ... Never was there even one victory in the campaigns of that province for which my intervention was not necessary because without my taking up arms, nothing could have been done ...[11]

Other accounts confirm Njai's contribution to Portuguese success in the early period of his alliance with the colonial power.

Era of the 'pacification' campaigns, 1912-1915

In October 1910 the Republicans took power in Portugal and introduced significant changes both in the colonies and the metropole. One historian, Gervase Clarence-Smith, claimed that, "[T]he rulers of the first republic, from 1910 to 1926, were committed to a more rational exploitation of empire. They conquered the indigenous peoples of the empire, disarmed them, imposed taxation, forced labor and forced cultivation on them ..."[12] By 1913, a Republican government in Portugal was prepared to implement this apparently "more rational" colonial policy in Guinea. However, the irony of Portuguese policy was that even with the assistance of Abdul Njai and others like him, Portugal could only administer part of the territory they claimed. Some six years after his intervention in the military subjugation of the Kasanje region of Angola, Teixeira Pinto made these observations of Portuguese Guinea:

> ... notwithstanding the heroic battles of some Portuguese, after setbacks and cruel massacres to our prestige, our [Portuguese] colony of Guiné had returned to being a simple occupation of fortresses, which was threatened by the consequences of a new revolt more complete or more violent.[13]

Because of this situation, policy makers in Lisbon determined to launch an all-out offensive against the remaining rebellious zones — Mansoa, Oio, Cacheu, Bissau and the Balanta territories.[14] Predictably the republican officer selected to lead the campaigns and to serve as *Chefe do Estado Maior* (Commander-in-Chief) was João Teixeira Pinto — the very same man who had salvaged the monarch's colonial ambitions in Angola in 1907. A seasoned colonial officer, Teixeira Pinto led a series of successful military campaigns in Guinea between 1913 and 1915 that earned him the esteem of republican officials and the title of *pacificador da Guiné*.

Teixeira Pinto's military victories, however, were very much the result of the assistance he received from Abdul Njai. Limited financial support from Lisbon insured the minimum amount of intervention from the Ministry of Colonies. Hence the assistance of Abdul Njai's irregulars was the determining factor in the military campaigns that Teixeira Pinto led. Teixeira Pinto was compelled to give Abdul Njai some credit for the success of the campaigns, but for obvious reasons his description of the achievements of the African irregulars was much concerned to point out their apparently ancillary relationship to the prosecution of the war:

> Amongst them [the auxiliary troops] Abdul Injai stands out [and] deserves to be noted in the history of Portuguese expansion as a hero, as one of those admirable *auxiliaries* who the Portuguese always know could rouse the people of occupied and colonized lands for the glory of Portugal.[15]

While Njai was described as a "hero" in Teixeira Pinto's account, his formal position as an officer and administrator of Portuguese Guinea was not referred to. Perhaps a more accurate description of the reality was Njai's claim that the Portuguese never had any victorious campaigns without his support.[16] Teixeira Pinto's omission was a portent of the gradual but deliberate traducement of African collaborators under the new republican colonial policy.

As early as 1913 Abdul Njai's irregulars combined with Teixeira Pinto's forces in the first campaigns against African communities in the Mansoa and Oio regions. Much like the Mandinka *Farim Cabos* of Kaabu and Alfa and Musa Molo of Fuladu, the Portuguese colonial administration was not able to subjugate the peasantry of these two backland regions in a manner that would allow for the consistent collection of annual hut and poll taxes. The peasants of Oio were particularly notorious in this regard. Part of their notoriety derived from the skewed and ambiguous field of power and authority in the backlands of Guinea south of the Cacheu River in the 1880s and 1890s. In 1897, for example, a Portuguese force from Farim on the northern bank of the river defeated the peasants of Oio. Following the defeat the leadership of Oio peasants crossed the river and travelled to the Portuguese fort at Farim to ask for a "pardon" as the Portuguese governor at Bolama put it. According to the governor, who was more than 70 miles south of the actual occurrence on the island of Bolama, "the pardon is just and all of Oio will be completely submissive".[17] However, what the pardon was for remained unclear — particularly since Musa Molo had not suffered any major defeat at the hands of Portuguese forces at the time and was prosecuting a war against the French in the north. Doubtless the visit of Oio's leadership to the Portuguese fort was a means of assessing the strength of the garrison, while they speculated on the capacity of the Portuguese to repulse Musa Molo if his armies began marching south again. Indeed given the failure of both the French and Portuguese to subjugate Fuladu, the prospect of Musa Molo's armies marching south was more a question of "when" rather then "if" until 1903. Peasant anxieties were not put to rest even after Musa Molo's defeat and subsequent flight into the Gambia in 1903, in as much as the immediate defeat of Musa Molo's army had been achieved by the French far to the north of Oio. Consequently, Molo's defeat did not significantly enhance Portuguese authority in the southern backlands between the Cacheu River and the administrative capital at Bolama. If anything, it drew greater attention to the shortcomings of the Portuguese colonial administration and encouraged a wider range of peasant resistance to the administration's fiscal demands. Such was the political context in which the Portuguese military campaigns of 1913 through 1915 in the Guinean backlands were pursued.

Oio's economic importance lay in its agricultural potential and the fact that all the commercial routes going from the coast of Guinea to the upper Casamance region passed through its territory. An enforceable taxation policy at Oio therefore was the touchstone of a more comprehensive regional taxation policy. Teixeira Pinto, unlike some of his colleagues, was keenly aware of Oio's importance for a more systematic Portuguese fiscal policy. As a result, he endeavored to learn about Oio's people at close hand. Disguised as an agent for Casa Soller, the German trading house for which Abdul Njai had worked,

Teixeira Pinto travelled across Oio to Farim familiarizing himself with the strategic and commercial importance of the territory.[18] As he himself explained,

> My desire to occupy Mansoa and Oio regions resulted from this study [of the occupation and pacification of the province] and from exchanging impressions about the local political scene at various times with His Excellency [the Governor of Portuguese Guinea] because occupying them will bring good results for the economy and development of the Province and will raise the prestige of the military forces in service here ...[19]

What Teixeira Pinto did not say was that he had hoped to reduce Portuguese dependence on African irregulars attached to Abdul Njai for transport, logistical purposes and combat. But that was not to be. Abdul Njai and his troops weighed in and made a Portuguese victory possible. Njai was promoted to the rank of lieutenant. He was also given authority to collect taxes in Oio on behalf of the Portuguese government. As payment for his services, Njai was allowed to keep ten percent of the tax revenue.[20] Such an arrangement probably did not suit Teixeira Pinto or the Portuguese governor at Bolama; for establishing the administrative machinery of Portuguese colonial rule on the basis of collaboration with local Africans appeared to violate the spirit of the new republicanism. More immediately, it undermined Teixeira Pinto's position as chief military officer in the area and provisional head of administration in the occupied areas. With fewer than a thousand Portuguese troops, however, Teixeira Pinto was compelled to keep his own counsel about his misgivings.

After successfully completing military operations in Mansoa and Oio, the Portuguese turned their attention to the Cacheu region from late December 1913 to March 1914. The Portuguese fighting force was relatively small and many advised Teixeira Pinto not to embark on such an ambitious offensive. But after Lieutenant José Nunes' murder during a routine tax tour in Cacheu, the Portuguese military was obliged to make a show of force. To do otherwise at that precise moment would have caused the Portuguese to lose face in recently occupied Oio and Mansoa and sparked new instances of resistance there. But despite his eagerness to avenge the murder of Nunes and quell the rebels at Cacheu, Teixeira Pinto had his own reservations about the success of the scheduled military operation in Cacheu:

> I had various requests not to proceed with such an insignificant force [five hundred men] ... they made this request because in 1904, the Governor's column ... of eighteen hundred men could not do anything in Xudo ... and [they wanted me to] think hard [about my decision] considering that, if the small force under my command was defeated, then the rebels would destroy Cacheu.[21]

Assisted by Abdul Njai and his men, Teixeira Pinto entered the operation fully confident of victory. Once the Portuguese were able to claim control of a large portion of the littoral region, located between the Cacheu and Mansoa rivers, resistance collapsed. As in other, conquered portions of the Guinean backland, Abdul Njai and his retainers speedily collected weapons and forced local inhabitants to pay hut taxes several weeks after the occupation.[22] Unlike his predecessors, Teixeira Pinto understood that conquest for conquest's sake was not enough. He called upon the newly installed republican government to provide more soldiers from the metropolitan country in order to enforce Portuguese authority and to begin to expand Portugal's administrative infrastructure in the region. Several things were needed immediately: telegraph lines to link the various administrative posts; schools to educate the chiefs' sons; and civilian clerks and tax collectors. Teixeira Pinto's sense of urgency about the need for a more efficient administrative infrastructure was seconded by the fact that in the interim post sergeants were to serve as school teachers in the conquered regions, and few of the latter had much more than basic literacy.[23]

After the fall of Cacheu in March 1914, just before the beginning of the rainy season, Teixeira Pinto convinced Abdul Njai to reverse the thrust of the previous military campaigns and move eastward toward the confluence of the Geba and Impernal Rivers. Teixeira Pinto was determined to establish a military post at Nhacra, a point in the very center of the rich agricultural lands watered by the two rivers. There were several obvious advantages associated with a military post at Nhacra. To begin with, the Balanta peasantry of this region had been diverting the waters from the confluence of the two rivers into a series of canals for centuries, thus increasing the amount of arable land at their disposal. The area around Nhacra could not only provide an immediate windfall for the government's tax coffers, but could also serve as a kind of model area for the rest of the backlands. Secondly a military post at Nhacra, midway between Farim in the north and Bolama in the south, would divide the job of policing the backlands into two more manageable sub-regions. The value of such an arrangement was seconded by the fact that the backland population was so highly dispersed, except at Oio, Mansoa, and the region around the two rivers in question. Finally, and most immediately, continued military incursions in the areas west of Mansoa and Oio without first shoring up a relatively permanent east-west supply line of food and equipment for troops would have compromised the value of the previous Portuguese military victories — particularly since the military campaigns threatened to continue well into the rainy season.[24]

The political currency that the Portuguese acquired as a result of their military victories prior to March 1914, the commencement of the rains, and the highly dispersed population of the Guinean backlands, forced subsequent African resistance to the Portuguese to assume a protracted and defensive posture. The heavy rains of April and May also put a decided brake on the use of firearms by the African opposition, since most of the rifles in their possession were breechloading muskets or single-shot hunting rifles. There were, of course, more of these weapons in the hands of African rebels than the Portuguese forces imagined; and, after the conclusion of hostilities the wholesale seizure of firearms and the licenses of European merchants who trafficked in firearms with Africans acquired a logic of its own. But the fact remains that large scale use of these weapons by the rebels at the outset of the eastern campaigns was not great. Doubtless because the rebels fully appreciating their limited use and even liability of such weapons in heavy rains, stored them underground or in the hollows of dead trees until more propitious times. Those times never came, however, because the combined force of Abdul Njai's irregulars and Teixeira Pinto's conscripts, many of whom were disaffected Fulbe and Mandinka, scored their most decisive victories before June 1914.

The initial force under the joint command of Teixeira Pinto and Abdul Njai was composed of about six hundred men. That initial six hundred was increased to eight hundred on the basis of local levies. The bulk of the local levy was taken on at the end of May 1914, just as Njai and Pinto's men began their relentless foraging for hidden firearms.

Even with the construction of the military post at Nhacra, Teixeira Pinto continued to feel uneasy. He continued to argue for the timely intervention of the metropolitan government in order to give coherence to the economic exploitation of the backlands — in much the same way that the mulatto republican Honório Baretto had done almost three generations before. Most immediately, despite his implicit belief in free trade, Teixeira Pinto was concerned about the increasing amount of firearms in the hands of putative colonial subjects. In a memorandum to the Governor in July 1914 he minuted, "all of the work of the occupation is lost as long as the sale of gunpowder, muskets and swords is not prohibited ... Thus I consider it would be advantageous to prohibit importation of these articles ..."[25] He stated further that the commercial houses should only sell firearms to merchants with licenses issued by the government, and that such merchants should have their place of business and residence near a Portuguese military post. Such merchants should also be obliged to give monthly accounts of their stock to the local military officer. Teixeira Pinto, like other military officers who preceded him, called on the government to provide more boats to transport goods as well as soldiers along the colony's rivers, which still functioned as the colony's the main highways.[26]

Between June and July 1915 Teixeira Pinto and Abdul Njai prosecuted the last of the series of wars associated with the definitive Portuguese occupation of Guinea.[27] This last phase of the Portuguese military offensives of 1913-1915 took place on the island of Bissau and was designed to guarantee the compliance of the Island's inhabitants with new tax laws. Njai himself mobilized sixteen hundred auxiliary troops. The commercial houses on the Island provided much of the logistical support — including boats, medical supplies, food and money. Njai claimed that this campaign was the bloodiest and cruellest of all the battles he fought in. In the end, however, he "obliged the people to deliver all of their gunpowder, and disarmed them".[28]

Abdul Njai later claimed that in this and other campaigns he spent his own money providing for his soldiers' maintenance and transportation fees. Even though the colonial government provided more support for these campaigns than it had in the past, Njai absorbed some of the campaign expenses, including recruiting and transportation costs. The French consul at Bolama confirmed Abdul Njai's account of these circumstances in a letter to the French Ministry of Foreign Affairs in the same year, "... the Portuguese government advised him [Abdul Njai] formally of the promises to reimburse all [that he spent] and to give him a sufficiently large sum as a reward".[29] Predictably the Portuguese failed to make good on the promises they made to Abdul Njai. Consequently, Njai and his men tried to support themselves by seizing as much booty as possible in subsequent campaigns, including people (to use as laborers), cattle and goats.[30] This booty was not enough for Njai and his men, who understood their central importance to the Portuguese war effort. Once again a French administrator in the service of the Portuguese colonial government, one M. Hostains, sustained Abdul Njai's point of view:

> ... it is Abdoul Ndiaye and he alone who submitted, pacified, [and] disarmed the country and gave it as he says to the Portuguese, who never had been not ever would have been capable, [perhaps] not ... of subduing [the place] but of establishing a relative security there ...[31]

On the other hand, Teixeira Pinto was strangely silent about this conjuncture between fiscal problems of governing Guinea and the prosecution of wars of pacification. As we shall see, this Portuguese failure to reimburse Njai was just one of several issues that drove a wedge between him and his sponsors.

Changing relations between Abdul Njai and the Portuguese, 1915-1919

After completing the campaign in mid-1915 against Bissau Island, Njai's relationship with the Portuguese gradually began to turn sour. Initially Portuguese unwillingness to carry out the promises they had made caused this deterioration. Njai did receive his lieutenant's title as well as the Oio region to govern. To be sure, during the military campaigns Njai and his retainers took a respectable portion of the spoils. But when the wars ended, Njai lost this critical source of revenue. The Portuguese had promised Njai ten per cent of the

the taxes collected in areas he helped to conquer, and this revenue would have replaced the booty no longer available. However, once the Portuguese administration had seized the numerous stores of firearms distributed in the backlands it felt confident enough to withdraw its initial offer. The administration's decision to withhold Njai's share may have been due to its inability to collect as much as it anticipated. It is more likely, though, that the desire to cast off Njai and his retainers was part of the new image that the Portuguese colonial administration sought to cultivate for itself under the aegis of new republican government in Portugal itself. Eventually the colonial administration's stance compelled Abdul Njai to carve out a constituency of sorts among the very people he had helped to subjugate. In time this new independent stance turned into open revolt.[32]

The Portuguese had made Abdul Njai a "warrant chief" in Oio before the disastrous events that followed the subjugation of Bissau Island in 1915. But unlike the new warrant chieftaincies in the British colonies in West Africa those in the Portuguese possessions were not formally linked to the creation of a new array of local courts that would have combined the administrative and judicial powers of the chieftaincies while moderating the chiefs' execution of such powers. Such courts would have been a concession to local custom and would have given the indigenous people some measure of participation in determining the administrative procedure under Portuguese rule.[33] Instead — at least from the vantage point of the local inhabitants of Guinea — the only legitimacy Abdul Njai and his retainers had was the result of conquest. In fact the brute force with which he ruled the central backlands was memorialized in songs and local oral histories of Oio and Mansoa. Unlike the harsh circumstances of the closing years of Musa Molo's rule, however, the cruelty associated with the Abdul Njai's rule was not perceived as a consequence of *baraka* or a force of nature.[34] Rather, Abdul Njai's tenure was associated with license and plunder underscored by the greed of the Portuguese and a general escalation of violence in the region. Cherif Hamed Ben Salah, a Muslim cleric from Casamance, who visited areas that were under Njai's control in 1919, claimed that pressures from Abdul Njai and the Portuguese were "eating" the people.[35] "... for a long time, he and the people attached to his fortune have constituted the principal police force of the local government ..."[36]

Abdul Njai committed numerous abuses against the people of the Guinean backlands; but the general abdication of the Portuguese from enforcing the law, except in instances of the possession of firearms or tax default, made instances of cattle theft, extortion, forced cultivation and murder on the part of Njai and his retainers all the more striking. In 1919, on the basis of testimony of Guinea refugees in the Casamance, French officials claimed:

> ... he [Abdul Njai] has tapped for his own profit the tax of his territory which the people already had deposited with the local authorities; he has

had some Peulh killed under what pretext I do not know; he turned to the Balanta territory outside of his boundaries; he deposed a village chief the Portuguese had just installed and named another of his choice; the governor sent for him to go to Bissau many times but without success ...[37]

The Portuguese colonial government was put in an awkward position. And once the apparent toll of abuse began to be recounted in official foreign circles, its representatives attempted to distance themselves from Njai's misdeeds:

> ... the native ruler Abdul Njai continues practicing all kinds of abuses, seizing, extorting and penalizing in manifest disobedience ... What will become of the [Portuguese colonial] authority's prestige if this ruler is not castigated? Abdul must not remain as the ruler of Oio, he must not even remain in the Province. His attitude is contemptuous and [that] of one who is resolved to do all to maintain his prestige in Oio and amongst the people conquered by him ...[38]

The Portuguese had fought the "pacification" campaigns of 1913-15 to increase their control over the people of Guinea and ensure the systematic economic exploitation of the region. Even though the Portuguese had been aware of Njai's excesses as early as 1913, they allowed them to continue because of his importance to the "official" campaign of repression.[39] After such campaigns ended, Njai's usefulness to the colonial cause diminished. The Portuguese had not fought the campaigns to bolster Njai's position, but given the logistics of the war such a "bolstering" was very nearly inevitable.

By 1919, numerous inhabitants of Oio and Mansoa preferred to flee north to the Casamance rather than continue to be victimized by the excesses of Njai and his auxiliaries. However, on occasion, Njai's raids extended into the Casamance and other portions of the neighboring French colony of Senegal. Yet the French never took action against Njai and his supporters.[40]

Njai's armed retainers enabled him to maintain his independence for four years after he returned from the Bissau campaign in 1915. Many of his recruits had come from various regions of Senegal itself such as Ziguinchor, Sedhiou and Sine-Saloum. Described by Portuguese and French officials as *réfractaires*, *mercenaires*, *mécontents* and *déserteurs*, Njai's recruits were the precipitate result of the frequent but small scale wars of the previous fifty years. Some were deserters from the Senegalese *tirailleurs*, auxiliary troops that the French used in their own "pacification" campaigns.[41] Others were soldiers who fought in the 1890s with Musa Molo and Fode Kaba. And still others were the victims or the children of the victims of the chain of violent events associated with these two men. These men joined Njai for a myriad of reasons — revenge, religious piety, fear, and so on.[42] A large portion of the soldiers recruited were, like Njai himself, nominally Muslim. Doubtless religious affiliation made it easier for Njai to attract soldiers across ethnic lines, even though there is no evidence to suggest that Njai and his forces believed themselves to be waging a *jihad*. For the majority of these soldiers the choice to join Njai was governed by less pious motives, although religious piety cannot be ruled out as a source of solidarity once these disparate persons became a cohesive group. Similarly one cannot rule out the possibility that some of these men might have seen in Njai the last chance at least to constrain European control.

Cherif Hamed Ben Salah, mentioned above, visited Njai's *royaume* in Oio. Ben Salah's observations of 1919 about the tenor of life in the central Guinean backlands under Abdul Njai were not destined to remain an obscure account taken down by an isolated French colonial official.[43] In August 1919 the Governor-General of all of French West Africa had sent Ben Salah's description of Oio to Albert Sarrat, the French Minister of Colonies. In turn, Ben Salah's account bolstered French doubts about Portuguese claims to sovereignty over Guinea. Well before the despatch of Ben Salah's account to France in August, the French consul at Bolama had observed:

> ... it seems difficult to take [seriously] their [Portuguese] title of sovereignty of a government which after more than four hundred years of domination allows itself to be held at bay for more than a year by a native chief [Abdul Njai], and finds itself forced to mobilize all of the resources at its disposal to try to subdue him without being sure of the result ...[44]

Abdul Njai's *de facto* control over central Guinea simultaneously threatened the indigenous population of Oio, Portuguese authority, and the French colonial regime in neighboring Casamance. Because the majority of Njai's retainers were from Senegal, French officials feared they might decide to return to their homelands. Anxiety over this prospect gave rise to a certain amount of political schizophrenia among French colonial officials. On the one hand, by June 1919, the French consul at Bolama was secretly writing to the Foreign Minister that, "In case of an uprising, [Njai's people] who only want to make a good thing of it, would plunder the French just as willingly as the Portuguese ..."[45] While on the other, the Governor-General of French West Africa gave the French representative in Bissau orders to maintain the strictest neutrality in issues involving the Portuguese government and Njai. Moreover, the Governor of Senegal received instructions to take whatever measures necessary to disarm Njai immediately if he sought refuge in the territory.[46]

French fears about Abdul Njai's return to Senegal were not without substance. His powerful base in central Guinea had given him a degree of confidence that belied his formal status as a Portuguese colonial subject. Njai supposedly declared "... that having already conquered the country once for the Portuguese, he would now take it from the Portuguese to give to France ..."[47] A significant number of French colonial officials believed that Njai could carry out such a plan, but they wanted no part of it. French anxieties about Abdul Njai's ambitions were also tied to their fear that he and Musa Molo, who was in exile in the Gambia, might form a kind of coalition that would threaten to sweep the Portuguese and the French out of the Senegambia. Musa Molo, for example, had repeatedly petitioned British, Portuguese and French authorities to allow him to settle at Kansala, then a part of Portuguese Guinea, near the grave of his father, Alfa Molo. French officials were intrigued by the possible consequences of a Musa Molo-Abdul Njai alliance, but in the end determined that their best strategy was to maintain the status quo while keeping both men under careful surveillance.[48] By 1919, the support given by Abdul Njai and his forces to the Portuguese in the previous decade had become a profound embarrassment for them. Like other African collaborators elsewhere, Njai himself had become "redundant".[49]

At the outset of June 1919, a new governor, Captain de Sousa Guerra, arrived in Guinea with orders "to take control of the indigenous chief Abdoul Ndiaye in one way or another ..."[50] Much like his predecessors, de Sousa Guerra called Njai to both Bolama and Bissau several times. As he had done on similar occasions, Njai curtly refused. He did, however, agree to meet de Sousa Guerra at Farim — less than 20 miles from his own seat of power at Oio and on the northern bank of the Cacheu River. Farim was less than 12 miles from French territory and more than 70 miles north of the Portuguese capital at Bolama. The fastest route to Farim from Bolama passed through territory controlled by Abdul Njai. Certainly the symbolism of this gesture was not lost on the new Portuguese governor. Moreover, Abdul Njai brought an entourage composed of over two hundred of his best soldiers to meet the governor. Predictably, de Sousa Guerra and Njai could not strike a compromise. Njai's entourage left the meeting before that of the governor's — forcing the latter to take the more circuitous route back to Bolama rather than risk the embarrassment of passing through Njai's territory once again.

In late June 1919 de Sousa Guerra requested Njai's presence at another meeting closer to Oio at the garrison town of Mansaba. Njai made five demands of de Sousa Guerra: (1) a sixty per cent reduction in the military force in Mansaba; (2) complete removal of the military force in Farim; (3) disarmament of the force in Bissoram; (4) the right to select the local officials in annexed zones; and (5) compensation for his expenditures during the "pacification" campaigns.[51] In effect Njai was demanding the removal of virtually all the vestiges of Portuguese authority in central Guinea. de Sousa Guerra, of course, refused to negotiate on any of these points. Consequently, by the beginning of July 1919 relations between the Portuguese and Njai had deteriorated to a point just short of war. By the end of July 1919 Njai's retainers were cutting the telegraph lines that connected them to Bolama. And by August 1919 the Portuguese military commander at Farim noted that refugees from Oio were beginning to make their way north again:

After this [meeting] the situation became more depressing because the robberies were even more frequent, and the cutting of the telegraph wires succeeded at each juncture, because of which the Oincas [the people of Oio] abandoned agricultural work going definitively to Farim ...[52]

Governor de Sousa Guerra dispatched all available troops to Mansaba, as well as several armed boats to enforce Portugal's decision to destroy its erstwhile ally. Njai failed to appreciate the extent of the Portuguese desire to eliminate him and his army.

On 1 and 2 August 1919, the conflict between the Portuguese and Njai began with two days of intense combat in Mansaba. On 3 August Njai surrendered and was taken into custody. Afterwards Portuguese anxiety over Njai's course of action quickly turned to derision:

... this same Abdul [Njai] who said that this time he would die but would not be taken prisoner, surrendered pitifully after two days of cruel combat in which he lost the majority of his people ...[53]

On 4 August the Portuguese took Njai to Farim and from there to Bolama on 16 August. He was subsequently deported to Cape Verde and tried by a tribunal of the republican government. Deportation left Njai incredulous: "For the immeasurable service [I] performed for the state, spending a great deal of money and losing horses ... the reward I receive is deportation to the Province of Cape Verde ..."[54]

Prior to his deportation a heated discussion ensued about the legal options available to Njai. Local European traders and government officials wanted to see Njai tried in front of the war council as a lieutenant in the army. On the other side of the debate, a group of urban residents, Cape Verdians and *Grumetes*, believed Njai should be tried under civil law. These people formed a nationalist group, *Parti Cap-Verdien*, which wanted to create a separate republic along the lines of Liberia. In relation to Njai's trial, they wanted to ensure the harshest penalty possible and to strip him of any political power. The *Parti Cap-Verdien*'s supporters were passionate about the trial and fought with African troops loyal to the Portuguese in the streets of Bissau until the Portuguese deported Njai without a trial.[55] Some sources indicate that Njai preferred a trial in a military court. Njai, however, claimed he did not care whether his trial was in a military or civilian court. He wanted justice upheld, "I only ask for justice and I only ask I be judged by a competent court. If I am guilty, I may be rigorously castigated and if not, I may be free ..."[56] Njai's emotional plea for justice is ironic since he had been totally unconcerned with justice for his subjects for many years.[57]

One report mentions that some of the traditional authorities whom Njai displaced wanted to take advantage of his deportation to re-establish their own control. These former rulers were unable to carry out this objective because of

155

the Portuguese plan to set up the colonial system designed to exploit the local people for the benefit of the Portuguese.[58] These rulers, like Njai, failed to understand the new and larger colonial program the Portuguese wanted to implement. The First World War was over and the Portuguese were ready to begin their systematic exploitation of the colony through regular tax collection, forced peanut cultivation, and forced labor.[59] For the Portuguese, the traditional authorities were useful only if they could facilitate the new economic goals by mobilizing labor, collecting taxes and encouraging cash crop cultivation for the Portuguese state. Njai was no longer valuable to the Portuguese because he had conquered the rebellious groups, and his presence in the colony had become a threat to the new colonial ideals. Therefore his elimination was an urgent necessity.

Once deported, Njai, like his counterparts elsewhere in Africa, received a small pension "sufficient for him to live with his family of one wife and two children".[60] This settlement did not reflect the reality of Njai's social situation. He left many more wives, children and dependents in Oio, but of course the Portuguese did not recognize them. Njai failed to understand the new circumstances of the Portuguese presence. Believing himself to have been completely betrayed by the Portuguese, his sense of injury was enormous:

> ... deported to Cape Verde for having revolted against Portuguese sovereignty in that Province [Portuguese Guinea], when it is certain and incontestable that it would have been conquered by terrible people if, even one time only, I had avoided taking part in whatever operation that [the Portuguese] ... carried out against them ...[61]

Even so, his sense of injury could not have been greater than the misfortune for which he had been the instrument. Njai died in 1922, several years after his deportation, but too early to have the last laugh on the government that had imprisoned and deported him. Four years after his death, in 1926, Portugal's republican government was overthrown by the fascist dictatorship of António Salazar.

Abdul Njai's story illuminates a neglected dimension of the African past. Stories of warlords who fought against and/or co-operated with Europeans in the initial phases of the conquest exist. Less is known, however, about the latter period of the conquest, the "pacification" era. During the first two decades of the twentieth century, Njai, and his counterparts elsewhere in Africa, facilitated the final colonial occupation. In Portuguese Guinea, between 1913 and 1915 in particular, Njai was directly responsible for the successful campaigns against some of the last strongholds of resistance to Portuguese authority. As a reward for his services, the Portuguese granted Njai the Oio province. As an outsider, Njai had no traditional legitimacy within this area. Consequently, he used force to establish himself as a ruler. Njai was interested only in personal gain. His army enabled him to win battles for the Portuguese at first and then later for himself. The colonial administration quickly realized that Njai's presence prevented them from exploiting their territory for their own benefit. They had to remove Njai from the scene in order to establish themselves as the sole authority. In 1919, the Portuguese successfully eliminated Njai, their former ally, who by then had become their most dangerous enemy.

Notes

1. Administrador de Farim to Governador 18 November 1915, *BCGP* 6, 21, January 1951, p. 124.

2. ANS, 13G67: Lt. Gouverneur de Sénégal to W. Ponty, Gouverneur-Général de l'Afrique Occidental Française, 17 August 1914.

3. See Teixeira da Mota, *Guiné*, 2, p. 34; and Ronald H. Chilcote, *Portuguese Africa*, Englewoods Cliffs, N.J., Prentice-Hall, 1967, p. 98.

4. Amadeu Nogueira, "Figuras da Ocupação: Abdul Injai", *BCGP*, IV, 13, January 1949, p. 50.

5. Abdul Injai, *Relatório: Os meus feitos na Guiné Portuguesa, desde 1894 a 1919, data em que por uma acusação falsa, fui deportado para a provincia de Cabo Verde*, Praia, 1920, p. 3. Even though Njai wrote this account in his own defence after his deportation, it contains useful information. For more information on Njai's early career see also ANS, 2F14: L'Administrateur en Chef, M. Hostains (Bissau), No. 49 to M. le Consul de France à Lisbonne, 22 February 1921 (?). One report claims Njai was an agent for the German commercial firm, Soller, but it seems that this relationship developed later in his career. See: *A Defeza das Victimas da Guerra de Bissau — O Exterminio da Guiné*, Lisbon, 1916 and James Cunningham, "The Colonial Period in Guiné", *Tarikh*, VI, 4, 1980, p. 36.

6. Nogueira, "Figuras", p. 51. *Marabouts* performed a variety of functions: they were Muslim clerics who were spiritual leaders, social organizers, healers and warriors.

7. Amadu Jobarteh, Banjul Series Tape 3 (Serekunda) 12 May 1978; and Jali Kemo Kuyateh, Banjul Series Tape 3 (Banjul) 13 June 1978.

8. Injai, *Relatório*, p. 3.

9. Amadu Jobarteh, Banjul Series Tape 3 (Serekunda), 12 May 1978; and Mamadou Falai Baldeh, Banjul Series Tape 14 (Sankulikunda), 25 June 1978.

10. Injai, *Relatório*, p. 3.

11. Injai, *Relatório*, p. 5; Cunningham, "Colonial Period", p. 33.

12. Clarence-Smith, *Third Portuguese Empire*, p. 12.
13. Teixeira Pinto, *Teixeira Pinto*, p. 10. At a subsequent point in his book even Clarence-Smith points out that in 1910 when the Republicans gained power, "the Portuguese probably controlled no more than a tenth of Angola, Guinea and Timor, and the situation was much the same in northern Mozambique". See: Clarence-Smith, *Third Portuguese Empire*, p. 139.
14. At best a united opposition could have temporarily stalled the Portuguese advance. For an insightful discussion of the situation in Mozambique see Allen F. Isaacman, *The Tradition of Resistance in Mozambique: Anti-Colonial Activity in the Zambesi Valley, 1850-1921*, London, Heinemann, 1976; and Allen F. Isaacman, "Social Banditry in Zimbabwe (Rhodesia) and Mozambique, 1894-1907: an Expression of Early Peasant Protest", *Journal of Southern African Studies*, IV, 1, October 1977, pp. 1-30. See also E.J. Hobsbawm, *Bandits*, London, Weidenfeld and Nicolson, 1969; reprinted 1981; and E.J. Hobsbawm, *Primitive Rebels*, Manchester, Manchester University Press, 1959.
15. Teixeira Pinto, *Teixeira Pinto*, p. 12. Other African commanders mentioned in various documents include Samba-ly, Bacari Suncaro, Malali Sisse, Mamadu Sisse and Mamadu Diallo. These auxiliaries supported Njai and carried out his orders. Unfortunately neither written or oral sources discuss their roles in the campaigns in specific detail.
16. Injai, *Relatório*, p. 5. See also Alberto Soares, Commandante Militar do Commando Militar dos Balantas to Commandante Militar das Regiões de Farim, Mansaba, Balantas e Bissoram, 12 August 1919, "Documentos sobre a campanha contra Abdul Injai", *BCGP*, VI, 21, January 1951, p. 86.

17. AHU, Guiné, Past 417: Governador em Bolama, No. 147 to Ministro e Secretário d'Estado dos Negócios da Marinha e Ultramar, 25 May 1897.
18. Teixeira Pinto, *Teixeira Pinto*, p. 179.
19. Teixeira Pinto, *Teixeira Pinto*, p. 31, 171.
20. Injai, *Relatório*, p. 6; Teixeira Pinto, *Teixeira Pinto*, p. 90; and ANS, 2F14: L'Administrateur en Bissau, M. Hostains, No. 49 to M. le Consul de France à Lisbonne, 22 February 1921(?). Njai maintained his ties with Cuor even after he assumed control of Oio. He actually returned to Cuor to live between November 1916 and March 1917. For more information see Caetano Barbosa, Administrador de Circunscrição de Farim to Governador da Província, 16 July 1919, "Documentos sobre a campanha contra Abdul Injai", *BCGP*, VI, 21, January 1951, pp. 92-3.
21. Teixeira Pinto, *Teixeira Pinto*, p. 98.
22. Injai, *Relatório*, pp. 6-7; and Teixeira Pinto, *Teixeira Pinto*, p. 113.

23. Teixeira Pinto, *Teixeira Pinto*, pp. 111-13. The 1911 Portuguese census showed a 77 to 79 per cent illiteracy rate in Portugal: see A.H. de Oliveira Marques, *History of Portugal*, 2, *From Empire to Colonial State*, New York and London, Columbia University Press, 1972, p. 134; and Douglas L. Wheeler, *Republican Portugal — A Political History, 1910-1926*, Madison, University of Wisconsin, 1978, p. 162.

24. Teixeira Pinto, *Teixeira Pinto*, p. 127. For other examples, see Timothy C. Weiskel, *French Colonial Rule and the Baule Peoples: Resistance and Collaboration, 1889-1911*, Oxford, Clarendon Press, 1980. For information on eastern Nigeria see A.E. Afigbo, *The Warrant Chiefs: Indirect Rule in Southeastern Nigeria, 1891-1929*, London, Longman, 1972 and J.C. Anene, *Southern Nigeria in Transition, 1885-1906*, Cambridge, Cambridge University Press, 1966.

25. Teixeira Pinto, *Teixeira Pinto*, p. 141.

26. For more information on the river system, see Teixeira da Mota, *Guiné*, 1, pp. 57-73.

27. *Grumete* refers to Africans who worked for Portuguese traders in the urban centers of the Upper Guinea Coast during the era of the slave trade. *Grumetes*, the boat builders, stevedores and caulkers of these coastal communities, made European trade possible. Their descendants remained in towns like Bissau and Cacheu after the abolition of the slave trade, and continued to perform skilled and unskilled jobs for Luso-African and European traders. For more information on *Grumetes*, see Rodney, *Upper Guinea Coast*.

28. Injai, *Relatório*, p. 7. See also Teixeira Pinto, *Teixeira Pinto*, p. 178, 185 and 218-19.

29. ANS, 2F14: Le Vice-Consul de France en Guinée Portugaise, No. 25 to Ministre des Affaires Etrangères à Paris, 26 June 1919.

30. ANS, 2F14: L'Administrateur en Bissau, M. Hostains, No. 49 to M. le Consul de France à Lisbonne, 22 February 1921(?). See also *A Defeza das Victimas*, pp. 36-7.

31. ANS, 2F14: L'Administrateur en Bissau, M. Hostains, No. 49 to M. le Consul de France à Lisbonne, 22 February 1921(?).

32. ANS, 2F14: L'Administrateur en Bissau, M. Hostains, No. 49 to M. le Consul de France à Lisbonne, 22 February 1921(?); ANS, 2F14: M. Merlin, Service des Affaires Civiles, No. 1971 to Afrique Occidentale et Equatoriale, Ière Section-Paris, 16 October 1919; ANS, 2F14: Gouverneur-Générale de l'A.O.F. to M. le Ministre des Colonies, 24 September 1920; ANS, 2F14: L'Administrateur Supérieur de la Casamance (Ziguinchor), M. Benquey, No. 227 to Lt. Gouverneur du Sénégal à St. Louis, 24 June 1919; and Amadu Jobarteh, Banjul Series

Tape 3 (Serekunda), 12 May 1978. For an example of another warlord who developed his own "empire" within a colonial state and who resented the broken promises of colonial administrators, see the history of Semei Kakunguru in A.D. Roberts, "The Sub-imperialism of the Baganda," *JAH*, III, 3, 1962, pp. 435-50.

33. For more information on the warrant chief system see Afigbo, *Warrant Chiefs*, p. 100.

34. See, for example, Amadu Jobarteh, Banjul Series Tape 3 (Serekunda), 12 May 1978; Jali Kemo Kuyateh, Banjul Series Tape 3 (Banjul), 13 June 1978; and Mamadou Falai Baldeh, Banjul Series Tape 14 (Sankulikunda), 25 June 1978.

35. ANS, 2F14: L'Administrateur Supérieur de la Casamance (Ziguinchor), M. Benquey, No. 227 to Lt. Gouverneur du Sénégal à St. Louis, 24 June 1919.

36. ANS, 2F14: Gouverneur-Général de l'A.O.F. to Ministre des Colonies, 24 September 1920.

37. ANS, 2F14: Administrateur en Chef de Ière Classe des Colonies, Hostains to Gouverneur-Général de l'A.O.F., 20 April 1919. See also ANS, 2F14: Gouverneur-Général de l'A.O.F. to M. le Ministre des Colonies, August 1919 and "Documentos sobre a campanha contra Abdul Injai", *BCGP*, VI, 21, January 1951, pp. 53-126.

38. Caetano J. Barbosa, Administrador da Circunscrição de Farim, No. 43 to Secretária Geral do Governo, 20 February 1919, "Documentos sobre a campanha contra Abdul Injai", *BCGP*, VI, 21, January 1951, p. 112. See also INIC, Documentos Diversos 1917-18: Presidente da Associação Commercial, Industrial e Agrícola de Bissau to Governador, 16 June 1917; and ANS, 2F14: Gouverneur-Général de l'A.O.F. to M. le Ministre des Colonies, August 1919.

39. Caetano J. Barbosa, Administrador da Circunscrição de Farim to Encarregado do governo, 19 October 1912, "Documentos sobre a campanha contra Abdul Injai", *BCGP*, VI, 21, January 1951, p. 125; and ANS, 2F14: L'Administrateur Supérieur du Casamance, "Rapport supplémentaire confidentiel joint au Rapport 122 du 23 Mai 1917".

40. ANS, 2F14: Gouverneur-Général de l'A.O.F. to M. le Ministre des Colonies, 20 September 1920. See also *A Defeza das Victimas*.

41. ANS, 2F14: Le Vice-Consul de France en Guinée Portugaise, No. 25 to Ministre des Affaires Etrangères à Paris, 26 June 1919; ANS, 2F14: Gouverneur-Général de l'A.O.F. to M. le Ministre des Colonies, 24 September 1920; ANS, 2F8: Le Vice-Consul de France en Guinée Portugaise to Gouverneur-Général de l'A.O.F., 18 November 1916; ANS, 2F14: L'Administrateur Supérieur de la Casamance (Ziguinchor), M.

Benquey, No. 227 to Lt. Gouverneur du Sénégal à St. Louis, 24 June 1919; and Ousmane Sisse, Banjul Series Tape 4 (Banjul), 10 June 1978.

42. Alhaji Kawsu Sillah, Banjul Series Tape 17 (Sankulikunda), 9 August 1978 and Mamadou Falai Balde, Banjul Series Tape 14 (Sankulikunda), 25 June 1978.

43. ANS, 2F14: Gouverneur-Général de l'A.O.F. to M. le Ministre des Colonies, August 1919.

44. ANS, 2F14: Le Vice-Consul de France en Guinée Portugaise, No. 25 to Ministre des Affaires Etrangères à Paris, 26 June 1919.

45. ANS, 2F14: Le Vice-Consul de France en Guinée Portugaise, No. 25 to Ministre des Affaires Etrangères à Paris, 26 June 1919.

46. ANS, 2F14: Gouverneur-Général de l'A.O.F. to M. le Ministre des Colonies, 24 September 1920; ANS, 2F14: Gouverneur-Général de l'A.O.F. to M. le Ministre des Colonies, August 1919; ANS, 2F14: L'Administrateur Supérieur de la Casamance (Ziguinchor), M. Benquey, No. 227 to Lt. Gouverneur du Sénégal à St. Louis, 24 June 1919; and ANS, 2F14: L'Administration Supérieur de la Casamance, "Rapport Supplémentaire Confidential joint au rapport 122 du 23 May 1917".

47. ANS, 2F14: Administrateur en Chef de Ière Classe des Colonies, Hostains to Gouverneur-Général de l'A.O.F., 20 April 1919.

48. ANS, 13G67: Lt. Gouverneur du Sénégal, No. 171 to Gouverneur-Général de l'A.O.F., W. Ponty, 17 August 1914; ANS, 13G67: Gouverneur-Général de l'A.O.F., W. Ponty, to Lt. Gouverneur du Sénégal, 8 September 1914; and ANS, 13G67: Gouverneur-Général de l'A.O.F. to Lt. Gouverneur du Sénégal, January 1915.

49. Roberts, "Sub-Imperialism", p. 440.

50. ANS, 2F14: Le Vice-Consul de France en Guinée Portugaise, No. 25 to Ministre des Affaires Etrangères à Paris, 26 June 1919. Governor de Sousa Guerra was one of three governors who served in Guinea in 1919. The rapid succession of administrators contributed to the weakness of the Portuguese state and reflected metropolitan politics. Political life in the metropole was unstable during the Republic. In its sixteen year existence there were forty-five governments — each lasted about four months. There was a *coup d'état* or attempted *coup d'état* every year and five hundred individuals held ministerial posts between 1910 and 1926. Ten governors served in Guinea during this period. See Richard Allen Hodgson Robinson, *Contemporary Portugal — A History*, London and Boston, Allen & Unwin, 1979, p. 36 and Clarence-Smith, *Third Portuguese Empire*, pp. 116-42. For more detail see: Wheeler, *Republican Portugal*; David Birmingham, *A Concise History of Portugal*, Cambridge, Cambridge University Press, 1993; Tom Gallagher, *Portugal:*

A Twentieth Century Interpretation, Manchester, Manchester University Press 1983; Machado Santos, *A Revolução Portuguesa 1907/1910*, Lisbon, Assírio e Alvim, 1982; and Carlos Ferrão, *História da Ia República*, Lisbon, Terra Livre, 1976.

51. Augusto José de Lima Junior, Commandante militar das regiões de Farim, Balantas e Bissoram, to Governador da Provincia da Guiné, 18 August 1919, "Documentos sobre a campanha contra Abdul Injai", *BCGP*, VI, 21, January 1951, p. 59.

52. Ibid., p. 64.

53. Ibid., p. 70. This account of Njai's losses is biased, but oral sources verify his surrender.

54. Injai, *Relatório*, p. 7.

55. ANS, 2F14: M. Merlin, Service des Affaires Civiles, No. 1971 to Afrique Occidental et Equatoriale Ière Section — Paris, 16 October 1919; and ANS, 2F14: Gouverneur-Général de l'A.O.F. to M. le Ministre des Colonies, August 1919. The *Parti Cap-Verdien* was related to an earlier party, the *Liga Guinéense*, that was formed immediately after the Republican take-over. Portuguese officials dissolved the *Liga Guinéense* in 1915 — accusing it of supporting the *Grumete* and Papel rebels in the Bissau Island campaign that year. The *Liga*, like the *Parti Cap-Verdien*, opposed Portuguese occupation and Njai's alliance with the colonial power. Many members of both parties were independent merchants who understood that the new Portuguese economic policies, especially taxation laws, would undermine their own positions. For more information on the *Liga Guinéense*, see Cunningham, "Colonial Period", pp. 33-6. The activities of these parties fits into the more general pattern of "creole" politics during the Republican era. See Clarence-Smith, *Third Portuguese Empire*, pp. 137-38; Gregory Alonso Pirio, "Race and Class in the Struggle over Pan-Africanism: a working paper on the Partido Nacional Africano, the Liga Africana and the Comintern in Portuguese Africa" (paper delivered at the conference on "The Class Basis of Nationalist Movements in Angola, Guinea-Bissau and Mozambique", Minneapolis, 25-27 May 1983); and Robert A. Hill, ed., *The Marcus Garvey and Universal Negro Improvement Association Papers*, Vol. VIII: March 1917-June 1921, Berkeley and Los Angeles, University of California Press, 1995.

56. Injai, *Relatório*, p. 9.

57. ANS, 2F14: Gouverneur-Général de l'A.O.F. to M. le Ministre des Colonies, 24 September 1920.

58. ANS, 2F14: M. Merlin, Service des Affaires Civiles, No. 1971 to Afrique Occidentale et Equatoriale, Ière Section — Paris, 16 October 1919.

59. Forced cultivation and forced labor in Guinea often were related to taxation. To pay their taxes, peasants had to produce cash crops, primarily groundnuts. If they failed to produce enough or refused to pay, they were forced to work for the state.

60. ANS, 2F14: Gouverneur-Général de l'A.O.F. to M. le Ministre des Colonies, 24 September 1920.

61. Injai, *Relatório*, p. 11.

7 Conclusion

In 1903 a visitor to the Senegambia, travelling southward from, say, Georgetown to the Rio Grande, would have looked out on extensive patches of charred and smoldering landscape: rivers, which had once sped commerce and information, were now choked with dead trees and mangrove roots at crucial junctures; peasants, who had once cultivated commercial and subsistence crops on the wide alluvial plains of the Forria and along the banks of the Rio Grande, were now huddled in small, tentative settlements in the most remote portions of the rocky upland and mangrove swamps; waged and formerly bound African laborers — the "Manjaco" of the *relatórios* and plaintive *testamunhas* of the European and Afro-European planters — were now clandestinely making their way northward toward the relative security of the Fulbe and Mandinka settlements in the British colony of Gambia. Finally, there were the petulant French and Portuguese colonial administrators, who, in time, came to curse their pyrrhic victory over Musa Molo's army; for they had neither the will nor inclination to create a new and more comprehensive infrastructure in the countryside. Consequently subsistence for the peasantry and the prospect of a dynamic regeneration of commercial agriculture languished.

Meanwhile, much of the economic transformation that took place during the "long nineteenth century" had grown out of the 1807 British decision to abolish the slave trade and to use its navy to enforce this decision. By the 1840s the new demands and constraints would compel merchants and traders to make choices that they would have previously never broached. Although some traders continued to sell slaves clandestinely, many traders chose to recycle slaves bound for Brazil or Cuba as "laborers" on the *feitorias* or plantations, along the banks of the Rio Grande and on Bolama Island. Such traders, who had been steered in the direction of "legitimate commerce" by the increasing size and power of the British naval squadrons, discovered that commercial peanut production could also be profitable. However, a significant factor in increasing profit margins was the redefinition of former slaves as nominally free laborers or "Manjacos" in subsequent official estimates. Consequently, as early as the 1840s, the new demands placed on African producers were at odds with the contradictory conceptions of the labor force. The clash of the two provoked smaller instances of the upheavals that would eventually engulf the entire region two generations later.

By midcentury the more prosperous traders were entering into a diverse set of labor arrangements in order to get the annual crop of peanuts to international markets. Peasant households were sometimes contracted as a group. Individuals were also recruited by the subalterns of the traders. And of course, there were the "Manjaco". But, once selected portions of Senegambia became profitable again, the differences among peasant sharecroppers, freely recruited laborers and bound dependent laborers became increasingly blurred. Despite the general disarray in the Senegambia, peanut exports often exceeded a million bushels a year.[1]

Like European traders elsewhere in the Senegambia, those in Portuguese Guinea exported peanuts to Europe in a raw, unprocessed state. Peasant sharecroppers were particularly disadvantaged. Peasants entered the production cycle as partial owners; yet they had no direct access to the international market or information about its changing requirements. As a result, given the nature of their contractual relationship, they absorbed a disproportionate amount of the risk associated with such enterprises. For example, traders readily passed their own losses to sharecroppers in the form of the purchasing price they offered to peasant producers. As a result, peasants in the Portuguese spheres of influence were often compelled to accept payment in kind, which took the form of waterlogged muskets and trade goods or cast-off military uniforms. In view of such shabby forms of remuneration African peasants sometimes chose to flee farther into the backlands.

In order to meet the increased European demand for peanuts, traders and land owners did have need of a reliable source of labor. The reserves of former slaves were not sufficient, however. Peasants readily voted with their feet if traders were not willing to guarantee them something beyond the effort price of their labor once they had committed their entire household and moveable property to peanut production. Finally, there were the Manjaco from Costa de

165

Baixo and the Forria. Such laborers remained reliable as long as war, political upheaval, and economic conjuncture did not threaten their home areas.

During the Atlantic slave trade some Manjaco men worked for European and Afro-European traders in the coastal towns and on their shipping vessels. Thus, the notion of hiring out one's labor was not entirely new to the Manjaco. However, those who left their homelands in the Costa de Baixo region to work on the *feitorias* went on contracts and never intended to settle permanently in the peanut producing regions.

Manjaco laborers were not tied to the land directly and thus had no desire to risk their lives for it. But many such workers had initially left their homelands because of local economic pressures. Hence for some, going home was difficult. Those who chose not to return often went to Senegal and Gambia to work as migrant laborers in the peanut fields. A dearth of willing hands would remain an enduring hallmark of Portuguese colonialism in West Africa until its demise in the 1970s.

Futa Jallon and other African polities were forced to reorganize their economies in the midst of the slave trade and the advent of "legitimate commerce". As noted in Chapter Two, during the eighteenth and nineteenth centuries, Futa Jallon actively traded slaves and local products with European and Afro-European merchants and their representatives. By the 1850s its economy was heavily dependent upon the revenues that the slave trade provided. Consequently, once the European nations decided to abolish the slave trade, Futa Jallon's economy began to contract. Futa Jallon also found it difficult to make the transition to the production of peanuts and rubber because of its inland location. Transportation costs to the coast amounted to a pointed disadvantage for Futa Jallon.

The Alfas Ibrahim and Yaya embarked upon a protracted but aggressive campaign of expansion in order to stave off economic collapse. Both rulers sought to incorporate all the lands to the northwest of the state's central provinces. Such a plan of expansion presaged the kind of transformation Futa Jallon and its hinterland would experience under European colonial rule. Futa Jallon's expansion resulted in the destruction of the centuries old Mandinka polity of Kaabu. After the 1850s, the Fulbe military advance was assisted by Kaabu's internal problems and an aristocracy that was unable to govern. In 1867, after the Battle of Kansala, three new spheres of Fulbe influence were created in the Senegambia region — Fuladu, Forria and Gabu.

The development of these new Fulbe polities exacerbated tensions between local Fulbe enclaves in the former state of Kaabu and the political and religious leadership of Futa Jallon. In Fuladu, Alfa Molo and his son, Musa Molo, who were *Fulbe-djiábe*, established themselves as rulers. They often installed *Fulbe-ribê* as provincial authorities, but as the cases of Kanadu, Kola and Sankolla illustrated, tensions between the *Fulbe-ribê* and *Fulbe-djiábê* continued to grow even after Kaabu's destruction. In Forria and Gabu, where *Fulbe-djiábê* groups fought side-by-side with *Fulbe-ribê* against their common enemies, the *Fulbe-djiábê* were determined to reap some of the benefits of the new political order. But *Fulbe-ribê* were just as determined to maintain the status quo. As a result, in all three areas, the various Fulbe groups tried to use the presence of Europeans to their advantage, thus complicating the situation even further.

In addition to destroying Kaabu, Futa Jallon's victory opened up the way for the spread of Islam throughout a larger portion of the Senegambia. New social categories and values emerged with the spread of Islam. But converts often only superficially adopted Islamic dress, food taboos, ritual obligations, and some Koranic principles and laws, while continuing to worship their ancestors. Senegambian Islam had a syncretic character drawing from both the Koran and traditional belief systems.[2] But many Senegambians chose exile or death over Islam. Those who refused to convert often became subject to enslavement.

At different times the Portuguese supported *Fulbe-djiábê* and *Fulbe-ribê* groups in their battles against one another. They often provided these groups access to arms and offered them whatever protection they could in their forts. The Fulbe who formed the alliances with the Portuguese failed to realize that these foreigners had imperial designs and that they had no interest in Fulbe independence.   Thus, the Fulbe groups aligned with the Portuguese miscalculated the new goals of these invaders. The Fulbe had no warning about the concerted European imperial advance. But even if they had understood the new plan of action, some Fulbe groups would have supported the Portuguese, believing that they represented a better alternative than subjugation under their enemies.

The Portuguese lacked a comprehensive plan for seizing the area that they claimed. They often operated without sufficient information about the local political and social realities.   Because of the lack of manpower and supplies, Portuguese officials on the spot had to rely on support from African allies to achieve their goals. Consequently, local conflicts often threatened to range out of Portuguese control. Despite their confusion and the vagaries of their colonial policy, the Portuguese still managed to hang on to the small portion of the Senegambia that they claimed for themselves.

Cultivating loyal allies among the Fulbe was a difficult task for the Portuguese. The lack of funds and supplies inhibited their ability to reward their supporters. In addition, the Portuguese administration was unstable. As noted in Chapter Three, in the first ten years of Portuguese Guinea's existence as a separate colony (1879-1889) seven governors and five secretary generals served.[3]   Consequently, few had the time or the interest to learn very much about the people or their history. There was little continuity in policy from one administration to another. The constant changes in the administration had an adverse effect on Portuguese endeavors: "From the confusion of the Government of the Province, from the lack of method and logic in its administration, the result was that agriculture [which was] relatively prosperous, declined appreciably, native conflicts completely worsened and jeopardized commerce".[4] Contrary to their claims of neutrality, these administrators entered into local conflicts. Like their French and British counterparts elsewhere in Senegambia, they wanted to cultivate allies and the only way to achieve their goals was to "divide and conquer" the local people. The Portuguese used their African supporters in their campaigns against rebellious groups. The Fulbe became the most important Portuguese allies — fighting in the "pacification" campaigns and supporting the Portuguese throughout the colonial period.

By the 1880s, African societies in the portion of the Senegambia that became Portuguese Guinea also had to confront a more concerted European presence. Even though the Portuguese established economic relations with coastal Senegambian communities as early as the fifteenth century, by the 1880s their goals and aspirations were different. In 1884-85, at the Berlin Conference, the European powers agreed that each country claiming territories in Africa had to prove "effective occupation". But Portuguese control in Guinea only amounted to a series of small forts in Bolama, Bissau, Geba, Farim, Cacheu and Buba. Moreover, local people constantly challenged Portuguese control of these forts.

Although the European powers agreed on several common goals at the Berlin Conference, competition on the local level often persisted between different countries. In the area that Portugal claimed in the Senegambia rivalry between Portugal and France continued even after they agreed to the Luso-French Agreement of 1886 in which they delineated the boundaries.[5] The competition between Portugal and France revolved around claims of control over the Casamance, Nunez and Cacine Rivers. Even though Portugal continued to claim the Casamance River until it signed the 1886 Agreement, France controlled commerce on this river throughout much of the nineteenth century. Portugal's claim to the Casamance focused on the fort that they maintained in Ziguinchor. This fort, which was located on the left bank of the river, was between two French posts, Carabane at the mouth of the river, and Sedhiou, further up the river.[6] This arrangement left Portugal in a rather precarious position. If Portuguese vessels wanted to carry goods from Ziguinchor to the coast, they had to pass through the French customhouse in Carabane where they had an obligation to pay duties. The French vessels on their way to and from Sedhiou had to pass through Ziguinchor, but the Portuguese lacked the manpower and firepower necessary to enforce the customhouse duties. Consequently, most French vessels escaped without paying any fees to the Portuguese. The French trading houses in Sedhiou and Carabane also diverted trade from the Portuguese posts in Cacheu and Farim by offering a wider selection of trade goods at reasonable rates. These commercial firms could sell imported items for less because they did not have to pay the heavy import duties required of Portuguese traders.[7] Thus even before the 1886 Agreement, Portugal had no control over the Casamance.

Portugal also claimed the Rio Nunez and Rio Cacine regions, but again French commercial firms exercised economic control in these areas. After the 1886 Agreement, the Rio Nunez officially became part of the French territory Rivières du Sud.[8] The Rio Cacine region remained a contested zone. Although Portugal claimed the area for herself, there were no customs officials along the river. Consequently, contraband flourished and a general state of confusion existed. French and British merchants from the Rivières du Sud and Sierra Leone, respectively, benefitted from the contraband trade. The French, Portuguese and Afro-European merchants established along the river, as well as the local Nalu rulers, suffered as the volume of contraband trade increased.

As a result of the illegal trade in tobacco especially, Portugal's representatives in Bolama called for the reorganization of the customhouse and the immediate occupation of the region.[9] Tobacco was used as a local currency. "[I]t is the principal article of exchange with the natives. Its absence affects not only commerce, and therefore, finances, but also actual native politics".[10] When tobacco was scarce, local traders often walked long distances to the French establishments in the Casamance or Rivières du Sud to exchange their produce for tobacco.[11] Tobacco was usually readily available and the prices were reasonable.[12] These traders returned to Portuguese-claimed territories and introduced this tobacco as contraband.[13] Thus, the Portuguese wanted to stifle this trade. In the end, Portugal managed to hold onto the Rio Cacine region but her influence in the region remained weak throughout the colonial period.[14]

France's victory over Futa Jallon in 1897 and her capture of Samori Touré in 1898 contributed to an improvement in relations between France and Portugal. These victories enabled France to begin consolidating her position in West Africa and designing a program that would allow her to exploit her colonies more efficiently. Competition between France and Portugal declined. France realized that territorial control of Portuguese Guinea was not essential, because she actually controlled the colony's economy. Thus, France allowed Portugal to hold onto Guinea and hoped that firms French nationals owned would maintain their dominant economic position.

Portugal's new offensive to establish "effective occupation" from the 1880s and 1890s and her policy of "divide and conquer" resulted in a series of campaigns across what became Portuguese Guinea. The Portuguese fought wars against Fulbe groups that Musa Molo and his generals led, as well as those that Bakar Quidali, Mamadu Paté Coiada and other leaders commanded. At the same time, the Portuguese faced stiff opposition on Bissau Island, the effective administrative center of the colony. Given the paucity of Portuguese resources, these wars were especially menacing for the Portuguese. Because they were fighting wars on several fronts simultaneously, as tensions flared up in different parts of the region, the Portuguese constantly had to move soldiers from one theater of war to another. As a result, the African rebels often found themselves in a stronger position. There were few Portuguese victories until Abdul Njai, an African commander, and João Teixeira Pinto, a Portuguese officer, teamed up to wage a series of "pacification" campaigns between 1913 and 1915.

From the 1890s forward, political and economic pressures in Portugal resulted in the Republican revolution in 1910-1911. The republicans expelled the monarchy, but as Douglas Wheeler points out,

> The 1910 Revolution did not usher in the millennium or a social revolution. The men who took power on 5 October [1910] were largely middle-class intellectuals and professional men, some of whom were ambitious for public office ...[15]

Many in Portugal saw the new republican regime as a solution to some of the problems that had plagued Portugal for generations,

> ... the "republic" was a remedy for a sick country, a fourth rate power aspiring to a higher station among nations. To those concerned with progress, it was a "leap forward", *o salto em frente*, in an era of general disillusionment.[16]

In fact, the new regime was rather moderate, and little changed for the average person. Although the republicans had some support outside of the capital, Lisbon was the focal point of the revolution. The new republican regime failed to recognize that "the well-being of the people depended on agrarian renewal and not on the petty squabbles of class factions in the cities..."[17]

In terms of the colonies, the republicans never considered liberating them. As Wheeler points out for Angola, the republican regime inherited "...the tasks of military conquest, expansion of authority and the implementation of a colonial policy, but tradition and vested interests set limits on its effectiveness...and ...no sweeping changes came before its demise in 1926".[18] By 1910-11 in Guinea, Abdul Njai had established his position as an indispensable ally in the Portuguese attempt to achieve "effective occupation". The most significant change in colonial policy occurred when the new republican government in the metropole embarked upon a series of "pacification" campaigns in 1913.

Although Abdul Njai continued to play a critical role, the Portuguese selected a new officer to lead these campaigns, João Teixeira Pinto. He was a veteran of previous army operations in Angola. Like other junior officers and enlisted men, Teixeira Pinto supported the republican cause. These soldiers hoped that the revolution would bring some relief, specifically better pay and improved working conditions, as well as a more professionalized officer corps. Many of these junior officers, known as the "Young Turks", and their allies among the enlisted men, were dissatisfied with the unprofessional nature of the officer corps. The majority of their superiors were royal appointees or noblemen who went into the army. These officers were often corrupt. Consequently, the men under them, who saw themselves as professionals, were outdone by their superiors. These contradictions led to various forms of insubordination which in some cases resulted in mutiny. Unlike the more senior military men, junior officers, including Teixeira Pinto, and enlisted men felt the weight of the "pacification" campaigns and the First World War. The protests against military policy culminated in two attempted military coups in October 1914 and January 1915. These coups "occurred on the very days when army units were about to embark on ships for military service in Angola and Mozambique against German colonial forces..."[19] Ultimately, the African campaigns and the First World War strengthened the position of the military officers who did not support the republican cause and enabled them to seize power in 1926.

Despite their intentions, the republicans failed to bring order to the government. In fact, in the fifteen years that the republicans ruled, 1910-1926, there were 45 governments. The results of this political instability in the metropole were felt in the colonies as well. In Guinea, Abdul Njai understood that this political instability meant that there were few checks on his reign. The Portuguese granted him control over Oio region as a reward for his loyal service. Njai ruled with brute force. The Portuguese did nothing to stop Njai until after the end of the First World War, when they began to focus their attention on the colonies. By 1919, the Portuguese wanted to eliminate Njai from the political equation in order to guarantee maximum return from their colonial subjects. Njai's subjects hoped that his defeat would bring them relief. Most failed to realize that Portuguese colonial rule would continue to exploit them in an even more deliberate and brutal way.

Notes

1. See Chapter Five.
2. One of the clearest examples of Islamic syncretism are the *marabouts* or the Islamic clerics who supplied believers with charms and amulets for their protection. Using charms violates orthodox Islamic tenets, but this practice was and continues to be very much a part of life for Muslims in this region.
3. *Anuário da Guiné Portuguesa*, 1946, p. 24.
4. Correia e Lança, *Relatório*, p. 7.

5. Teixeira da Mota, *Guiné*, 1, pp. 3-4. The final delineation of the borders was not completed until 1905. Border disputes continue to plague the contemporary state of Guinea-Bissau.

6. AHU, Guiné, Pasta 409: Secretária do Governo em Bolama to Ministro e Secretário d'Estado dos Negócios da Marinha e Ultramar, 12 March 1881; AMNE, Guiné, Caixa 73 (1101): Ministro e Secretário d'Estado dos Negócios da Marinha e Ultramar to Ministro e Secretário d'Estados dos Negócios Estrangeiros, 21 October 1881.

7. AHU, Guiné, Pasta 365: Pedro Inácio de Gouveia, Governor to Secretário da Commissão Parlamentar, 29 September 1883.

8. Prior to the establishment of a separate colony called Rivières du Sud in 1890, the Rio Nunez area came under the jurisdiction of Senegal. See: AHU, Guiné, Pasta 413: Interim Governor to Ministro e Secretário d'Estado dos Negócios da Marinha e Ultramar, 20 January 1890.

9. AHU, Guiné, Pasta 390: Interim Governor to Ministro e Secretário d'Estado dos Negócios da Marinha e Ultramar, 19 March 1889.

10. AHU, Guiné, Pasta 391: Augusto Rogério Gonçalves dos Santos, Governor to Ministro e Secretário d'Estado dos Negócios da Marinha e Ultramar, 26 February 1890.

11. AHU, Guiné, Pasta 391: Augusto Rogério Gonçalves dos Santos, Governor to Ministro e Secretário d'Estado dos Negócios da Marinha e Ultramar, 26 February 1890.

12. AHU, Guiné, Pasta 391: Interim Governor to Ministro e Secretário d'Estado dos Negócios da Marinha e Ultramar, 21 January 1890.

13. AHU, Guiné, Pasta 319: Augusto Rogério Gonçalves dos Santos, Governor to Ministro e Secretário d'Estado dos Negócios da Marinha e Ultramar, 16 June 1890.

14. The people of the southern districts near the border of the Republic of Guinea rallied behind the national liberation movement, *Partido Africano da Independência da Guiné e Cabo Verde* (PAIGC), during the war (1963-73). Without their support the PAIGC's struggle would have been more difficult.

15. Wheeler, *Republican Portugal*, p. 59.

16. Wheeler, *Republican Portugal*, p. 38.

17. Birmingham, *Concise History*, p. 152.

18. Wheeler and Pélissier, *Angola*, p. 109.

19. Wheeler, *Republican Portugal*, p. 113.

Bibliography

A. Archival Sources

I. Arquivo Histórico Ultramarino (AHU), Lisbon, Portugal

Guiné, Pasta 363 (1879-1891), 1ª Repartição: Diversas
Pasta 364 (1890-1892), Officias
Pasta 365 (1883-84), 1ª Repartição: Relatórios (1887-88)
Pasta 374 (1934), Relatório do Governador Luis António de Carvalho Viegas
Pasta 385, Documentos Diversos de Guiné e São Tomé e Principe
Pasta 387 (1882-1885), Direcção do Ultramar 2ª Repartição
Pasta 388 (1886), Direcção do Ultramar 2ª Repartição
Pasta 389 (1887), Direcção do Ultramar 2ª Repartição
Pasta 390 (1888), Direcção do Ultramar 2a Repartição
Pasta 391 (1890), Direcção do Ultramar 2ª Repartição
Pasta 392 (1891), Direcção do Ultramar 2ª Repartição
Pasta 393 (1892), Direcção do Ultramar 2ª Repartição
Pasta 394 (1893), Direcção do Ultramar 2ª Repartição
Pasta 395 (1894), Direcção do Ultramar 2ª Repartição
Pasta 396 (1895), Direcção do Ultramar 2ª Repartição

Guiné, Pasta 397 (1896), Direcção do Ultramar 2ª Repartição
   Pasta 398 (1897-98), Direcção do Ultramar 2ª Repartição
   Pasta 399 (1898-99), Direcção do Ultramar 2ª Repartição
   Pasta 406 (1880-1893), Sinopses de Correspondência
   Pasta 409 (1879-1885), 1ª Repartição
   Pasta 411 (1888), 1ª Repartição
   Pasta 412 (1889), 1ª Repartição
   Pasta 413 (1890), 1ª Repartição
   Pasta 414 (1891), 1ª Repartição
   Pasta 415 (1892-1894), 1ª Repartição
   Pasta 416 (1895), 1ª Repartição
   Pasta 417 (1896/1898-99), 1ª Repartição
   Pasta 418 (1900-1904), 1ª Repartição
   Pasta 419 (1905-1918), 1ª Repartição
Guiné, 6382
   6387, Processo 24
   6388, Processo 23
   6390, Processo 6
   6398, Processo 5
   6399, Processo 8
   6404, Processo 12
   6407, Processo 20
   6409, Processo 26
   6410, Processo 9
   6412, Processo 21
   6413, Processo 13
   6415, Processo 3
   6416, Processo 2
   6417, Processo 10
   6418, Processo 18
   6419, Processo 17
   6420, Processo 16
   6421, Processo 11
   6429, Processo 15
   6434, Processo 25
   6479, Processo 19
Cabo Verde, Pasta 63 (1849-50)
   Pasta 64 (1851-52)
   Pasta 65 (1853-1855)
   Pasta 66 (1856)
   Pasta 67 (1857)
   Pasta 68 (1857)

Cabo Verde, Pasta 69 (1868)
    Pasta 70 (1859)
    Pasta 71 (1860)
    Pasta 72 (1860)
    Pasta 73 (1862)
    Pasta 74 (1863)
    Pasta 75 (1868)
    Pasta 76 (1865)
    Pasta 77 (1866)
    Pasta 78 (1867)
    Pasta 79 (1868)
    Pasta 80 (1869)
    Pasta 81 (1870)
    Pasta 82 (1871)
    Pasta 83 (1872)
    Pasta 84 (1873)
    Pasta 85 (1874)
    Pasta 86 (1875)
    Pasta 87 (1877)
    Pasta 88 (1878)
    Pasta 93 (1879-1881)
    Pasta 126 (1879)
Miscelânea, Maço 715, Indígenas (1901-1908)
    Maço 774, Cabo Verde (1838-1855)
    Maço 775, Escravatura (1842-1866)
    Maço 781, Cabo Verde e Guiné (1830-1859)
    Maço 782, Cabo Verde e Guiné (1835-1879)
    Maço 789, Escravos (1833-1873)
    Maço 790, Cabo Verde (1840-1864)

II. Arquivo do Ministério dos Negócios Estrangeiros (AMNE), Lisbon, Portugal.

Guiné No. 73 (1101)

III. Archives Nationales Section Outre-Mer (ANSOM), Paris, France

Sénégal et Dépendances III
    Dossier 11: Exploration et Missions (1880-1887)

Sénégal et Dépendances IV
   Dossier 106: Expansion territoriale et politique indigène en Casamance
   Dossier 107: Expansion territoriale et politique indigène en Casamance
   Dossier 108: Expansion territoriale et politique indigène en Casamance
   Dossier 128: Expansion territoriale et politique indigène (1895-1904)
   Dossier 129: Expansion territoriale et politique indigène (1886)
   Dossier 131: Expansion territoriale et politique indigène (1903)
Sénégal et Dépendances VI
   Dossier 5: Affaires Diplomatiques: Portugal (1840-60)
   Dossier 14: Affaires Diplomatiques: Portugal (1881-85)
   Dossier 25: Affaires Diplomatiques: Angleterre (1) (1890-95)
   Dossier 27: Affaires Diplomatiques: Portugal (1890-95)
Sénégal et Dépendances XIII
   Dossier 11: Agriculture, Commerce, Industrie (1815-1895)
Afrique Occidnetale Française IV
   Dossier 6: Expansion territoriale et politique (1913)
Guinée III
   Dossier 1: Exploration et Missions (1889-1892)
   Dossier 2: Exploration et Missions (1893-95)
   Dossier 3: Missions et Voyages (1895-1901)
Guinée IV
   Dossier 1: Expansion territoriale et politique indigène (1889-1895) Rio Nunez
   Dossier 5: Expansion territoriale et politique indigène (1889-95) Fouta Djallon
   Dossier 6: Expansion territoriale et politique indigène (1891-1900) Affaires Musulmanes
Guinée VI
   Dossier 3: Affaires Diplomatiques (1890-1904)
   Dossier 5: Affaires Diplomatiques (1897-1902)
Guinée VII
   Dossier 6: Administration Générale et Municipale (1907-08)
Guinée XIII
   Dossier 7: Agriculture, Commerce, Industrie (1896-1903)

IV. Public Record Office (PRO), London, England

Colonial Office (CO) 87 (Gambia)/79, 85, 108, 128, 129, 130, 131, 132, 136, 137, 141, 142, 144, 146, 149, 151, 153, 158, 163, 166, 168, 169, 170, 171, 174, 175, 178, 181, 182, 183, 184, 185, 191, 200, 206

V. Instituto Nacional de Investigação Ciêntífica

Documentos Diversos (1878-1936)

VI. Archives Nationales du Sénégal (ANS)

Série B: Correspondance général (1779-1895)
   Sous-Série 1B: Correspondance du Ministre au Gouverneur du Sénégal (1779-1895)
   Sous-Série 2B: Correspondance, Depart du Gouverneur du Sénégal au Ministre (1816-1896)
Série F: Affaires Etrangères (1809-1920)
   Sous-Série 1F: Gambie (1820-1920)
   Sous-Série 2F: Guinée Portugaise, Portugal et Iles du Cap-Vert (1820-1920)
Série G: Politique et Administration Générale (1782-1920)
   Sous-Série 1G: Etudes Générales: Mission, Notices et Monographies (1818-1921)
   Sous-Série 7G: Affaires Politiques, Administratives et Musulmanes: Guinée (1839-1919)
   Sous-Série 13G: Affaires Politiques, Administratives et Musulmanes: Sénégal (1882-1919)
   Sous-Série 15G: Affaires Politiques, Administratives et Musulmanes: Soudan (1821-1920)

B. Oral Sources

Oral Interviews were conducted in Guinea-Bissau and The Gambia in 1977 and 1978. They were done under the auspices of the Instituto Nacional de Investigação Ciêntífica in Bissau and the Gambian Cultural Archives in Banjul. The recordings of these interviews are on file in the respective archives. The major informants for this study were:

Ibrahima Koba Casama. An Islamic scholar in Bijini, Guinea-Bissau, who read a Tarikh about Kaabu and Bijini. This Tarikh is a major source for the history of Kaabu and has also been recorded by B.K. Sidibe and was presented at the "Colloque International sur les Traditions Orales du Gabu," Dakar, May 1980.

Alhaji Irama Sisse. The imam in Contuboel, Guinea-Bissau, and an Islamic scholar with a considerable amount of information on Musa Molo, Kaabu, Oio, and other related subjects.

Sori Sane. An elder in Cambore, Guinea-Bissau, offered considerable information on Fulbe history.

Buli Galiça. A well-known griot attached to the Embaló family in Gabú. His information on Kaabu and the area of Portuguese colonial rule was helpful.

Alhaji Mamangari Djaló. The imam in Cambore and a famous Islamic scholar. He is very knowledgeable about Kaabu and Fulbe history. His tarikh was very useful for background information on the Fulbe.

Mamadou Falai Baldeh. An Islamic scholar and grandson of Musa Molo who lives in Yorobelikunda, The Gambia now. He is the most important source for the official Baldeh family version on Alfa Molo and Musa Molo's story. He was very helpful and his story is the basis of the history presented here.

Alhaji Kawsu Sillah. An Islamic scholar with extensive information about Alfa Molo and Musa Molo. He has traveled throughout the Gambia, Senegal, and Guinea-Bissau. His mother was one of Musa Molo's daughters. He lives in Brikama although he also has a compound in Sankulikunda, The Gambia.

Ousmane Ceesay. An Islamic scholar in Sukuta, The Gambia. He has a great deal of information about Alfa Molo and Musa Molo. He lived in Guinea-Bissau before settling in The Gambia and knows about the Portuguese in Portuguese Guinea.

Mansajang Banja. The former market master in Bansang, The Gambia. He is the son of one of Musa Molo's generals. He is very knowledgeable about Musa Molo's period.

Jali Kemo Kuyateh. A well-known griot in The Gambia whose stories about the "pacification" period in Portuguese Guinea are interesting.

Arafang Tombong Tambajan. Respected and learned scholar in Bansang, The Gambia.

Tansangkung Jabi. An elder in Libras who shared his knowledge about Alfa Molo and Musa Molo.

Jali Sanejang Kuyateh. A griot from Kerewan, The Gambia, connected to the Baldeh family. He recited the story of Alfa Molo and Musa Molo.

Bakoyo Suso. Son of Bamba Suso, the famous griot in The Gambia.
He recited Alfa Molo's story and also stories about the fall of Kaabu
at his home in Latrikunda, The Gambia.

Amadu Jobarteh. A well-known griot with good information about
Portuguese activities in Portuguese Guinea, especially in the early
twentieth century.

C. Works Cited

Afigbo, A.E. (1972), *The Warrant Chiefs: Indirect Rule in Southeastern
Nigeria, 1891-1929*, Longman, London.

Alexandre, Valentim (1979), *Origens do Colonialismo Português Moderno
(1822-1891)*, Sá da Costa, Lisbon.

Almada, Alvares de (1964), "Tratado Breve dos Rios de Guiné", in Brasio,
António (ed.), *Monumenta Missionaria African-Africa Ocidental
(1570-1600)*, 2d ser., vol. 3., Agência Geral do Ultramar, Lisbon.

Amir, Samir, ed. (1974), *Modern Migration in Western Africa*, Oxford
University Press, London.

Anene, J.C. (1966), *Southern Nigeria in Transition, 1885-1906*, Cambridge
University Press, Cambridge.

Anuário da Guiné Portuguesa (1946).

Arcin, André (1907), *La Guinée Française: races, religions, coutumes,
production, commerce*, Challamel, Paris.

Arpoare, Henrique d'. (1882), "Exploração agronômica em Cabo Verde e
Guiné", *BSGL* 6, pp. 362-69.

Astrié, Max. (1885), "La Guinée Portugaise", *BSGL* 9, pp. 564-68.

Azevedo, M. Ennes (1894), "Chronica Geral", *Portugal em Africa*.

Bah, Thierno Mouctar (1971), "Architecture militaire traditionelle et
poliorcétique dans le Soudan Occidental (du XVIIè fin du XIXè siècle)",
Thesis, 3ème cycle, Paris.

Blade, Mamadou Saliou (1975), "L'Esclavage et la guerre sainte Fuuta
Jalon", in Meillassoux, Claude (ed.), *L'Esclavage en Afrique
Précoloniale*, François Maspero, Paris.

Balde, Chiakhou (1939), "Les associations d'âge chez les Foulbé du Fouta
Djalon," *BIFAN* 1 (January), pp. 89-109.

Barahona e Costa, and Cesar da Silva, Francisco (1901), "Comissão (Uma)
de engenharia militar na Guiné Portugueza", *Revista de Engenharia
Militar*, 6 (February), pp. 53-69.

Barbosa, Octavia C. Gomes (1946), "Breve notícia dos caracteres étnicos
dos indígenas da tribo biafada", *BCGP* 1 (April), pp. 205-71.

Barre, H. (1898), "Les Colonies Portugaises", *Bulletin de la Sociéte de Geographie de Marseille* 22, pp. 117-42.

Barreto, Honório Pereira (1843), *Memoria Sôbre o Estado Actual de Senegambia Portuguesa--causas de sua decadencia e meios de a fazer prosperar*, Lisbon.

Barreto, João (1938), *História da Guiné: 1418-1918*, Edição do Autor, Lisbon.

Barros, Augusto de (1947), "A invasão fula ao circumscrição de Bafata--Queda dos Beafadas e Mandingas--Tribos 'Gabu' Ngabé", *BCGP* 2 (July), pp. 737-43.

Barros, A.F. de (1883), "A praça e porto de Buba no Rio Grande de Bolola", *As Colonias Portuguezas* 1 (1 May), pp. 51-2.

Barros, Marcelino Marques de (1882), "Guiné Portuguesa: breve notícia sobre alguns usos, costumes, línguas e origens dos seus povos", *BSGL* 12, pp. 117-21.

Barrows, Leland Conley (1974), "The Merchants and General Faidherbe: Aspects of French Expansion in Senegal in the 1850s", *Revue française d'historie d'outre-mer*, Tome LXI, No. 223 (2e trimestre), pp. 236-283.

Barry, Boubacar (1983), "The Expansion of Fuuta Jallon Towards the Coast and the Social and Political Crises in Southern Senegambia during the First Half of the Nineteenth Century", Unpublished Paper.

_____. (1988), *La Sénégambie du XVe au XIXe Siècle — Traite Négrière, Islam e Conquête Colonial*, Éditions L'Harmattan, Paris.

Beaver, Philip (1805), *African Memorandum: Relative to an Attempt to Establish a British Settlement on the Island of Bulama...in the year of 1792*, C.R. Bladwin, London.

Bérenger-Feraud, L. J. B. (1879; 1973), *Les Peuplades de la Sénégambie: Histoire-Ethnographie-Moeurs et Coutumes, Legendes, etc.*, Ernest Leroux; reprinted Kraus Reprint, Nendeln, Germany.

Birmingham, David (1993), *A Concise History of Portugal*, Cambridge University Press.

Bocandé, Bertrand (1849), "Notes sur la Guinée Portugaise ou Sénégambie Meridonale", *Bulletin de la Sociéte de Geographie* (Paris), 3d ser., no. 11 (May and June 1849), pp. 265-350.

_____. (1849), "Notes sur la Guinée Portugaise ou Sénégambie Meridonale", *Bulletin de la Société de Geographie* (Paris), 3d ser., no. 12 (July and August), pp. 57-93.

Bonvalet, E. (1893), "Manjacques, Feloups, Balantes", *Bulletin de la Société Geographie de Lille*, 19, pp. 294-302.

_____. (1893), "Manjacques, Feloups, Balantes. Sur le Rio Cacheo--L'Esclavage en Guinée Portugaise--Moussa Molo", *Bulletin de la Société de Goegraphie de Lille* 19 (June), pp. 406-15.

Bouet-Willaumez, E. (1848), *Commerce et traite des noirs aux côtés occidentales d'Afrique*, Paris.

Boulège, Jean (1968), "La Sénégambie du milieu du XVè siècle au debut du XVIIè siècle", Thesis, 3ème cycle, Faculté des Lettres et Sciences Humaines de l'Université de Paris.

Bowman, Joye L. (1986), "Abdul Njai: Ally and Enemy of the Portuguese, 1895-1919", *JAH*, 27, pp. 463-79.

_____. (1987), "'Legitimate Commerce' and Peanut Production in Portuguese Guinea, 1840s-1880s", *JAH*, 28, pp. 87-106.

Brito, Raquel Soeiro de. (1966), "Guiné, Cabo Verde e São Tomé e Principe: alguns aspectos da terra e dos homens", in *Cabo Verde, Guiné, São Tomé e Principe*, Universidade Tecnica, Instituto Superior de Ciências Sociais e Política Ultramarina, Lisbon.

Brooks, George E. (1980), "'Artists' Depictions of Senegalese Signares: Insights Concerning French Racist and Sexist Attitudes in the Nineteenth Century", *Genève-Afrique*, XVII, pp. 75-89.

_____. (1973), "Bolama as a Prospective Site for American Colonization in the 1820s and 1830s", *BCGP* 28 (April), pp. 5-21.

_____. (1993), *Landlords and Strangers: Ecology, Society, and trade in Western Africa, 1000-1630*, Westview Press, Boulder, Colorado.

_____. (1980), *Luso-African Commerce and Settlement in the Gambia and Guinea-Bissau Region*, Boston University, African Studies Center Working Papers, no. 24, Brookline, Mass.

_____. (1983), "A Nhara of the Guinea-Bissau Region: Mãe Aurélia Correia", in Robertson, Claire C. and Klein, Martin A. (eds.), *Women and Slavery in Africa*, University of Wisconsin Press, Madison.

_____. (1975), "Peanuts and Colonialism: Consequences of the Commercalization of Peanuts in West Africa, 1830-1870", *JAH* 16, pp. 29-54.

_____. (1976), "The Signares of Saint Louis and Goreé: Women Enterpreneurs in Eighteenth-Century Senegal", in Hafkin, Nancy J. and Bay, Edna G. (eds.), *Women in Africa: Studies in Social and Economic Change*, Stanford University Press, Stanford, Calif.

Brosselard, H. (1889), "La Guinée Portugaise et les Possessions françaises voisines", *Bulletin de la Société e Geographie de Lille* 11, pp.381-434; 12, pp. 8-64.

Brosselard-Faidherbe, Henrique (1889), "Voyage dans la Senegambie et la Guinée Portugaise", *Le Tour du Monde* 57, pp. 97-144.

181

Cabral, Amilcar (1974), "Brief Analysis of the Social Structure in Guinea-Bissau", in *Guinea-Bissau: Toward Final Victory!-Selected Speeches and Documents from PAIGC*, LSM Press, Richmond, B.C., Canada.

Cameron, Rondo (1985), "A New View of European Industrialization", *Economic History Review*, 38, 1 (February), pp. 1-23.

Cannadine, David (1984), "The Present and Past in the English Industrial Revolution, 1880-1980", *Past and Present*, no. 103, pp. 131-172.

Caroço, Jorge Vellez (1948), *Monjur: O Gabú e a Sua História*, Centro de Estudos da Guiné Portuguesa, no. 8, Bissau.

Carreira, António (1966), "Aspectos históricos da evolução do Islamismo na Guiné Portuguesa (achegas para o seu estudo)", *BCGP* 21 (October), pp. 405-55.

_____. (1983), *Documentos para a História das Ilhas de Cabo Verde e "Rios de Guiné" (Séculos XVII e XVIII)*, Lisbon.

_____. (1963), "Duas Cartas topográficas do Graça Falção (1894-97) e a expansão do Islamismo no Rio Farim", *Garcia de Orta*, 11, pp. 189-212.

_____. (1964), "A etnonimia dos povos entre o Gambia e o estuário do Geba", *BCGP*, 19 (July), pp. 233-275.

_____. (1947), *Mandingas da Guiné Portuguesa*, Centro de Estudos da Guiné Porgutuesa, no. 4. Bissau.

_____. (1961), "Organização social e economica dos povos da Guiné Portuguesa", *BCGP* 16 (October), pp. 641:736.

Carreira, António, and Martins de Meireles, A. (1959), "Notas sobre os movimentos migratórios da população natural da Guiné Portuguesa", *BCGP* 14 (January), pp. 7-19.

Castel-Branco, João Bentes (1891), *Guia do Colono para a Africa Portugueza*, Typ. da Empreza Litteraria e Typographica, Porto.

Castro, Armando (1978), *O Sistema Colonial Português em Africa (meados do século XX)*, Editora Caminho, SARL, Lisbon.

Chilcote, Ronald H. (1967), *Portuguese Africa*, Prentice-Hall, Englewood Cliffs, N.J.

Cissoko, Sékéné Mody (1966), *Histoire de l'Afrique Occidental-Moyenâge et temps modernes VIIè siècle-1850*, Presence Africaine, Paris.

_____. (1972), "Introduction à l'histoire des Mandingues de l'ouest: l'empire de Kabou (XVIè-XIXè siècle)", Paper presented to the Conference on Manding Studies, SOAS, London.

_____. (1969), "Traits fondementaux des sociétés du Soudon Occidental du XVIIè au debut du XIXè siècle", *BIFAN*, séries B, 31, pp. 1-30.

Clarence-Smith, Gervase (1985), *The Third Portuguese Empire 1825-1975: A Study in Economic Imperialism*, Manchester University Press, Manchester.

Clark, Samuel (1984), "Nobility, Bourgeoisie and Industrial Revolution in Belgium", *Past and Present*, no. 105, pp. 140-175.

Colvin, Lucy, et. al. (1980), *The Uprooted of the Western Sahel: Migrants' Quest for Cash in the Senegambia*, Praeger, New York.

Contribuição para uma Biblografia sobre a Guiné-Bissau (1977), Centro de Documentação e Informação, Lisbon.

Cooper, Frederick (1977), *Plantation Slavery on the East African Coast*, New Haven, Yale University Press.

_____. (1979), "The Problem of Slavery in African Studies", *JAH*, 20, pp. 103-25.

_____. (1980), *From Slaves to Squatters: Plantation Labor and Agriculture in Zanzibar and Coastal Kenya, 1908-1925*, Yale University Press, New Haven.

Corriea e Lança, Joaquim da Graça. *Relatório da Provincia da Guiné Portugueza-Referido ao anno Económico de 1888-89*, Imprensa Nacional, Lisbon.

Crowder, Michael (1968), *West Africa Under Colonial Rule*, Evanston, Northwestern University Press.

Cunningham, James (1980), "The Colonial Period in Guiné", *Tarikh*, 6, 4, pp. 31-46.

Curtin, Philip D. (1975), *Economic Change in Precolonial Africa: Senegambia in the Era of the Slave Trade*, 2 vols., University of Wisconsin Press, Madison.

_____. (1971), "Jihad in West Africa: Early Phases and Interrelations in Mauritania and Senegal", *JAH*, 12, pp. 11-24.

Defeza (A) das Victimas da Guerra de Bissau-O Exterminio da Guiné (1916), Lisbon.

Demougeot, A. (1944), *Notes sur l'Organization Politique et Administrative du Labe avant et depuis l'Occupation Française*, Memoires de l'Institut Français d'Afrique Noire, no. 6, Librairie Larose, Paris.

Derman, William (1973), *Serfs, Peasants and Socialists: A Former Serf Village in the Republic of Guinea*, University of California Press, Berkeley.

Diallo, Thierno (1972), *Les Institutions Politiques du Fouta Dyalon au XIXè Siècle*, IFAN, Dakar.

Dinis, António J. Dias (1946, 1947), "As tribos da Guiné Portuguesa na História", *Portugal em Africa*, 2d ser., 3, pp. 206-15; 4, pp. 88-95, 129-238.

"Documentos sobre a campanha contra Abdul Injai", *BCGP*, 6, 21 (January), pp. 53-126.

Eltis, David (1987), *Economic Growth and the Ending of the Transatlantic Slave Trade*, Oxford University Press, Oxford.

Ferrão, Carlos (1976), *História da Ia República*, Terra Livre, Lisbon.

Fisher, Allan G. B., and Humphrey J. Fisher (1970), *Slavery and Muslim Society in Africa*, C. Hurst & Co, London.

Fonseca, Alfredo Loureiro da (1910), *Guiné–Finanças e Economia*, Typographia da Cooperative Militar, Lisbon.

Fonseca, Joaquim Machado da (1915), "O Amendoim na Guiné Portuguesa", *Revista Agronomica*, 2d ser., 2, pp. 31-35.

Gable, Edward Eric (1990), "Modern Majaco: The Ethos of Power in a West Africa Society", Ph.D. dissertation, University of Virginia.

Gallagher, Tom (1983), *Portugal: A Twentieth Century Interpretation*, Manchester University Press, Manchester.

Geraldes, Francisco António Marques (1887), "Guiné Portugueza–Communicação à Sociedade de Geographia sobre esta provincia e suas condições actuaes", *BSGL*, 7, pp. 465-522.

Girard, Jean (1963), "De la communauté traditionelle à la collectivité moderne en Casamance", *Annales Africaines*, pp. 135-65.

Goerg, Odile (1986), *Commerce et colonisation en Guinée, 1850-1913*, François Maspero, Paris.

_____. (1981), "Echanges, réseaux, marchés: l'impact colonial en Guinée (mi-XIX-1913)", Thèse de 3ème cycle, Université de Paris VII.

Gomez, Michael A. (1992), *Pragmatism in the Age of Jihad: The precolonial state of Bundu*, Cambridge University Press, Cambridge.

Grace, John (1975), *Domestic Slavery in West Africa–with particular reference to the Sierra Leone Protectorate, 1896-1927*, Frederick Muller Ltd, London.

Gray, J. M. (1940, reprinted 1966), *A History of the Gambia*, The University Press, Cambridge; Cass, London.

Greenberg, Joseph Harold (1970), *The Languages of Africa*, 3d ed. Indiana University Press, Bloomington.

Griffith, Robert R. (1971), "The Dyula Impact of the Peoples of the West Volta Region", In *Papers on the Manding*, Hodge, Carelton T. (ed.), Indiana University Press, Bloomington.

"Guiné Portugueza–De Geba ao Indornal–Documentos Officiaes" (1882), *BSGL*, 11, pp. 689-94.

"Guine (A) Portugueza em ruínas", *As Colonias Portuguezas*, 5, pp. 99-100.

Hall, Trevor (1992), "The Role of Cape Verde Islanders in Organizing and Operating Maritime Trade between West Africa and the Iberian Territories, 1441-1616", Ph.D. dissertation, Johns Hopkins University.

Hargreaves, John D. (1963), *Prelude to the Partition of West Africa*, Macmillan, London; St. Martin's Press, New York.

_____. (1974), *West Africa Partition–The Loaded Pause, 1885-1889*, Vol. 1, University of Wisconsin Press, Madison.

Hequard, Hyacinthe (1855), *Voyage sur la côte et dans l'interieur de l'Afrique Occidentale*, Imprime de Bernard et Cie., Paris.

Hill, Robert A., ed. (1995), *The Marcus Garvey and Universal Negro Improvement Association Papers*, Vol. VIII: March 1917-June 1921, University of California Press, Berkeley and Los Angeles.

Hobsbawm, E.J. (1975), *The Age of Capital, 1848-1875*, Charles Scribner's Sons, New York.

_____. (1987), *The Age of Empire, 1875-1914*, Weidenfeld and Nicolson, London.

_____. (1969; reprinted, 1981), *Bandits*, Weidenfeld and Nicolson, London.

_____. (1959), *Primitive Rebels*, Manchester University Press, Manchester.

Hodge, Carelton T. (1971), *Papers on the Manding*, Indiana University Press, Bloomington.

Hopkins, A.G. (1973), *An Economic History of West Africa*, Columbia University Press, New York.

Injai, Abdul (1920), *Relatório: Os meus feitos na Guiné Portuguesa, desde 1894 a 1919, data em que por uma acusação falsa fui deportado para a provincia de Cabo Verde*, Praia.

Innes, Gordon (1976), *Kaabu and Fuladu–Historical Narratives of the Gambian Mandinka*, SOAS, London.

Isaacman, Allen F. (1977), "Social Banditry in Zimbabwe (Rhodesia) and Mozambique, 1894-1907: an Expression of Early Peasant Protest", *Journal of Southern African Studies*, 4, 1 (October), pp. 1-30.

_____. (1976), *The Tradition of Resistance in Mozambique: Anti-Colonial Activity in the Zambesi Valley, 1850-1921*, Heinemann, London.

Kennedy, Paul (1987), *The Rise and Fall of the Great Powers*, Random House, New York.

Khan, Muhammad Zafrulla (1975), *The Quran–The Eternal Revelation vouchsafed to Muhammad–The Seal of the Prophets*, 2d rev. ed., Curzon Press, London.

Kiernan, V.G. (1988), *History, Classes, and Nation-States*, Polity Press, Cambridge; Blackwell, New York.

_____. (1995), *Imperialism and its Contradictions*, Routledge, New York.

Klein, Martin A. (1971), "Slavery, the Slave Trade, and Legitimate Commerce in late Nineteenth-Century Africa", *Etudes d'Histoire Africaine*, 2, pp. 5-28.

_____. (1969), *Islam and Imperialism in Senegal: Sine-Saloum, 1847-1914*, Stanford University Press, Stanford.

_____. (1972), "Social and Economic Factors in the Muslim Revolution in Senegambia", *JAH*, 13, pp. 419-41.

Last, Murray (1973), "Reform in West Africa: Movements of the 19th Century", In *History of West Africa*, Ajayi, J. F. and Crowder, Michael (eds.), Vol. 2, Columbia University Press, New York.

Law, Robin, ed. (1995), *From Slave Trade to "Legitimate" Commerce–The commercial transition in nineteenth-century West Africa*, Cambridge University Press, Cambridge.

Leary, Frances Ann (1972), "Gabu in the 19th Century: A Study of Futa Jalon-Firdou-French Relations", Paper presented to the Conference on Manding Studies, SOAS, London.

_____. (1970), "Islam, Politics and Colonialism: A Political History of Islam in the Casamance Region of Senegal, (1850-1914)", Ph.D. dissertation, Northwestern University.

Legrand, René (1912), "Fouladou", *La Geographie*, 26, pp.241-53.

Lloyd, Trevor (1972), "Africa and Hobson's Imperialism", *Past and Present*, no. 55, May, pp. 130-53.

Lovejoy, Paul E. (19), "The Characteristics of Plantations in the Nineteenth-Century Sokoto Caliphate (Islamic West Africa)", *American Historical Review*, 84, 4, pp. 1267-92.

_____. (1981), *The Ideology of Slavery in Africa*, Sage Publications, Beverly Hills, CA.

_____. (1983), *Transformations in Slavery–A History of Slavery in Africa*, Cambridge University Press, Cambridge.

Machat, J. (1906), *Les Rivières du Sud et le Fouta-Djallon: Geographie Physique et Civilisations Indigènes*, Paris.

Madrolle, Claude (1890), *En Guinée*, Paris.

_____. (1894), *Notes d'un Voyage en Afrique Occidental–de la Casamance en Guinées par le Fouta Diallo*, Librarie H. Le Soudier, Paris.

Magalhaes, Vasco de Sousa Clavet de (1916), *Provincia da Guiné–Relatório apresentado pelo Administrador da Circumscrição Civil de Geba, 1914*, Porto.

Manding: Focus on an African Civilization (1972), Papers presented to the Conference on Manding Studies, 3 vols., SOAS, London.

Mane, Mamadou (1978), "Contribution à l'Histoire du Kaabu, des origines au XIXè siècle", *BIFAN*, 40, série B, no. 1 (January), pp. 88-159.

_____. (1974-75), "Contribution à l'Histoire du Kaabu des origines au XIXè siècle", Memoire de Maitrise, Thesis, Université de Dakar.

Martins, João Augusto (1921), *Madeira, Cabo Verde e Guiné*, Editions Ernest Leroux, Paris.

McCall, Daniel F., and Norman R. Bennett, eds. (1971), *Aspects of West African Islam*, Boston University Papers on Africa, vol. 5, African Studies Center, Boston University, Boston.

McCarthy, Joseph M. (1977), *Guinea-Bissau and Cape Verde Islands–A Comprehensive Bibliography*, Garland Publishing, New York and London.

McGowan, Winston Franklin (1975), "The Development of European Relations with Futa Jallon and the Foundation of French Colonial Rule 1794-1897", Ph.D. dissertation, SOAS.

McPhee, Allan (1926; reprinted 1970), *The Economic Revolution in British West Africa*, London; New York.

Meillassoux, Claude (1986), *Anthropologie de l'esclavage: le ventre de fer et d'argent*, Presse Universitaire de France, Paris.

_____, ed. (1975), *L'esclavage en Afrique pré-coloniale*, François Maspero, Paris.

Miers, Suzanne, and Kopytoff, Igor, eds. (1977), *Slavery in Africa– Historical and Anthropological Perspectives*, University of Wisconsin Press, Madison.

Monteil, Charles (1953), "La légende du Ouagadou et l'origine des Soninké", In *Mélanges Ethnologiques*, Mémoires de l'Institut Français d'Afrique Noire, no. 23, IFAN, Dakar.

Moraes e Castro, Armado Augusto Gonçalves de (1925), *Anuário da Provincia da Guiné do anno de 1925*, Imprensa Nacional, Bolama.

Morazé, Charles (1976), *The Nineteenth Century, 1775-1905*, Allen & Unwin, London.

_____. (1966), *The Triumph of the Middle Classes*, Weidenfeld and Nicolson, London.

Moreira, José Mendes (1948), *Fulas do Gabú*, Centro de Estudos da Guiné Portuguesa, no. 6, Bissau.

_____. (1964), "Os Fulas da Guiné Portuguesa na panorâmica do mundo Fula", *BCGP*, 19 (July), pp. 289-327; 19 (October), pp. 417-32.

Mouser, Bruce L. (1975), "Landlords-Strangers: A Process of Accomodation and Assimilation", *International Journal of African Historical Studies*, 8, 3, pp. 425-40.

_____. (1971), "Trade and Politics in the Nunez and Pongo Rivers, 1790-1865", Ph.D. dissertation, Indiana University.

_____. (1983), "Women Slavers of Guinea-Conakry", In *Women and Slavery in Africa*, Robertson, Claire C. and Klein, Martin A. (eds.), University of Wisconsin Press, Madison.

Nogueira, Amadeu (1949), "Figuras da Ocupação: Abdul Injai", *BCGP*, 4, 13 (January), pp. 49-60.

Obichere, Boniface I. (1971), *West African States and European Expansion: The Dahomey-Niger Hinterland, 1895-1898*, Yale University Press, New Haven.

Olanigan, Richard Adeboye (1969), "The Anglo-Portuguese Dispute over Bulama: A Study in British Colonial Policy, 1860-1870", Ph.D. dissertation, Georgetown University.

Oliveira Marques, A.H. de (1972), *History of Portugal: From Empire to Colonial State*, vol. 2, Columbia University Press, New York.

O'Sullivan, John Michael (1976), "Developments in the Social Stratification of Northwest Ivory Coast during the 18th and 19th Centuries: From a Malinké Frontier Society to the Liberation of Slaves by the French–1907", University of California.

Paige, Jeffery M. (1975), *Agrarian Revolution: Social Movements and Export Agriculture in the Underdeveloped World*, Free Press, New York.

Pehaut, Yves (1976), *Les Oléagineaux dans les pays d'Afrique Occidentale Associés au Marché Commun: la production, le commerce et la transformation des produits*, 2 vols., Editions Honoré Champion, Paris.

Pélissier, Paul (1966), *Les paysans du Sénégal: les civilisations agraires du Cayor à la Casamance*, St. Yrieix.

Pélissier, René (1978), "Guinea-Bissau: Physical and Social Geography", In *Africa South of the Sahara 1978-79*, Europa Publications Ltd., London.

Pereira, Carlos Almeida (1914), *La Guinée Portugaise*, Lisbon.

Person, Yves (1968-75), *Samori–Une Revolution Dyula*, 3 vols., IFAN, Dakar.

Pinheiro Chagas (1890), *As Colonias Portuguesas no Século XIX (1881-1890)*, Lisbon.

Pinheiro Chagas, Frederico (1910), "Povos da Guiné Portugueza", *Anais do Club Militar Naval*, 41, pp. 86-96.

Pirio, Gregory Alonso (1983), "Race and Class in the Struggle over Pan-Africanism: a working paper on the Partido Nacional Africano, the Liga Africana and the Comitern in Portuguese Africa", paper delivered at the conference on "The class basis of nationalist movements in Angola, Guinea-Bissau and Mozambique", Minneapolis.

"Provincia da Guiné Portugueza (Abandono completo das suas fazendas agrícolas)" (1887), *As Colonias Portuguezas*, 5 (31 December), p. 137.

Puvel, Pierre (1909-10), "A Agricultura no Coconda", *Revista Portuguesa Colonial e Maritima*, 13, pp. 145-56.

_____. (1910), *Rapport de (...) sur ses propriétés de Kacondo sur le Rio Cassini*, Brussels.

Quinn, Charlotte A. (1972), *Mandingo Kingdoms of the Senegambia: Traditionalism, Islam and European Expansion*, Northwestern University Press, Evanston.

_____. (1971), "A Nineteenth Century Fulbe State", *JAH*, 12, pp. 427-40.

"Relatório de 1882–Governador Pedro Inácio de Gouveia" (1952), *BCGP*, 7 (April), pp. 403-76.

Roberts, A.D. (1962), "The Sub-imperialism of the Baganda", *JAH*, 3, 3, pp. 435-50.

Roberts, Richard L. (1987), *Warriors, Merchants and Slaves: The State and the Economy in the Middle Niger Valley, 1700-1914*, Stanford University Press, Stanford.

Roberts, Richard and Klein, Martin (1980), "The Banamba Slave Exodus of 1905 and the Decline of Slavery in the Western Sudan", *JAH*, 21, pp. 375-95.

Robertson, Claire C. and Klein, Martin A. (eds.), (1983), *Women and Slavery in Africa*, University of Wisconsin Press, Madison.

Robinson, David (1975), *Chiefs and Clerics: Abdul Bokar Kan and Futa Toro 1853-1891*, Clarendon Press, Oxford.

_____. (1985), *The Holy War of Umar Tal: The Western Sudan in the Mid-Nineteenth Century*, Clarendon Press, Oxford.

Robinson, Richard Allen Hodgson (1979), *Contemporary Portugal–A History*, Allen & Unwin, London and Boston.

Robinson, Ronald and Gallagher, John (1961), *Africa and the Victorians*, Macmillan, London; St. Martin's Press, New York.

Roche, Christian (1976), *Conquête et resistance des peuples de Casamance (1850-1920)*, Les Nouvelles Editions Africaines, Dakar.

Rodney, Walter (1966), "African Slavery and Other Forms of Social Oppression on the Upper Guinea Coast in the Context of the Atlantic Slave Trade", *JAH*, 7, pp. 431-43.

_____. (1970), *A History of the Upper Guinea Coast: 1545-1800*, Clarendon Press, Oxford.

_____. (1968), "Jihad and Social Revolution in Futa Djalon in the Eighteenth Century", *Journal of the Historical Society of Nigeria*, 4 (June), pp. 269-84.

Rouch, Jean (1960), "Problèmes relatifs à l'étude des migrations traditionelles et des migrations actuelles en Afrique occidentale", *BIFAN*, Ser. B, 22, pp. 369-78.

Rude, George F.E. (1972), *Debate on Europe, 1815-1850*, Harper and Row, New York.

Rudebeck, Lars (1974), *Guinea-Bissau: A Study of Political Mobilization*, Scandinavian Institute of African Studies, Uppsala.

Sanneh, Lamin O. (1979), *The Jakhanke: The History of an Islamic Clerical People of the Senegambia*, International African Institute, London.

Santos, Machado (1982), *A Revolução Portuguesa 1907/1910*, Assírio e Alvim, Lisbon.

Searing, James F. (1993), *West African Slavery and Atlantic Commerce: The Senegal River valley, 1700-1860*, Cambridge University Press, Cambridge.

Sidibe, B[akary] K. (1974), "A Brief History of Kaabu and Fuladu, 1300-1930: A Narrative Based on Some Oral Traditions of the Senegambia", Unpublished manuscript.

_____. (n.d.), "The Nyanchos of Kaabu", Mimeographed, Gambian Cultural Achives.

_____. (1972), "The Story of Kaabu: Kaabu's Relationship with the Gambian States", Paper presented to the Conference on Manding Studies, SOAS, London.

_____. (1972), "The Story of Kaabu: Its Extent", Paper presented to the Conference on Manding Studies, SOAS, London.

_____. (1972), "The Story of Kaabu: The Fall of Kaabu", Paper presented to the Conference on Manding Studies, SOAS, London.

Sidibé, Mamby (1959), "Les Gens de Caste ou Nyamakala au Soudan Français", *Notes Africaines*, 81 (January), pp. 13-17.

Silva, J.D. and Teixeira da Mota, A. (1973), *Honório Barreto, Português da Guiné*, Lisbon.

Silva, Francisco Teixeira da (1889), *Relatório do Governo da Provincia da Guiné Portugueza com referência a 1887-88*, Typ. Minerva Central, Lisbon.

Silva Loureira, António da (1934), *Tributo de Sangue: Monografia das Campanhas Militares para a Occupação da Guiné*, Edições da Exposição Colonial Portuguesa.

Simões, Landerset (1935), *Babel Negra*, Porto.

Smith, H.F.C. (1961), "A Neglected Theme of West African History: The Islamic Revolutions of the 19th Century", *Journal of the Historical Society of Nigeria*, 2, pp. 169-95.

Smith, Thomas C. (1959), *The Agrarian Origins of Modern Japan*, Stanford University Press, Stanford.

Socrates da Costa, Alexio Justiniano (1885), "Provincia da Guiné Portuguesa", *BSGL*, 4, pp. 94-112; 146-60; and 188-203.

Sousa Monteira, José Maria de, "Estudos sobre a Guiné de Cabo Verde", *O Panorama*, 10 (1853), pp. 50, 63, 66, 77, 87, 102, 126, 140, 148, 214, 230, 236, 244, 271, 278, 366, 373, 383, 389, 402, and 420; 12 (1855), pp. 60, 66, 74, 85, 146, 158, 165, 174, 398, 407, and 409; 13 (1856), pp. 151, 154, 165, 174, 181, 191, 205, 216, 223, 231, and 242.

Sow, Mamadou Samba (n.d.), "La Region de Labe (Fouta-Djallon) au XIXè e au debut du XXè siécle", Diplome d'Etudes Supérieures Université.

Suret-Canale, Jean (1970), "The Fouta Djalon Chieftaincy", In *West African Chiefs: Their Changing Status Under Colonial Rule and Independence*, Ajayi, J.F.A. and Crowder, Michael (eds.), Columbia University Press, New York.

_____. (1972), "The Western Atlantic Coast 1600-1800", In *History of West Africa*, Ajayi, J.F.A. and Crowder, Michael (eds.), Vol. 1, Columbia University Press, New York.

Swindell, Ken (1980), "Serawoolies, Tilibunkas and 'Strange Farmers': The Development of Migrant Groundnut Farming Along the Gambia River, 1848-95", *JAH*, 21, pp. 93-104.

Tauxier, Louis (1937), *Moeurs et Histoire des Peuls*, Payot.

Teixeira da Mota, A. (1974), "Actividade Maritima dos Bijagós nos séculos XVI e XVII", In *Memoriam António Jorge Dias*, Instituto de Alta Cultura; Junta de Investigações Cîentíficas do Ultramar, Lisbon.

_____. (1950), "A agricultura de Brames e Balantas vista através de fotografia aéres", *BCGP*, 5 (April), pp. 131-72.

_____. (1969), "Un document nouveau pour l'histoire de Peuls au Sénégal pendant les XVème et XVIème siècles", *BCGP*, 24 (October), pp. 781-860.

_____. (1970), *Fulas e Beafadas no Rio Grande no Século XV (Achegas para a Ethnohistória da África Ocidental)*, Agrupamento de Estudos de Cartografia Antiga, Série Separatas no. 60, Junta de Investigação do Ultramar, Lisbon.

_____. (1954), *Guiné Portuguesa*, 2 vols., Agência Geral do Ultramar, Lisbon.

_____. (1947), *Inquérito Ethnográfico*, Bissau.

_____. (1948), Introduction to *Fulas do Gabú* by José Mendes Moreira, Centro de Estudos da Guiné Portuguesa, no. 6, Bissau.

_____. (1948), "Um Relatório de Sousa Lage", *BCGP*, 3 (April), pp. 329-52.

Teixeira de Barros, Alberto Xavier (1896), *Breves Apontamentos sobre a História do Forria*, Imprensa Nacional, Lisbon.

Teixeira Pinto, João (1936), *A Ocupação Militar da Guiné*, Divisão de Pulblicações e Biblioteca, Agência Geral das Colónias.

Travassos-Valdez, Francisco (1861), *Six Years of a Traveller's Life in Western Africa*, 2 vols., London.

Udo, Reuben K. (1978), *A Comprehensive Geography of West Africa*, Africana Publishing Company, New York.

Valdausa, Marquis de Liveri de (1910), *Notice sur la Guinée Portugaise*, Biarritz.

Valkhoff, Marius F. (1966), *Studies in Portuguese and Creole*, Witwatersrand University Press, Johannesburg.

Vasconcellos, Ernesto J. de Carvalho e. (1971), *Guiné Portuguesa: Estudo Elementar de Geografia Física, Económica e Política*, Tip. da Cooperative Militar, Lisbon.

Viegas, Luiz António de Carvalho (1936, 1939 and 1940), *Guiné Portuguesa*, 3 vols., Lisbon.

Walter, Jaime (1947), *Honório Pereira Barreto*, Centro de Estudos da Guiné Portuguesa, no. 5, Bissau.

Watts, Michael (1989), "Manufacturing Dissent: Culture and Production Politics in a Peasant Society", Paper presented to the seminar "Political Economy and Popular Culture in Africa", Hoover Institution, Stanford University.

Weil, Peter M. (1984), "Slavery, groundnuts and European capitalism in the Walé Kingdom of Senegambia, 1820-1930", *Research in Economic Anthropology*, 6, pp. 77-119.

Weiskel, Timothy C. (1980), *French Colonial Rule and the Baule Peoples: Resistance and Collaboration, 1889-1911*, Clarendon Press, Oxford.

Westermann, Diedrich, and Bryan, M.A. (1970), *The Languages of West Africa*, Dawsons of Pall Mall for the International African Institute, Folkestone and London.

Wheeler, Douglas L. (1978), *Republican Portugal: A Political History, 1910-1926*, University of Wisconsin Press, Madison.

Wheeler, Douglas L. and Pélissier, René (1971), *Angola*, Pall Mall Press, London.

Willis, John Ralph (1967), "Jihad Fi-Sabil Allah: Its Doctrinal Basis in Islam and Some Aspects of Its Evolution in 19th Century West Africa", *JAH*, 8, pp. 395-415.

Wilson, W.A.A. (1962), *The Crioulo of Guiné*, Witwatersrand University Press, Johannesburg.

Wright, Donald R. (1977), *The Early History of Niumi: Settlement and Foundation of a Mandinka State on the Gambia River*, Ohio University Center for International Studies, Africa Series, no. 32, Athens, Ohio.

Index

Gambia 4, 11-13, 16, 34, 38-40, 42, 44, 51, 55, 56, 58, 61, 75, 77, 79-81, 87, 90-94, 121, 125-127, 146, 154, 164, 166
Grant, Ulysses S. 123
grumetes 149, 155

hunters, role of 53-54
"hut" tax 144

Ibrahima, Alfa (Labe)
  Berekolong, Battle of 55-56
  relationship with Forria 105-106
Industrial Revolution 2, 20
Islam 1-4, 14, 15, 17-19, 22, 32, 40-45, 48, 49, 52, 54-58, 60, 73-76, 81, 89, 91, 95, 104, 106, 121, 126, 131, 167
  as unifying force 95
  spread of 2, 4, 11, 18, 19, 21, 44, 48, 127, 167

Jahnke Wali 38, 40, 52, 58, 59
jihad 17, 41-47, 49, 54-57, 75, 103, 104, 106, 111, 131, 153

Kaabu 3, 10, 12, 13, 17, 32, 34, 35, 37, 38, 40, 41, 43, 47-60, 73, 74, 76, 103-105, 107, 146, 166, 167
  economy of 3, 38-39, 47
  Futa Jallon's invastion of 49
  Kansala, Battle of 58-59
  koringo 35, 37, 40, 41, 57
  Mane and Sane families 35
  Nyancho 34-41, 52, 53, 55, 56, 59, 108
  political power 3, 10, 39, 76, 155
  provinces 11, 34, 35, 37-40, 46, 48, 49, 52-55, 57, 74, 76, 79, 84, 85, 87, 88, 90, 91, 93, 94, 102, 124, 166
Kaarta 56, 57

Kanadu 52, 74, 75, 77, 81-84, 86, 88, 102, 103, 166
Kankelifa 89
Kansala, Battle of 58-61
Kantora 12, 13, 34, 40, 90
Kolla 84-86, 88
  commercial importance of 147
  rebellion against Musa Molo 84-86

Labe 42-46, 48, 49, 55-58, 104, 105, 108
"legitimate commerce" 1-3, 5, 10, 32, 80, 105, 122, 125, 132, 165, 166
Liga Guineénse 162

Mamadu Paté Bolola 108-110, 112
Mamadu Paté Coiada 109, 113, 169
Mandinka 3, 4, 8, 10, 12-18, 32, 34-37, 39-44, 49, 51-55, 58, 59, 73, 90, 102-105, 107, 108, 146, 149, 164, 166
  age groups 14
  agricultural practices 13, 15
  caste system 14-15
  connection to ancient Mali 12-13, 32, 34
  role of elders 14
  slavery among 14-15
  states among 13-14
  women 13-15, 35, 39, 41, 53, 59, 77
Manjaco 8, 10-12, 34, 125, 126, 164-166
  class structure 11
  confusion about name 10-11
  Council of Elders 11, 46
  economic activities 39, 85
  migrant laborers 10, 12, 125, 126, 130, 166
Molo Eggue (Alfa Molo)
  Berekolong, Battle of 55-56

death of 40, 74, 75, 104, 106, 107
Futa Jallon, relationship with 60
introduction to Al-hajj Umar Tal 53-55
Islam 1-4, 14, 15, 17-19, 22, 32, 40-45, 48, 49, 52, 54-58, 60, 73-76, 81, 89, 91, 95, 104, 106, 121, 126, 131, 167
Jimara's defeat 57
Kansala, Battle of 58
Musa Molo 60, 73, 75-81, 83-95, 110, 113, 146, 152, 154, 166, 169
coalition with Abdul Njai 153-154
conflict with Bakary Demba 75-79
conflict with Nbuku Nyapa 81-83
economy 1, 4, 12, 13, 20, 21, 32, 39, 46, 47, 80-83, 88, 105, 110, 123, 127, 129, 143, 147, 166
exodus to British territory 92
perception of Portuguese 78-81
relationship with British 91-93
relations with Europeans 76-77
succession to throne 75-77
ties to the French 86-87, 89-94
treaties with the French 78, 89
treaties with the Portuguese 83-84
war against Bamba Dalla 89-90

N'Dorna 74, 75, 77
Nbuku Nyapa 74, 75, 81-85
as Portuguese ally 85
relationship with Musa Molo 90
Nhara 121, 122
Nozolino, Caetano José 121-124

Oio Region 141, 150, 171

Pachisse 88, 89, 91, 113
French campaign and Musa Molo 89-90
palm products 2, 81, 105
Parti Cap-Verdien 155

peanuts 2-4, 12, 15, 20, 21, 47, 76, 77, 80-82, 93, 105, 108, 119, 121-124, 126-130, 165, 166
abandonment of food crops 4
"political economy" 1
Portugal 2, 8, 19, 20, 50, 51, 76, 77, 83, 90, 123, 124, 127-129, 132, 143-145, 148, 151, 154, 169-171

Qadiriyya 43

Republican government 145, 148, 151, 155, 156, 171
Republican revolution 2, 170
rice 4, 6, 12, 13, 15, 39, 46, 47, 77, 109, 122, 123
river system 5, 6, 149
Rivières du Sud 109, 121, 169, 170, 186
rubber 2, 15, 80-82, 105, 113, 127, 143, 166

Salazar, António 156
Sambel Serandim 75
Sankolla 40, 53, 55, 84-86, 88, 167
commercial importance of 147
rebellion against Musa Molo 84-86
slave labor 3, 14, 81, 125, 126
slave trade 1-4, 10, 13, 15, 18, 20, 32, 39, 44, 47, 80, 105, 106, 121-125, 131, 149, 164, 166
slavery 1, 3, 4, 12, 15, 19, 35, 74, 80, 121, 122, 125
"strange farmers" 93, 125

Teixeira Pinto, João 170-171
Tijaniyya 43, 54
tobacco 2, 3, 38, 39, 41, 109, 111, 127, 169
Traoré, Tiramang 32, 34-35